Photographic realism

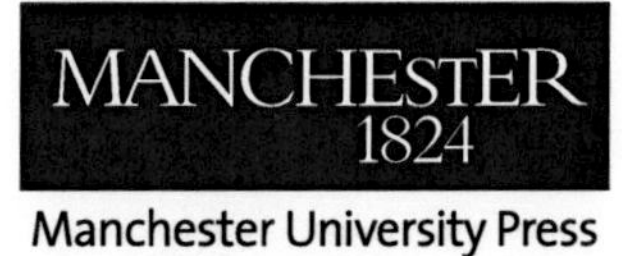

Manchester University Press

Photographic realism

Late twentieth-century aesthetics

JANE TORMEY

Manchester University Press

Published by Manchester University Press
Altrincham Street, Manchester M1 7JA, UK
www.manchesteruniversitypress.co.uk

British Library Cataloguing-in-Publication Data
A catalogue record for this book is available from the British Library

ISBN 978 1 5261 0672 8 *paperback*

This edition first published 2017

Typeset in Perpetua by
Koinonia, Manchester
Printed in Great Britain by
TJ International Ltd, Padstow

Contents

Figures

Part I

Introduction

Photographic realism: late twentieth-century aesthetics discusses uses of photography in the context of art practice, and relates it to the wider cultural debate described as post-structural. Focusing on a range of photographic projects between 1970 and the turn of the century, it addresses the exchange between theories and practice and draws parallels between them. First, the book aims to provide a theoretical overview of the post-structural dimensions of photographic practice. Second, by talking about theories and practice in tandem, it presents photographic practice as providing a discursive means to explore ideas. Third, looking beyond formal analysis, it outlines different perspectives from which to respond to photographs and which encourage an informed and expansive engagement with ideas. Above all, it promotes the photograph's capacity to provoke thought – philosophically, culturally and politically.

Photographic realism develops different conceptions of realism to provide structure and focus for a discussion of the photograph's reference to the 'real' world. It provides a historical review of post-structural ideas that have affected cultural practices since the 1960s and outlines the influence of some of its key thinkers – such as Jacques Derrida, Michel Foucault and Julia Kristeva – who have disturbed traditional philosophies and attitudes to subjectivity and representation. At a point when postmodernism is contested and post-structuralism is questioned as perpetuating art as 'text', this book appraises a post-structural aesthetic as a dynamic phase in photography's history. As such, it discusses a historical era of practice with regard to the legacies of 1960s–80s thinking, and before the assimilation of later influences such as Jacques Rancière's readdress to aesthetics and politics, or Nicolas Bourriaud's 'relational' practice.

Photographic realism examines developments in photographic aesthetics by spotlighting an era in photographic history and its predominant preoccupation with issues of representation. The book's focus is 'realism' so that, rather than using examples that have developed in painterly ways following the application of digital technologies, I deliberately choose to examine photographic projects that reference the world directly and which offer a number of possibilities in responding to it. I consider the different sorts of reality that photography can present. Discussion is organised thematically and does not aim to present a comprehensive survey of individual photographers, or to feature all the major figures of the time. Emphasis is given to the use of photographs, rather than photographers and, strictly speaking, when I use the term 'photography', I mean *uses* of photography. And in discussing its use, I assume the assimilation of the medium of photography into mainstream fine art practice. The book aims to consider abstract theory in relation to specific instances of art practice and to move back and forth between them. To that end, I avoid discussing a photographer's oeuvre, so structure the book in terms of ideas rather than photographic genres. In some instances, one photographer's work will occur across several chapters with reference to a different aspect of their practice. In considering the structure of photographs, I avoid focus on formal analysis or the photographer's artistry and aim to stress the development of ideational content. I give emphasis to the photograph's unique manner of making pictures; how photographs 'speak', construct ideas and promote thought.

The photographs used are predominantly from the 1990s, characterising a particular era following the use of photography as a record of conceptual work, and signalling a direction for developments in the twenty-first century. This era marked a point of transition from the concern to assert photography as a valid art form to one which not only established photographic methods as valid, but offered an alternative medium with which to address subjects that challenged dominant art discourse. This is a period in which photographic practice introduced a response to, and a parallel engagement with, the wider critical debate. I use this era to demonstrate what photography can *do* – rather than what it *is*. In discussing practice as an identifiable aesthetic, the book serves as an alternative to, for example, Jonathan Friday's substantial analysis in *Aesthetics and Photography*, which discusses photographs from the nineteenth century through to 1974 and so does not include examples that have been digitally manipulated. *Photographic realism* moves substantially away from discussions that are restricted to the 'classic' domain of photography or which position 'normative aesthetics' as central, so that concerns are influenced by the underlying post-structural critique of established procedures, traditions and aesthetics. The book outlines a photographic aesthetic, which develops following conceptual art and the shift in thinking about authorship and difference. As the main thrust of the discussion focuses on conceptual ideas, the argument stresses that the post-structural aesthetic is concerned with a shared conceptualism, rather than one that is specific to photography and its ontology, marking a significant difference from modernist preoccupations. As its main concern is ideational content, it therefore assumes the difference that digitalisation makes to the fabrication of photographic images. The chapters build elements of practice by presenting a series of 'realisms' concluding with the *discursive*, which centres the development of an aesthetic that can provoke dialogue, can be critical and argue, and is characteristically rhetorical. Chapters feature a number of examples that involve both verbal and visual elements, which challenge the division between the discursive and the figural, and give momentum to the argument concerning the potential use of the photograph: whether it be political or aesthetic or both.

My context is the cultural exchange reframing practice and the development of the photographic aesthetic following modernism, which is largely determined by American photography and its extension in Europe. As I scrutinise the development of practices that deviate from the paradigms of modernist photography, photographers discussed emerge from a succession to this tradition either by birth or education in the US or Western Europe. It is notable that the influence of 'globalisation' (or more precisely Westernisation) extends increasingly to include Africa and Asia, most notably China, which features in the concluding section. Principally, discussion stresses changes to conceptions of practice that emerge in the 1970s and become established in the 1980s–90s, by which time art practice has assimilated the influence and *knowledge* of both conceptual art and models of post-structuralism. The book aims to acknowledge a considerable adjustment in photographic practice that develops alongside, and as a result of, post-structural influences. In doing this, it puts aside the label 'postmodern', often assigned to art-photography of this era and which tends to gather prejudice, and refers instead to 'post-structural photography' in order to look at more subtle developments.

Photographic realism provides a historical review of the critical debates that have influenced the nature of the photograph and its relation to realism and fine art practice. It reframes a body of critical thinking by its consideration specifically in relation to photographic practice. The book assumes an interdisciplinary approach and makes particular reference to photographic projects that engage with political or conceptual ideas. The theorists chosen for discussion, largely from French post-structuralism, adopt interdisciplinary modes of engagement, introducing the reading of culture (including the visual) as text, and redefining thinking in a way that questions assumptions. They each share a reaction to aspirations for absolute truth and rationalism by incorporating consideration of difference (race, gender, class), the irrational and the mutability of the subject. The texts used focus on challenges to Western thinking initiated in the 1960s and through the 1980s, by which time most had been translated into English. These decades also mark a point of change for photography with regard to attitudes to authenticity, authorship and meaning. An exception is made for some texts by Gilles Deleuze and Félix Guattari that were not available in translation until the early 1990s, but are introduced in Chapter Eight as a pertinent extension to ideas concerning the division between discourse and the figural, and as a useful direction for response and interpretation of photographic projects at the end of the century.

Prompted by undergraduate response to the potential of photography and students' interest in its more philosophical associations, my aim has been to discuss photography not as a separate domain, but as it relates to theoretical thinking more generally. I have tried to keep a balance between complex areas of theory and practice, and to show how photographic ideas parallel those in other practices, and ultimately contribute to that cultural thinking. In aiming to explain the ideas found in primary texts, I have not confused them with references to secondary commentaries that apply those texts. Whilst this book extends the possibilities for 'reading' photographs, it does not attempt to achieve any kind of manual for responding to images. Rather, it emphasises an open-ended approach that encourages discussion provoked by photographic ideas. I acknowledge the influence of some approaches that have provided a lead for how we might respond and write about art: examples that insert a dimension of criticism, which move across the humanities and between objective appraisal and subjective response. For example, John Roberts's critical examination (1998) of the relationship between photography, art and realism remains one of the most significant contributions to questioning practice; Mieke Bal's *reading* of art works (2002) is a useful model of responding to their provocation and is one that I extend; Yve Lomax's challenging approach (2000, 2005) describes the collision of art and theory as an adventure.

Structure

The book is divided into two sections: Part I provides a historical frame for understanding approaches to uses of the photograph during the late twentieth century and Part II asserts an argument about the direction of aesthetics during this period. Part I introduces the background essential to a discussion of theory and practice and its contribution to the disassembly of the assumed principles and traditions of modernist photography. Whilst it aims to provide an introduction to the key ideas, I suggest that readers new to the subject will gain more comprehensive understanding by following the suggested reading lists. By the same token, those who are familiar with this list may choose to skip this chapter and proceed to Chapter Two, which initiates discussion of photographs more directly. I have interspersed explanation of difficult concepts with their application in photographic practice. I deliberately pick up concepts throughout chapters as the book proceeds, so that, for example, Julia Kristeva's notion of the 'subject in process' introduced in Chapter Two is extended in Chapters Three and Five. I have used notes to clarify definitions or to indicate further study or sources of reference. Whilst I refer to a number of photographs to give context, I keep those photographs featured for extended discussion to a minimum. The internet provides easy access to the work of all photographers mentioned in the text, and I have suggested some useful websites for this purpose in the notes. I have used a number of subjective passages (indicated by italics) to give focus to the viewer's experience of the photograph. They serve as a reminder of the experiential nature of photographs and provide a break in the tone from the academic and philosophical to a response grounded in direct observation.

Chapter One, 'Photography's legacies' sets the scene for the exploration of the disturbance of photography's historical traditions in the following chapters, by introducing photography's inheritance of the key debates of 'reality', authenticity and objectivity. The chapter looks at conceptions of the photograph as a 'mirror to the world' and representation more generally, with reference to analyses by Nelson Goodman and Roland Barthes. It describes the theories that circulate around the debates of 'pictorialism' and 'realism', document and expression, all of which are characteristic themes in modernist photography. This chapter also introduces a background to the development of structural readings of the photograph, outlining the rhetorical codes inherited from Charles Sanders Peirce and Ferdinand de Saussure, and reviews the influences of some of the key commentators on photography, such as the 'photographic seeing' of Susan Sontag and the humanist approach of John Berger. Chapter two, 'Practice/theory exchange' outlines the influence of key thinkers, such as Derrida and Foucault, and their critique of the philosophies that strive to verify the world by categorisation and synthesis. It examines changing attitudes to the individual and subjectivity provoked by Barthes and Kristeva, which invite both subjective and objective perspectives. It outlines changes in attitudes to reading photographs, from that of interpretation to one of discourse. This chapter demonstrates key ideas as being paralleled in photographic practice, introducing the exchange between theory and practice as a direction for discussion in Part II.

In Part II specific photographic projects provide focus for the discussion of theoretical ideas in more depth. The chapters are conceived as a series of post-structural engagements with 'reality' and introduce approaches which challenge processes of thinking and incorporate a number of contrasting dimensions: emotional resonance, social condition, political value, bodily response, poetic or fictional space. Each chapter describes a mode of 'realism' by identifying a particular kind of engagement with the world, and a different perspective with which to approach discussion. For example, Derrida's demonstration of reading photographs in the *Right of Inspection*, Jean Baudrillard's photographic *irreal* and Kristeva's *dialogical matrix* provide starting points that extend earlier structural interpretations. Chapter Three, 'Dialogical realism', introduces a self-reflexive approach to responding to photographs. The notion of *dialogism* establishes the photograph as provoking a form of dialogue and presents alternative processes that 'play' with conventions of meaning and which counter existential phenomenological ideas. In considering different encounters with subjectivity, it focuses on a number of photographic series, loosely defined as 'portrait', and the nature of the exchange between the photographer, the subject and the reader. It introduces attitudes to 'others' discussed by Baudrillard and Emmanuel Levinas and relates them to the photographic portrait. Chapters Four, 'Poetic realism', and Five 'Fictional realism' focus on the manner in which meaning is constructed in images. 'Poetic realism' examines the mechanism of metaphor, from the different perspectives of literary theory and cognitive linguistics (George Lakoff); 'Fictional realism' outlines the role of detail and the metonymic power of photographic elements with reference to Barthes's analysis and Derrida's critique of Immanuel Kant. Using the analogy of the poem with reference to works by Gabriel

Orozco and Roni Horn, 'Poetic realism' explores the elusive and unlocatable aspects of photography's absent references; 'Fictional realism' confirms the photograph's alliance with fiction, and its rhetorical nature with reference to the works of Jeff Wall and Sophie Calle. It considers the narrative / counter-narrative dialectic and the psychological dimensions of the unconscious in the making and interpretation of photographic work with reference to Kristeva's discussion of desire and the aspirations of Surrealism.

The last three chapters establish a position for photographic practice as it moves towards the turn of the century. Chapter Six, 'Phenomenal Realism', focuses on our response to photographs from the perspectives of postmodernism and phenomenology. It considers the condition of 'reality' provoked by Baudrillard's discussion of representation, which confronts different relationships between 'subject' and 'object' with reference to examples by Beat Streuli and Nick Waplington. In contrast, it discusses developments in photographic ideas that upset the privileging of vision over other senses with reference to the ideas of Maurice Merleau-Ponty, and works by Lorna Simpson and Jean-Luc Mylayne. Chapter Seven, 'Political realism' discusses the influence of political theories on practice and the issues that divide political and aesthetic purpose. It extends discussion started in Part I of the documentary heritage of the photograph and considers photographic accounts that incorporate an awareness of authorship and representative modes, and which mirror the emphasis on 'difference' and individual experience brought to the forefront by feminist and post-colonial writers. It recollects the important contributions concerning social realism, and the political dimensions with reference to projects by Alfredo Jaar that address a responsible engagement with others or which provoke discussion (Tracey Moffatt). The final chapter, 'Discursive realism', outlines works by Allan Sekula and Jeff Wall that encompass implicit critique and geo-political aspects. It discusses the influences of conceptual art and the consequences of photographic representation that no longer needs to be authentic. It considers the influence of the thinking of Gilles Deleuze and Felix Guattari and the possibilities for an aesthetic that accommodates both ideological discussion and sensual response. A concluding section uses photography by the Chinese artists Zhang Huan, Xing Danwen and Wang Qingsong to summarise a post-structural aesthetic that underlines photography as a discursive practice.

1

Photography's legacies

This first chapter outlines the origin of photography's recurring themes and gives a brief overview of the photograph's aesthetic history with particular focus on modernism.[1] It introduces the applications of structural analysis that established a base for interpreting photographs. It aims to focus on photography's relationship with 'realism' and the traditional legacies that have continued to influence the use of photography and its interpretations.

Ontology

In 1839 photography, described as 'drawing with light', is understood as a physical consequence of light falling onto a light-sensitive surface. Since that time, photography's ontology, resulting from that physical process, has provided the foundation for its philosophies, theories and its aesthetic history. By ontology, I mean the ideas that emerge from what a photograph is or how it is made, what its defining characteristics are in referring to the real world.[2] The photograph, caused by a transference of light, is understood to be a natural form of realism that makes an authentic copy of the world. Photography attracts metaphorical and metaphysical alliances, such as Geoffrey Batchen's reference to it as a coalition of light, the sun, nature and God, and associated with history, human kind and culture (Batchen 1999: 101). The photograph functions as a metaphor for seeing and as a 'mirror to the world', which results in recurring debates concerning the photograph's apparent transparency and its capacity to document truth or to be expressive. The dominant faculty of vision, which the photographic process embodies, provides an extended metaphor for understanding, which is commonly expressed by 'I see what you mean' or 'seeing is believing'. Photographs confront the activity of looking because they appear to confirm what we see in front of us, and looking at the world contributes to our construction of what is seen as 'reality'.[3] And because 'looking' is conceived as providing verifiable documentation of the world, the photograph establishes its association with one of Western philosophy's fundamental preoccupations – that of naming and categorising things.

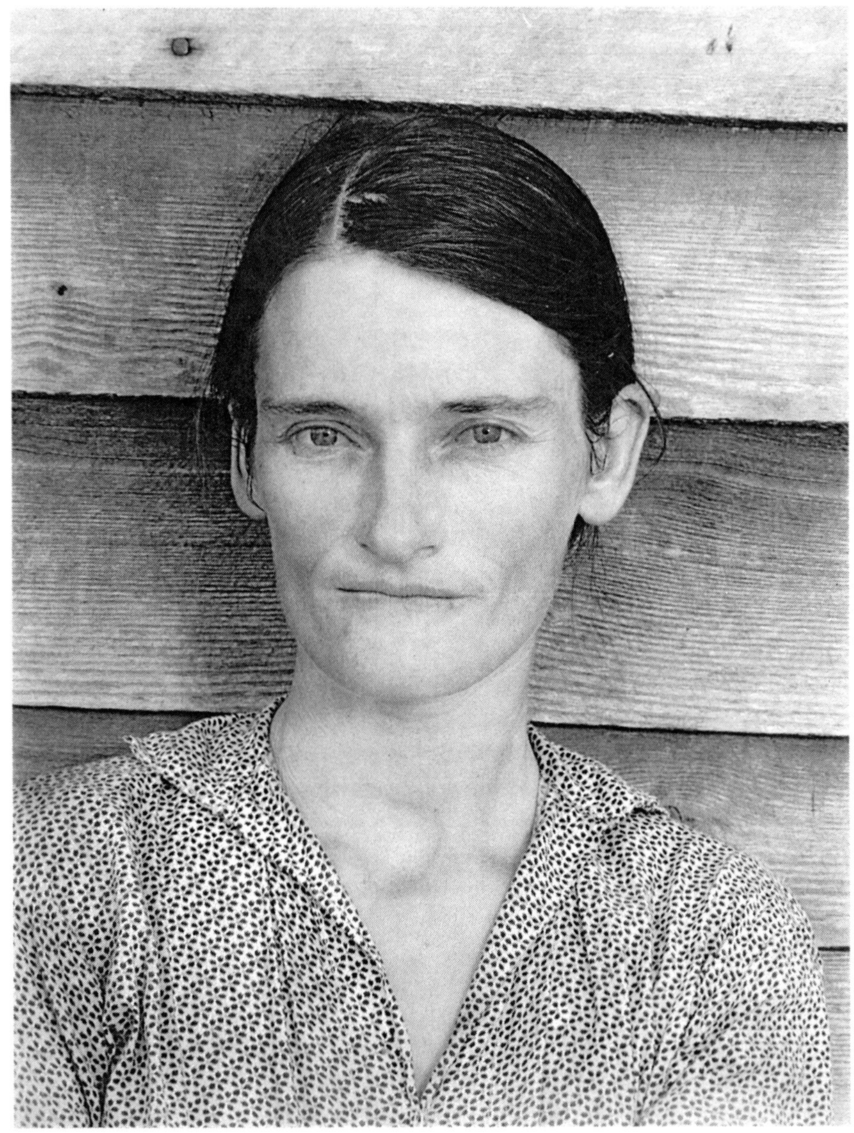

Figure 1 Walker Evans, *Allie Mae Burroughs*, 1936.

The function of naming derives from our fundamental desire to make sense of the world by defining objects in relation to ourselves. In the modern Western world, we assume that an interior psychological subjectivity centres our perceptual experience. The world is represented for us by a sense of a centred self ('I') that mediates experience and which, at the same time, confirms us as central to it. Experience appears to be direct and simple, but in apprehending the world I use reason to make sense of objects outside myself and to bring them into alignment with my own framework of understanding. This process of translation helps me to recognise what I know, to organise what seems complex and to dispel uncertainty. In this way, experience is translated into a logical activity that unifies the world so that it fits with my existing conception of the world. Similarly, in responding to images, unfamiliar objects are made familiar by naming and categorising, and in the course of this process a number of assumptions are made. For example, looking at Walker Evans's *Allie Mae Burroughs* (1936) (Figure 1):

I assume there is some truth to this document; I believe this woman was called Allie Mae and was photographed in 1936 because it is described as such, and I assume that the photographer has integrity; I categorise her in relation to what I can learn from her stance, her clothes and her expression; I calculate her character and make judgements on the basis of the limited visible information available: this is a woman who looks hard and determined and yet who appears vulnerable and less privileged than myself. [4]

Kendall Walton (1984) describes photographs as functioning transparently. Transparency is a consequence of our ability to imagine beyond what is in front of us; when I see a photograph, I 'see' also what it refers to so that when I look at the photograph of Allie Mae Burroughs, I see the woman and forget it is a photograph. However, the conception of the photograph as 'transparent' is problematic and theorists, such as Simon Watney (1982), have exposed the notion as a fallacy. To refer to the photograph as transparent takes little account of the thinking process that mediates our response to photographs or the associations provoked by the things depicted. Jonathan Friday discusses the implications for aesthetics in accepting the suggestion that it is the photograph's transparent rendition of the world that sustains interest and not the artistic sensibility in representing it (Friday 2002: 67–9). His argument refers to the photograph's representational structures, which are layered and immeasurable, and which cannot include expressive qualities, because they cannot be specifically located. By this account, expressive quality cannot form part of any transparent access to the real world. Photography can be understood as a physical manifestation of the filtering process that mediates our view of the world and which forms our ideas about it. Because we filter what we see according to our existing knowledge, an immediate connection with the world is not possible. And, if we accept that direct perception is mediated through our internal reference system and the ideological norms that influence us, a photograph must be translated similarly, via its mode of representation and the choices made by the photographer.

My response to the photograph of Allie Mae cannot be simple because it is coloured by my knowledge of Walker Evans's work and, once known, I cannot unknow *it. If I were not familiar with this series, I might assume that this was a simple individual 'portrait' that, by presenting the subject centrally in an oddly relaxed and tolerant manner, allows her character to be the focus. But because I am familiar with this image and therefore know the context of the Farm Security Administration (FSA, 1935–44), another dimension is added to my experience of it.*[5] *I know that photographers were hired to provide visual evidence that the FSA projects were meeting the needs of the poor in rural areas during the Great Depression. I know also that original publication of this photograph (In Praise of Other Men, 1941) used the pseudonym 'Mrs Gudger' and that we cannot therefore take the author's naming at face value.* As soon as we see another photograph that contradicts or extends our knowledge, or which shows an individual photograph in the context of the whole scene, it is shown to be merely a deceptive fragment and we have a different understanding; we are forced to reappraise what we have hitherto understood to be 'real'. As we see with *Allie Mae Burroughs*, the photograph presents apparently evidential truth together with the contradiction of possible deception, depending on the context and the spectator's knowledge.

Reality and realism

The desire to represent experience is associated with a visual imitation of physical reality, and the history of Western pictorial representation illustrates a sequence of different imitative models. The imitative illusion of reality in painting has been translated into a form of visual resemblance referred to as 'realism'. However, illusion alone is not thought to be enough for classification as 'art', and this imitative process has developed an additional assumption that painting (and now photography) must reveal something essential behind its superficial appearance. The prejudice that imitation masks a hidden reality originates in Plato's view that assumed the existence of an original truth and 'ideal forms', from which the world of representation and illusion removes us.[6] His dialogue [375 BC][7] reveals that representation is generally interpreted as an illusion that relies on little more than 'a mere phenomenal appearance' of objects rather than an experiential engagement with those objects through their use. Plato pointed out that appearance will always depend on the perspective from which something is viewed and is therefore incidental to what is being described (Plato 2003: 339–40). He suggested that appearance can only provide a one-dimensional and transitory view of reality that is not 'truth' in any lasting or meaningful sense. The persistent premise of capturing the 'essence' is dependent on the notion that there is an original or essential meaning to be found, beyond appearance. And running parallel with the impulse to translate reality is the desire to reveal what is hidden. Photography's aesthetic has emphasised the capacity of the medium to exploit this so that, in addition to copying nature, the photographer must insert something meaningful; the photograph is expected to beautify, to universalise qualities or to be expressive – for example by revealing the essential character of *Allie Mae Burroughs*.

Photographs inherit equivalence with realism, which has been at the centre of its history since 1839. And photography's history is founded on changing attitudes to translating reality. Realism, as a system of representation in general terms, refers to the desire to describe 'real' events of the everyday. The 'everyday' is a significant feature of modernism, and distinct from the idealism that was typical of the art in previous centuries. The 'everyday' suggests that what is truly meaningful is available to everyone and not just the privileged few. The nineteenth-century novel parallels many of the divisions in the history of photography – between conceptions of how a sense of reality could be achieved – either by striving to reflect unmediated nature, or by expressing a form of idealism in its appearance. The French Realists advocated truthful observation over the stylistic romantic themes that went before, and developed a plain manner of writing. Honoré de Balzac's representation of society and inner life gives a total vision of the world in which its appearances are mediated and revealed to us by the author's observations (Rignall 1992: 37), whereas Gustave Flaubert made efforts to describe details and facts in a distanced manner without expression or comment; this is an approach that Walker Evans later actively emulates. In an interview in 1971, Evans says of Flaubert: 'his realism and naturalism, and his objectivity of treatment; the non-appearance of author, the non-subjectivity. That is literally applicable to the way I want to use the camera' (Katz 1981: 360). Flaubert's 'deadpan narration' fragments the experience of the world and questions its certainty in appearances (Rignall 1992: 81–2). The history of photography's attitude to realism is similarly divided – between aspirations to naturalism or to idealise and aestheticise, and between the author's interpretation or distance. However, the photographic debate is further complicated by its physical resemblance to the world, which perpetuates a series of assumptions and a circulatory logic:

Realism is the equivalent of what things look like, which is equivalent to what is 'real'. Visual resemblance is equivalent to verisimilitude, can be verified by what I see, and so is equivalent to the real. So that whatever is depicted photographically is understood to be real, which in turn equates with 'truth', which is assumed to be found in visual evidence. In a photograph, the real appears as visually self-evident. Photographic descriptions verify the world's appearance, are simple and truthful, and can be universally recognised as confirming what is 'known', what is understood and what is familiar. In this way of thinking, a convincing conception of reality is constructed based on what is felt to be a direct experience of the world, and photographs appear to represent the world in a direct and transparent way.

André Bazin [1958] introduced a discussion concerning the consequences of 'mechanical reproduction' for our attitude to reality. His point about the intervention of the machine emphasised the automatic process of the camera, which can be thought to remove the photographer's subjective intervention:

> We are forced to accept as real the existence of the object reproduced, actually re-presented, set before us . . . in time and space. Photography enjoys a certain advantage in virtue of this transference of reality from the thing to its reproduction. (Bazin 1980: 241)

Bazin points out that, in freeing painting from its obsession with realism, photography assumes it for itself, and that the quarrel over realism in art stems from a confusion between what is considered to be aesthetic and the consequences of psychological need. What is understood as 'true realism' reflects the need to give significant expression to the world in terms of its appearance and in terms of what is seen as its essential value, and 'the pseudo-realism of a deception aimed at fooling the eye' satisfies that need (1980: 240). Photographic realism encourages us to forget the difference between reality and representation, a condition that increases expectations of realism. The significance of realism is doubly ironic for photography because its history has contributed to our knowledge and trained us to conceive the world in terms of modes of photography. For example, an encounter with 'landscape' is framed in the wake of familiarity with the work of 'Ansel Adams', which appears on so many calendars – for example, *Mount Williamson – the Sierra Nevada, from Manzanar, California*, 1945. His studies of landscape divide foreground, middle ground, background and sky in a perfectly proportioned conception of landscape that echoes Plato's 'ideal form'.[8]

Looking at the object

A dominant form of philosophy in the twentieth century – phenomenology – attempted to locate metaphysical questions in terms of our lived experience, as distinct from what the intellect conceives, by exploring how meaning comes to be, and how our consciousness develops a relationship to objects outside ourselves. Phenomenology establishes that human experience is always responding to something in the world that means something to us (Levinas 1986: 14). Traditional approaches to photography originate in phenomenological attitudes that rely on the centrality of the individual in attempting to describe our experience of the world and others. The relationship between the photographer and the photographed subject depends on our interaction with others and the principle of identifying and naming the things we encounter:

Because she looks back at me, I assume that she has agreed to be photographed; I assume the right to look at this woman. My attitude to the object of representation turns Allie Mae Burroughs into an object for discussion because she is now 'captured' in an image and therefore translated into an object available to us all.

The photographic portrait visualises the position of power that resides in the active role of the subject who 'takes the picture' of someone else (the object). Note that the object is often referred to as being 'taken' by the photographer and is implicitly at their mercy.

Jean Paul Sartre's description [1943] of a pure act of self-absorption in the process of looking is demonstrated by his story of looking through a keyhole to what is in the room beyond. He describes this as an act without self-consciousness, as if consciousness is the act of looking itself – until he becomes aware of being seen by someone else (Sartre 2001: 359). In looking at others, he is the subject, framing others in relation to his world. Being looked at by someone else reverses the process so that he becomes object and thus framed by others. The major factor in the constitution of self-awareness that defines our relation to others is the co-dependent position of 'being-as-subject' or 'other-as-object'.[9] Three implicit conditions of the encounter, as described by this existential phenomenology, contribute to notions of power and possession commonly associated with photographing people: first, the centrality of the 'I' as an individual; second, the inherent suspicion of others; third, the contradictory condition that, despite being free subjects, we are influenced by others. These attitudes, applied to photography in the writings of Roland Barthes and Susan Sontag, appear persistently throughout photographic theory and critique. In *Camera Lucida* [1980], which is dedicated to Sartre's *L'Imaginaire*, Barthes's description (1993b: 11) of his self-consciousness in being photographed translates Sartre's existentialist view to the specific instance of a personal encounter with the photographer. It extends the analogy of encounter to that of photography itself, so that the photographic pose represents our relationship with others generally. Barthes describes the experience of being photographed as so influenced by the photographer's intention, so immersed is he in the inevitable performance of posing, that he loses his sense of identity and becomes an 'object' and ex-posed (Sartre 2001: 259). Because, to maintain oneself as subject, consciousness and identity have to remain together, and once being-as-subject is contained in the 'landscape' of the photograph it is possessed, appropriated and no longer itself: 'once I feel myself observed by the lens, everything changes: I transform myself in advance of the image' (Barthes 1993b: 11). The camera serves as a mechanical metaphor for the existential look, and the photographer's penetrating look perpetuates the hierarchy of subject, notions of conflict, violation and constraint associated with the photographer's control. As vulnerable photographic-objects, when photographed and in fear of revealing too much, we erect a persona that masks our true selves. Traditionally, it is the photographer's task to reveal what is hidden behind the mask.

These processes of looking and naming indicate a number of principles that influence our attitude to photographs. They involve a series of oppositions: appearance and reality, truth and fallacy, subject and object, cause and effect. The peculiar properties of the photograph, resulting from light and vision, lead to assumptions in its use. The photographer's attitude to the object of representation influences the nature of authorship; the photograph, superficially seen to be transparent, leads us to consider it as a true document; the suspicion of appearance persuades us to search for an underlying 'truth'. It is difficult to remove metaphysical references from photography's history. Assumptions interweave with attitudes and judgements, so that photography's developing aesthetic is entangled with its ontological constituents. The themes – of reality and appearance, truth and artifice – echo phenomenological debates with regard to the relationship between reality and perception and the difference between a distanced objectivity and the construction of some sort of ideal. Photography's reference to the world circulates around the possibility of its objective representation of reality, and, because expectations of photography persistently rely on these values, the photographic aesthetic perpetuates its own metaphors. As a consequence, attitudes that emerge early in photography's history fall into one of two camps: idealism and overt authorship (pictorialism in photography's terms), or raw naturalism and the fundamental argument that asks questions about what reality is or can be (realism). Conceptions of photography described as a direct access to the essence of things, or the alliance of light with alchemy (Fox Talbot 1980 [1834]), or as the 'pencil of nature' (Fox Talbot 2011 [1844]) initiate these ontological themes very early on. Simplified, the trajectory of photography's aesthetic history follows four fundamental stages or four debates which provoke change: realism and pictorialism; pictorialism and modernism; modernism and conceptualism; postmodernism.

Early aesthetic history

Ideas about what photographs should do have developed in tandem with photographers' concern to establish photography as an art form. The photograph's distinguishing feature of copying the appearance of things by mechanical means has forced the history of photography to find ways that justify it as being art and not merely a physical process. Julia Margaret Cameron's aspirations [1864] described an extreme form of idealism, which included the full range of possible themes. She identified not only the discourse between realism and idealism but also the ambition to establish photography as an acceptable form of art: 'My aspirations are to ennoble Photography and to secure for it the character and uses of High Art by combining the real and the Ideal and sacrificing nothing of Truth by all possible devotion to Poetry and beauty' (quoted in Naef 1995: 72). In their aspiration to be considered artists, photographers emulated the appearance of painting, as with Cameron's symbolic use of her subjects. *Whisper of the Muse* (1865) is a photograph of the painter G. F. Watts, which shows him between two little angelic-looking girls: one looking out of the photograph at us and the other whispering in his ear. The surface is soft, diffused and ethereal. Admiration for Watts is symbolised in the suggestion that the artist is inspired by an otherworldly force – creativity – which is only available to 'great' artists. Reliant on the photographer's assumption that the photograph must express a sentiment that should be recognisable, the photograph was staged with the intention of expressing this ideal view.[10] Oscar Rejlander's *Two Paths of Life* (1857) and Henry Peach Robinson's *When the Day's Work is Done* (1877) are examples of photography which fabricate an ideal view: the first by staging an allegorical tableau akin to classical mythological painting, and the second by juxtaposing six different negatives to create a real-life scene recognisable for its reference to Dutch interior paintings. And so, in its early history, photography invented and used symbols and aspired to something more than raw reality. In his essay 'Idealism, Realism, Expressionism' [1896], Robinson describes the photograph as 'pure, unadulterated machine-made' and 'the most perfect specimen of realism the world could produce' (Robinson 1980: 96). He recognised the defining issue as being the interface between a scientific process, an automatic mechanism and the photographer's agency – 'man and instrument'. He was concerned with the potential of photography to be used and read in different ways. However, his suggestion that it was impossible to dispense with idealism altogether heralded an important consideration for interpretation, in indicating that ideas of nature are socially constructed and that notions of realism are interchangeable with our imagination:

> [Realism] is the fashion to yearn for Nature, and to select her as bare, bald, and ugly as she is made, the particular kind being that which is the outcome not of nature, but of the errors of civilisation. But when we examine the matter closely, we find that no art to be successful, however it may try, can entirely dispense with idealism. (Robinson 1980: 92–3)

Concerned that the camera's focus should equate with the principles of vision and our experience of looking, P. H. Emerson's position was one of 'naturalism' over idealism. He introduced the dialectic between the author's interference or aestheticisation of the object and a more documentary approach. However, his 'Hints on Art' [1889] betray not only a particularly idealistic attitude that promotes photography's aesthetic value, but an individual artistic vision with the implicit aim of truth:

> Do not call yourself an 'artist-photographer' and make 'artist-painters' ... laugh; call yourself a photographer and wait for artists to call you brother ...
> Be true to yourself and individuality will show itself in your work ...
> Do not mistake sentimentality for sentiment, and sentiment for poetry ...
> Do not mistake sharpness for truth, and burnish for finish ...(Emerson 1980: 100–2)

Photography's modernism

In the twentieth century, photographers continued their exploration of what might legitimise photography as an art form. Whilst painting, post-photography, was concerned with ridding itself of representational realism in ever increasing abstraction, photographers endeavoured to justify it. For example, Edward Steichen's blurry photographs (e.g. *Self Portrait*, 1901) imitate painterly surfaces and lighting effects, evoking atmosphere and 'visual poetry'. In his essay 'Pictorial Photography' [1899], Alfred Stieglitz emphasises the subjectivity in the photograph's making. His aspiration to establish the expressive photograph as authorial signature extends the debate about what engenders the photograph's authenticity: whether it is the artists' integrity or the objectivity of the photographic process. His 'expressive realism', an

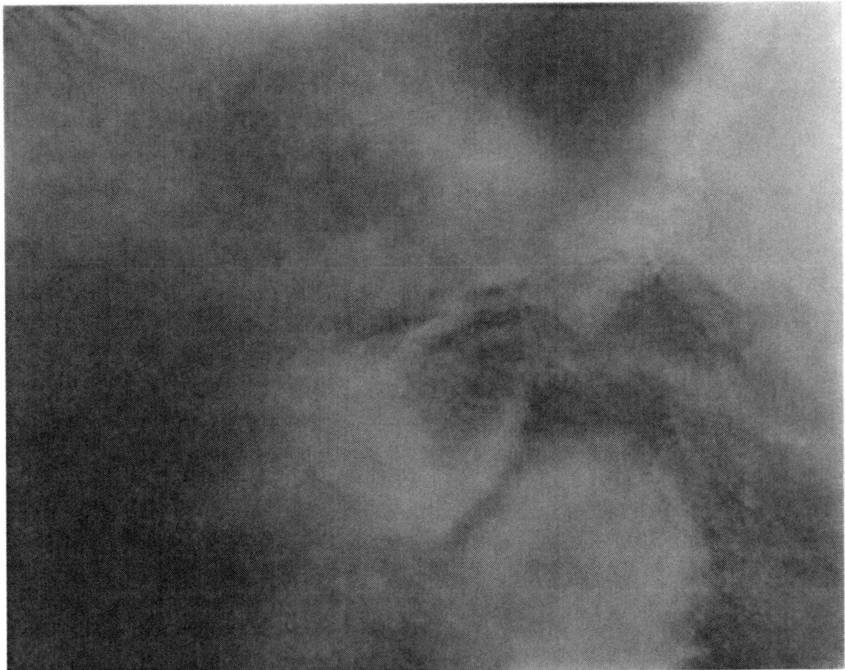

Figure 2 Alfred Stieglitz, *Equivalent*, 1923.

imitation of reality with feeling (typified by the *Equivalent* series, 1925–31),[11] aimed to demonstrate that the photograph can be seen as the visual equivalent to feeling, and thereby transcend its association as a mere physical copy of nature (Figure 2). Its ambition demonstrated the implicit aspiration for it to be recognisable as 'art'.

Each photograph in the Equivalent series has a common format that frames a cropped portion of cloud in the sky. But they do not describe cloud formations in an informative way that demonstrates their meteorological structure. They give me very little information – combinations of light and dark – that are near to abstraction. Neither can I see shapes in the clouds that suggest human form or any quirky resemblance to anything. They suggest content beyond the picture – the sky refers metonymically to the heavens, or they suggest states of being, which are presented metaphorically as – stormy, dynamic, oppressive. Stieglitz's intentions as an artist focus the dialectic concerning the photograph, conceived as 'document', and the photograph as an expressive medium for the artist's special vision (Stieglitz in Trachtenberg 1980: 115–24).

Elsewhere, other forms of modernism developed that rejected expressionistic approaches as being too artful. In Europe, the virtues and dangers of photography were a common subject for debate. László Moholy-Nagy [1927] asserted an experimental attitude that aimed to exploit the photography's unique visual properties:

> The fact of photography does not grow or diminish in value according to whether it is classified as a method of recording reality or as a medium of scientific investigation or as a way of preserving vanished events, or as basis for the process of reproduction, or as 'art'. The photographic process has no precedent among the previously known visual media. And when photography relies on its own possibilities, its results too, are without precedent ... the first and foremost issue is to develop an integrally photographic approach that is derived purely from the means of the photograph itself... (Moholy-Nagy 1989: 83)

Louis Aragon [1936] emphasised the photographic 'everyday' that celebrates its capacity to see 'what the eye fails to discern' (1989: 75). Alexander Rodchenko [1928] emphasised the photograph's ability to expand our understanding of the 'ordinary everyday object', for example, from different angles (1989: 247). El Lissitsky [1926] stressed how it can show us familiar things in a way that 'forces us to ponder them more deeply' (1989: 226). Each suggested the ordinary as metaphorically representing what is essential to life, a desire for recognition of the value in the everyday, and the camera as amplifying this phenomenological desire. The phenomenological method, which aims to understand our experience through self-reflection, is echoed in photography's concern to reveal what is hidden or neglected in ordinary things and thereby reveal what is beyond appearance. Traditionally, phenomenological methods attempted to put aside the personal and subjective in order to examine what was thought of as being universal, and to search for the certainty of pure perception or essential meaning. Similarly, Paul Strand's use of words [1917] such as 'absolute', 'honesty' and 'straight' and 'a real respect for the thing' being photographed, indicated a desire for a kind of purity. He asserted the photograph as 'an absolute unqualified objectivity. Unlike the other arts, which are really anti-photographic, this objectivity is the very essence of photography, its contribution and at the same time its limitation.' Strand advocated a 'straight' photography that was to amplify its strengths by avoiding manipulation of the process: 'The full potential power of every medium is dependent upon the purity of its use' and its fullest realisation will be without any manipulation or tricks but 'through the use of straight photographic methods' (Strand 1980: 141–2). The modernist photograph, and its search for purity in direct experience, underlies much of the ideal of 'straight' photography. 'Unadulterated' photographs have become a sign of objectivity and a purity of vision, just as a distanced objectivity has become a sign for a photographer with integrity and honesty. In Europe, between 1918 and 1933, Albert Renger-Patzsch presented a photographic realism with a sharply focused documentary quality. *Neue Sachlichkeit* (literally 'new dispassion') was concerned that photography should rely on 'its own means' and avoid emulating painterly effects because its 'secret ... resides in its realism' (Renger-Patzsch, 1989 [1927]: 105). This objectivity (the 'new objectivity' in Europe or the 'straight' photography of the United States) avoided manipulated effects and asserted a pure attitude, an integrity that adopted the most direct approach, but one that incorporated authorial expression. In America, Strand explored objectivity via a precise observation of simple objects and a belief in their potential to display poetic qualities. This tradition continued with Edward Weston, whose reverence of the object, purely displayed in a disinterested way, is exampled in photographs that treat the subject (peppers, shells or human torsos) in the same way (e.g. *Nude, Cristal Gang*, 1926, *Two Shells*, 1927).

Photographers have exploited the photograph's particular characteristics to reveal what we cannot see with our eyes or to 'capture' a fleeting moment in time. The privileging of the present and absolute moment, idealised by different accounts of phenomenology, is echoed in photographic ideals such as Henri Cartier-Bresson's 'decisive moment' [1952], which describes the vital moment as the point at which the photographer decides to press the shutter. The photographer, the camera and the shutter physically embody the fleeting transience of experience. Cartier-Bresson's *Gare St-Lazare* (1932)[12] equates the moment in which the photographer makes a decision and engages the automatic function of the camera with his artistry and vision.

I understand the extraordinary in the everyday as I notice with a surprising shock the man in mid-air as he leaps into what appears to be a still void. The ladder leads the figure nowhere as he is forever fixed in mid-air. In contrast to the leaping man, I notice the still, lone figure behind the railings watching. The glass-like surface mirrors and doubles the impact of the leap. The clock-face on the building behind registers the precise time of this moment. I anticipate disturbance to the stillness of the water that must happen in the next.

Cartier-Bresson's statement about the 'decisive moment' [1952] describes the collision of the transitory, objective moment with the photographer's subjective vision. He clearly articulates the expectation that this absolute unitary moment is dependent on the photographer's vision:

> Sometimes you have a feeling that here are all the makings of a picture except for just one thing that seems to be missing. But what one thing? . . . You wait and wait, and then finally you press the button – and you depart with the feeling (though you don't know why) that you really got something. (Cartier-Bresson 1981: 385)

Interesting divisions have developed between an attitude that photography can be objective, dependent on the automatic mechanism of the camera, and one that considers it to be wholly mediated by the photographer's agency; between an attitude that holds a certain reverence for the photographer who is assumed to be able to put subjectivity to one side, and one that insists on the photographer's artistic expression transforming the world for us. In the 1960s, a photographic aesthetic emerged that, to some extent, resolved the division between distance and objectivity and the desire for authorship and expression, and secured an authoritative position for photography as a serious alternative art form. This confidence was attributable in some degree to John Szarkowski's curation of the exhibition *The Photographer's Eye* at the Museum of Modern Art, New York in 1964, which promoted photography's potential to transform the everyday into a transcendent vision beyond the literal. The exhibition asserted photography's modernism as concerned with its own materiality, a photography that relies for its art on the author's instinct – the 'photographer's eye'. Szarkowski adopted Walker Evans's confident position as a flagship for what photography could become more generally. Evans's approach was at once intimate and distant, reconciling the duality of document and expression in what he termed *documentary style*: 'You see a document has use, whereas art is really useless. Therefore art is never a document, though it certainly can adopt a style' (Katz 1981: 364). Evans establishes an identity for photography that demonstrates it as art, marrying the physical and the spiritual, and a celebratory form of realism. He says: 'Unless I feel that the product is a *transcendence* of the thing, of the moment of reality, then I haven't done anything, and I throw it away' (362). In paradoxical fashion, 'high' photographic modernism developed a tradition of a restrained, functional and largely black-and-white aesthetic, which relied on its own physical properties. Aesthetic formalism, of the sort championed by Clement Greenberg (2005 [1960]), prioritises the medium over the subject-matter to the extreme position of banishing reference to the outside world altogether, as with abstract expressionist painting. Echoing Greenberg's call for painting to be true to the nature of its material and process, another form of idealism is established – photography's mid-century modernism of the 'straight' photographic document, which has the quality of objectivity, is true to its materiality *and* is imbued with the author's expression. Expressing the real, in the manner of 'straight' photography, became increasingly seen as authentic and, as is the way with photography's alliance with authenticity, was judged to be the most valid.

There were other uses of photography, which ran in parallel with the classic modernism described above. A series of avant-gardes – Futurism, Dada and Surrealism – each made use of photography and contributed particularly to the possibilities of collage and fragmentation, rather than realistic representational forms, and for that reason I do not describe them here except for the Surrealists' attitude to reality (to which I return in Chapter Five). Some aspects of collage anticipated developments later in the century, especially following the advent of digital processes. Significant for this discussion, since the influence of conceptual art practices in the 1960s, and their use of photography, is that two very separate histories (modernist photography and fine art) have converged. The processes of meaning inserted by conceptual art is particularly pertinent to photography because it promoted exchange between the use of language and the image and questioned the need for a work of art to be dependent on resemblance, which the photograph embodies. Sol LeWitt presented a version of art that placed the idea and the visual as being inter-dependent, where the process of conception and the process of visualisation are of equal importance. Kosuth's *One and Three Chairs* (chair, photograph and verbal definition) presents a visual expansion of Plato's idea of the one true and universal chair (Figure 3). Kosuth, in questioning aesthetic formalism, posited that the idea itself can be considered as art and shifted the emphasis from the material and visual to the conceptual content – a shift from looking to reading – exemplified by the work of the Art & Language

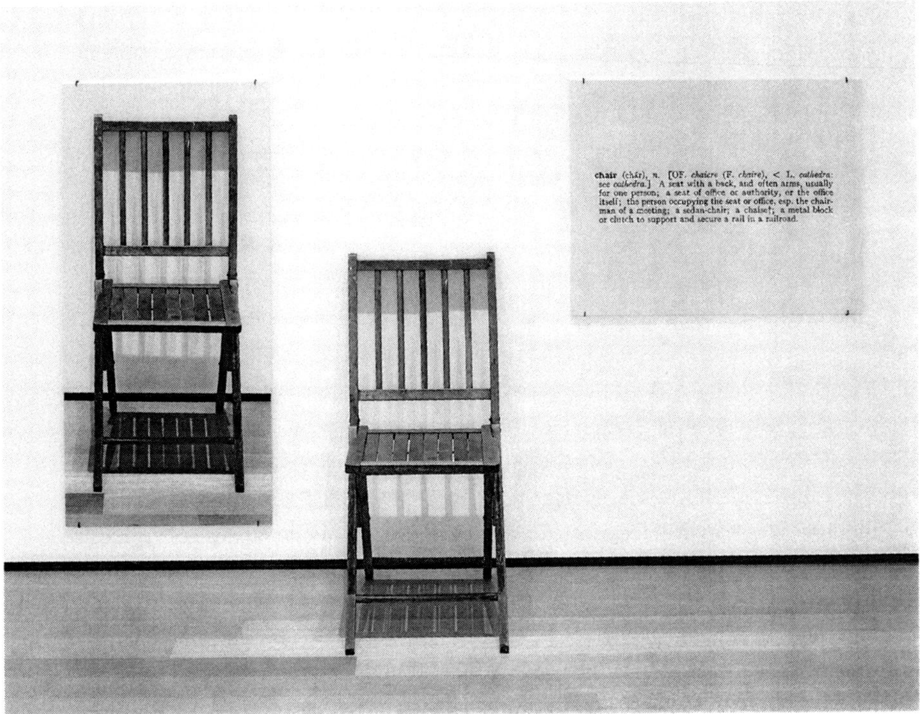

Figure 3 Joseph Kosuth, *One and Three Chairs*, 1965.

group, founded in 1967–68.[13] In addition, Andy Warhol's use of the photograph as a 'readymade' and Ed Ruscha's work introduced an anti-aesthetic of indifference to the skill and integrity of photographic conventions. For example, Ruscha's *Twentysix Gasoline Stations* (1963) is presented as a kind of topography in the form of a book. The photograph is positioned on the right-hand side, and on the left-hand side are the name of the station and the location. In this process, the photograph is used simply as a recording device, eliminating attempts at expression and for the most part only taking one shot of each station. However, aiming for a mass-produced object with a 'clear-cut machine finish', twenty-six frames sharing a common format were selected (Ruscha, quoted in Wolf 2004: 120). Conceptual art adopted photography to effect ideas and in many respects enabled photography to develop in other ways than candid realism. These attitudes will be seen as significant for the consideration of later examples of photographic realism in the chapters that follow.

Terminologies

A photograph features layers of meaning on a number of levels. In contrast to what may be popularly believed, there are few facts that one can attribute to a photograph. A photograph is more a display than description; it is ambiguous, possessing simultaneous properties that generate multiple associations and prohibit definitive interpretation (Goodman 1969: 26–30). Visual qualities, such as subtle variations of tone, texture or contrast, and numerous references lead us away from, and confuse, the more informative aspects. For example, *Equivalents* uses the literal description of clouds – the gradations of light and dark, the particular dynamic and character of the shape – to express feelings. Few photographic properties are merely informational and yet, with their facility to give us a likeness of things, we tend to consider a photographic image as fact when it is not; it is a representation. The development of visual semiotics has given us the terminology with which to talk about meaning in photography. Using the term 'reading' with regard to photographs does not imply that they can be translated literally into verbal text, but that they can necessitate a 'reading' that requires the reader to be more actively engaged than 'looking' passively, and can be considered in terms of an interrelation with aspects of theory. An active reading of representation has developed in response to structural systems of analysis that attempt to systemise the processes of meaning.

Nelson Goodman's *Languages of Art* (1969) gives a detailed explanation of the complex procedure of representation and the role of mediation in reading images. It clarifies distinctions between the different functions of meaning operating in an image: between referent (the object referenced in a photograph), property (the qualities in treatment of that object) and feeling, and the association with mood and character (what is provoked). Goodman's analysis identifies the key condition as being the relationship between different elements and the context in which they are found. For example, the closely cropped frame of *Allie Mae Burroughs* does not show us the conditions in which she lives. Thus a photograph possesses certain properties, refers to certain objects, leaves many factors out and expresses by provocation and projection. What the photograph refers to does not determine the kind of photograph it is or how we come to understand that representation. Representation depends on the kind of representational system within which a photograph is seen. For example, the systems of 'art' and 'journalism' are driven by different motivations and traditions. A deliberately obscure art-photograph may be ambiguous in appearance and invoke complex meaning. An apparently straightforward descriptive photograph may be less ambiguous in content, but may be more laden with intention, as with journalistic imagery, which may have a political agenda. In a supposedly informational context, such as journalism, a photograph may be understood as descriptive, but it is doubtful that any photograph can be merely informational and not influence the meaning that the selected frame and context implies. A photograph of someone, once recognised as a category of photograph, in the sub-category of 'portrait', will be qualified by the expectations of that genre; it is a 'representation-as' portrait, which influences the way we respond to it (Goodman 1969: 26–30). In the context and history of fine art, the appearance and *idea* of 'portrait' or 'documentary' will therefore act as a kind of constraint.[14] Goodman's procedure requires us always to ask two distinctly different questions: what is described and what is its agenda? Is it aiming to comment, as in journalism, or use the object of reference to describe inner feelings as with *Equivalent*, or to 'capture' a true likeness, as in the portrait?

The structural analysis of images owes its development to adaptations of Ferdinand de Saussure's theories of signs, *Course in General Linguistics* (1983 [published posthumously, 1916]), and Charles Sanders Peirce's *Collected Writings* (published posthumously 1931–55), which each contribute a different emphasis to understanding meaning production. Peirce's model has three elements: *representatum*, *interpretant* and *object*. In photographic terms these translate as the photograph, the sense or meaning in the photograph and what is referred to in the real world – what is commonly called the *referent*. Saussure's model has two elements (*signifier* and *signified*), which together constitute the *sign*. It does not have a term for the material object in the real world and refers to the 'mental image', which emphasises that representation is not to be confused with the real world and can only be constructed. Joseph Kosuth demonstrates the fact that there are many ways to represent something in *One and Three Chairs* (1965), which features a physical chair, a photograph of a chair and a dictionary definition of the word 'chair'. What they each provoke is the concept of a chair as a constant idea (Figure 3). Peirce's model does not assume that meaning is linguistic, and emphasises the relationship between its three elements and how they generate meaning in visual representations. Peirce identified a complex system of interrelating classifications defined in terms of the kind of relation between the sign and object. *Icon*, *index* and *symbol* are the most commonly referred to: *Icon* refers to a relationship that depends on some sort of resemblance or similarity, so that a photograph of a person, a 'portrait', is an *icon* of that person. *Index* refers to a factual or causal relationship between *sign* and what is *signified*; for example, smoke is an *index* for fire. A *symbol* is a *sign* that is conventionally or culturally recognisable as such (e.g. in Western culture, a red rose is a recognisable *symbol* of 'love'). Peirce's system focuses on meaning being dependent on interpretation rather than initial conception. In Saussure's model the physical *signifier* provokes a concept in our mind; it establishes the arbitrariness of the relationship between the *signifier* and the concept it refers to; it points to how one sign readily leads to another in a chain of signification. This importantly indicates that the production of meaning is dependent on the cultural context in which the photograph appears.

There are many terms used in semiotic analysis and, if used indiscriminately, they can be confusing. The frequently used term 'indexical' refers to the causative link between the chemical operation of light and the photograph, between the referent and its representation in a photograph. This is complicated by our general use of the terms *indication*, *indicate* and *indicative*. In photography, the *referent* is simply the concrete object in the real world that is depicted by the photograph. The relationship between the photograph and the *referent* is by denotation; the photograph denotes (indicates, refers to) the object (*referent*). But this term *referent* (whatever is referred to), can be confusing when it is used also to refer to actions, histories or relationships. Because a photograph also *signifies* concepts and associations, ideas and events as well as material objects, interpretation becomes complicated when photographs rely on knowledge of such contexts – as I discuss in the next chapter.

Readings and influences

Structuralism applied aspects of linguistic theory to the task of reading photographs and helped to establish the premise of looking at images as another form of reading. Umberto Eco's 'rhetorical codes' (1982 [1970]) present an extreme form of structural approach to understanding photographs which suggests that, because they are not natural but culturally coded, they are a readable language that we can learn to decipher. He emphasises the difference between looking at and interpreting the image, and looking at the same object in the real world. Examples of analyses such as Goodman's and Eco's lend clarification to the structure of meaning. However, as I will discuss in the next chapter, post-structuralism exposes structural classification as arguably inadequate because most photographic projects are complex amalgams of a number of categories and contexts. Goodman's definitions make sense within the parameters of structuralism, which aims to find a system for decoding images, but are limited when looking at photographs, which are, in his own terms, 'dense' and immeasurable.

A series of key theorists have contributed a range of perspectives with which to respond to photographs and which help us to understand the difference between what we see and what we understand: the object, the associations provoked by the photograph and the ideas attached to the object, so that the *Equivalent* series accesses clouds, and the weather and states of consciousness. There are different approaches to looking at photographs and none of them takes a photograph at face value, but all offer differing attitudes. I outline here contributions made by some key commentators on photography that will be important for discussion in following chapters.[15] Roland Barthes's writings are hugely influential in the development of 'photographic theory', from his earlier structural explanations to his last work *Camera Lucida* (1980), which applies a very subjective view to remnants of his own structuralism. Notions of 'reading photographs' are associated with Barthes's earlier essays, 'The Photographic Message' [1961], 'The Rhetoric of the Image' [1964] and 'The Third Meaning' [1970] in which he echoes the implications raised by Peirce's and Saussure's systems – notably the role of interpretation or context. These essays identify three levels of meaning in an image, ranging from informational to symbolic, to a third dimension which is difficult to define. His use of the terms denotation and connotation is useful. Denotation refers to what is discernible as informational meaning – the objects referred to, the focus of the image, the formal facts of position, lighting and shapes. Connotation is more 'obtuse' and refers to the historical, ideological and cultural, symbolic meaning or relates to a particular genre: reportage, landscape or family snapshot (Goodman's 'representation-as'). He describes 'connotative procedures' as those factors affecting the making of the image directly (e.g. lighting), and the more indirect 'gestures, attitudes, expressions' that endow the image with meaning because of the cultural context in which they are found.

Barthes's analysis exposes the photograph's naturalness, and transparency, as a myth. The photographer's interventions at the outset insert too much mediated content for the photograph to be used as a literal message (Barthes 1977: 44). There is no possibility of grasping the photograph in any immediate sense; rather, it is immersed in cultural connotation to such an extent that we cannot itemise distinctive elements because they are mediated by ideological and aesthetic values. He suggests that analysis using photographic codes – if presented as constant, universal or 'trans-historical' – can tell us more about the society in which they are found than the photographs to which they are applied. For example, a photograph that presents a shell or a pepper as beautiful tells us that the photographic community values simple form as a mark of quality. Barthes describes the photograph as a 'form of paradox', which transforms a 'mechanical art into the most social of institutions' (Barthes 1977: 31–6). His analysis concludes that photography is more allied to analogy (clouds = consciousness) than communication. Barthes asserts that the photograph resists definitive analysis of meaning and, because different levels of meaning are complex, the photograph as an art form is a 'rhetoric' that depends on the *relationships* between elements because there is no direct relation between sign and concept as there is with language. He differentiates between photographic objectivity, its reference to real things, and aspects that impart quality and which are more elusive as a result of its treatment, its genre and its aesthetic frame (Barthes 1977: 49–50). And, because a photograph is also subject to the constraints of context and time, it is unlikely that we could establish a complete inventory of all the meaning available to it. His discussion introduces questions about photographic signification that continue to be useful: 'How do we read a photograph? What do we perceive?' 'How does meaning get into the image? Where does it end? And if it ends, what is there beyond?' (Barthes 1977: 28, 49). Barthes's writing thus explores the 'real unreality of the photograph' and its lack of immediacy or presence. It anticipates many of the questions developed later by Derrida and Foucault, which I will discuss in Chapter Two and throughout Part II.

Walter Benjamin's classic texts 'A Short History of Photography' (1980 [1931]) and 'The Work of Art in the Age of Mechanical Reproduction' (2005 [1936]) introduce a number of contentious issues that confront the photographer's starting premise. Writing about photography well before Barthes, his ideas introduce more subtly political considerations. First, he discusses the photograph as fundamentally changing our attitude to what art might be, as it rids it of *aura*, the unique factor in a work of art that inspires awe in its presence. Second, he refers to the photograph's peculiar phenomenological capacity to present us with something past – its 'uniqueness and duration . . . closely entwined' (Benjamin 1980: 210), which Barthes later explores in his subjective expansion in *Camera Lucida*. Third, Benjamin points out the dangers of removing the photograph from context, which Allan Sekula, for example, later develops. Benjamin quotes Baudelaire's concerns about those that believe photography gives an 'exact reproduction of nature' (Benjamin 1980: 214). And he quotes Bertolt Brecht: 'A photograph of the Krupp works or of the A. E. G. reveals almost nothing about these institutions' – in other words photographs tell us little about the hidden politics involved (Benjamin 1980: 213). Benjamin points to the significant impact that the introduction of photography has on the notion of authenticity in art practice. In ridding the work of art of uniqueness, mechanical reproduction 'emancipates' it from its 'parasitical dependence on ritual', by which he means the conventions of originality, for example. Photography liberates painting and enables it to do something else than resemble the appearance of the world in illusion. On the other hand, photography provides the social function of making images more available to the masses, because it is so easily reproduced. From a photographic negative, for example, one can make any number of prints, so to ask for the 'authentic' print makes no sense. Potentially, the total function of art is reversed. Instead of being motivated by ritual conventions such as mastery or uniqueness, it has the capacity to be based on other principles such as politics. However, the reaction of art in the nineteenth century, in the face of 'the first truly revolutionary means of reproduction', was to reiterate its position as art for art's sake, which Benjamin terms 'a theology of art' (Benjamin 2005: 522). Benjamin's critique highlights the social function of art and importantly indicates a division that exacerbates the dilemma for photographic aesthetics. For photography, the instant the criterion of authenticity ceases to be applicable to artistic production, its potential becomes something else other than compositionally beautiful. But in the nineteenth century, photography's concern was to establish an equivalent position as an art form by assuming the same criteria as painting. It is not until later that photography becomes confident enough to assert its material potential. However, the potential that Benjamin envisaged was exploited, not in mainstream photography, but in avant-garde movements such as Surrealism and in the emergence, later in the 1970s, of a concern for the political responsibility of context and social function that is addressed in works by, for example, Allan Sekula, Martha Rosler, Victor Burgin and Jo Spence.

Susan Sontag's *On Photography* [1977] discusses the attempts of successive generations of photographers to show us reality through new, 'photographic eyes'. It anticipates most assumptions presented to us by photography, and articulates a view that demonstrates humanism as being the leading ideology because it hides the confusions of 'about truth and beauty underlying the photographic enterprise' (Sontag 1979: 112).

> Insofar as photography does peel away the dry wrappers of habitual seeing, it creates another habit of seeing: both intense and cool, solicitous and detached; charmed by the insignificant detail, addicted to incongruity. But photographic seeing has to be constantly renewed with new shocks, whether of subject matter or technique, so as to produce the impression of violating ordinary vision. For, challenged by the revelations of photographers, seeing tends to accommodate to photographs … . What it once took a very intelligent eye to see, anyone can see now. Instructed by photographs, everyone is able to visualise that once purely literary conceit, the geography of the body for example, photographing a pregnant woman so that her body looks like a hillock, a hillock so that it looks like the body of a pregnant woman. (Sontag 1979: 99–100)

Sontag argues that photographic seeing makes things appear 'normal' after a period of time. Once something has been shown to us in a new light, it soon becomes common-place and we look for another way of looking. One might say that photographers are constantly looking for new ways of seeing the world to shock us into noticing. Photographers are seen to be recyclers of visions, analogies and meaning, contributing to the production of cliché, and anaesthetising reality 'as a spectacle (for masses) and as an object of surveillance (for rulers) it substantiates a ruling ideology' (Sontag 1979: 178–9). Sontag emphasises the power of photographs to influence and deceive. Photographic images are powerful in their very ubiquity; leaving us bereft of discrimination; readily responding to, or ignoring, the beautiful, the pitiable and the horrific. She relates the ease with which 'an ugly or grotesque subject may be moving because it has been dignified by the attention of the photographer' (Sontag 1979: 15). It has become any purposeful photographer's obligation to cut through blandness and, in so doing, run the risk of elevating the subject, as the photograph can so easily transform a subject into an object of display, as with the beauty or the dignity of the poor or distressed (Sontag 1979: 102). Her later book (2003) offers a thorough account of the ability of the photograph to invoke sympathy or protest. Both she and later Jean Baudrillard are demonstrative in their acknowledgement of photography's ability to misrepresent and be used as a substitute for a real connection to the world.

John Berger has written in a lyrical way about photography and from a sociological, humanist perspective. He has emphasised a paradoxical feature of the tradition of documentary photography, which is founded on the motivation to tell the truth about a situation and inform the world. In *Another Way of Telling* [1982] he demonstrates the ambiguity of photographs, and examines how they can be seen as telling truth or lies. At its birth, photography was thought to provide the truth and it was believed that it would replace subjectivity 'and all that was dark and hidden in the soul would be illuminated by empirical knowledge' (Berger and Mohr 1995: 99). He questions the degree to which photographs can record definite fact, stating that facts do not constitute meaning. One photograph can lead us to completely different meanings and be taken out of context or driven by different agendas (Berger and Mohr 1995: 102). So, for example, *Allie Mae Burroughs* can be discussed, in the context of the FSA project, as evidence of the conditions of hardship in rural Alabama at the time; or it can be discussed in the context of its inscrutability as portrait; or it can be discussed from the point of view of the photographer's attitude to photographing people. Berger describes photographs as culture's constructions, which quote from appearances, rather than translate, and if they do not translate they cannot lie: 'The camera does not lie even when it is used to quote a lie. And so, this makes the lie appear more truthful' (Berger and Mohr 1995: 97). The fact that they do lie results from the fact that they only quote fragments and that the truth they tell is only limited. For example, the particular photograph of *Allie Mae Burroughs*, with which we are familiar, omits the background environment and focuses our attention on the subject's integrity, rather than her circumstances.

Given that photographs are deceptive and that semiological systems do not explain them adequately, Berger asks: 'How is it possible for appearances to "give birth" to ideas?' (Berger and Mohr 1995: 122) How do they give us meaning? How do they function? How do they move us? How do they endure? He suggests that the ambiguity lies in the 'abyss' of space and time, between the moment that the photograph is taken and the moment of looking at it (Berger and Mohr 1995: 89). He pursues the idea that a photograph effects a duration of meaning by 'unfolding' meaning, by telling a story, which develops as the viewer reads. He explores how 'appearances cohere', how they pull thoughts, memories and associations together, and lead to expectations, imaginations and possibilities. He speaks of the hidden 'photographic possibility' and the capacity of some photographs to 'extend the event beyond itself'. He concludes that a photograph articulates a general idea, by uniting the particular with the universal, which is what lends it 'duration' of meaning beyond appearance (Berger and Mohr 1995: 126). The generalising effect of the photograph will later be seen to divide thinkers: Berger, who celebrates the capacity of the photograph to do this, and Sekula and Tagg, who warn against the removal from context.

Discussion of photography presupposes metaphorical relationships – between camera and vision, vision and photography, photographer and 'subject', light and truth, truth and reality. Access to photographic meaning is not as simple as it might seem, not just a matter of what is there before us, and difficult to disentangle from the photograph's ontological and aesthetic history. Photography's ontology and approaches to analysis are allied to photography's recurring relationship with realism, and the 'reading' of photographs is dependent on different perspectives and contexts. These key metaphysical themes establish a base from which to explore the development of practice and aesthetic change, and the next chapter considers the ways in which traditional ideas about photographic relationships are disassembled.

Suggested further reading

Barthes, R. (1977) 'The Photographic Message' [1961] and 'Rhetoric of the Image' [1964], in *Image: Music: Text*, trans. S. Heath, Fontana Press, London

Bate, D. (2009) *Photography: The Key Concepts*, Berg, Oxford; New York

Berger, J. and J. Mohr (1995) *Another Way of Telling* [1982], Vintage Books, New York

Edwards, S. (2006) *Photography: A Very Short Introduction*, Oxford University Press, Oxford

Friday, J. (2002) *Aesthetics and Photography*, Ashgate, Aldershot

Sontag, S. (1979) *On Photography* [1973], Penguin, London

Trachtenberg, A. (ed.) (1980) *Classic Essays on Photography*, Leete's Island Books, New Haven

Wells, L. (ed.) (2000) *Photography: A Critical Introduction*, Routledge, London

Notes

1 Beaumont Newhall's *History of Photography: From 1839 to the Present* (1949) presents a modernist view of the history of photography.

2 See for example See Jeffrey 1992: 351–6; Iverson 1994, 450–64; Charlesworth 1995, 207–15.

3 When using terms such as 'truth', 'reality' and 'real', I have used quote marks to indicate that the term is disputed or relies on a raft of assumptions and values, or is dependent on the context in which it is used. From here on, after the first use of such a term, I relinquish the quote marks.

4 This is an example of text written in the first person (always indicated by italics) in which I describe a photograph – they can sit somewhere between description and reverie. The passages aim to emphasise the experience of viewing a photograph. They also provide a break in tone from the discursive sections. This establishes a practice of immediate response that describes what can be seen, which cannot be wholly objective but acknowledges the relevance of the viewer's subjective response. They also serve as examples of rhetorical argument, a device that will be developed as a theme in photography practice. Chapter Three will provide a precedent for this manner of writing with reference to Derrida's writing on photography. (See pp. 73–4)

5 Photographs by Walker Evans taken in 1936 of the Burroughs family can be viewed on the Library of Congress website: 'The photographs in the Farm Security Administration – Office of War Information Photograph Collection form an extensive pictorial record of American life between 1935 and 1944. This U.S. government photography project was headed for most of its existence by Roy E. Stryker, who guided the effort in a succession of government agencies: the Resettlement Administration (1935–1937), the Farm Security Administration (1937–1942), and the Office of War Information (1942–1944).' Search for Walker Evans and Burroughs at www.loc.gov/pictures/collection/fsa and http://memory.loc.gov/ammem/fsahtml/fsainfo.html, accessed 8 August 2010.

6 Plato's theory of forms refers to the idea of immutable states and timeless truths. For example, the 'concept' of a green leaf will always be green – it doesn't wither and turn brown as we know leaves do. When thinking about green leaves, we have in mind something that is common to all green leaves – whatever variety. See Gilbert Ryle, www.philosophicalsociety.com/Archives/Plato/

7 Square brackets are used to indicate date of original publication and before translation.

8 See www.masters-of-photography.com/A/adams/adams_clearing_storm_full.html, accessed 23 August 2012.

9 A hyphenated concept such as 'being-as-subject' is shorthand for the notion of someone looking at others as objects. I will refer to a number of these; for example, the 'photographic-subject' indicates anyone who is photographed, or 'representation-as-portrait' is shorthand for a representation carrying the history and conventions of portrait.

10 See the collection in the Victoria & Albert Museum – www.vam.ac.uk/images/image/4240-popup.html, accessed 8 August 2010.

11 See for example the collection in the Museum of Modern Art, New York –www.moma.org/collection/object.php?object_id=44200, accessed 23 August 2012.

12 This image can be found on many websites. See for example, http://collections.glasgowmuseums.com/viewimage.html?oid=164442&i=382183, accessed 23 August 2012.

13 Further discussion of the influences of conceptual art follows in Chapter Eight. See www.artandlanguage.co.uk (accessed 8 September 2010), and search 'conceptual art' on the Tate website: www.tate.org.uk..

14 Goodman's 'representation-as' refers to the far-reaching implications of Ludwig Wittgenstein's *Philosophical Investigation* (2001 [1953]), in which he considers how we see any thing in terms of something else.

15 Barthes's contribution is unavoidable as it covered structural analysis and introduced subjective response as valid, taking photography's discourse in a wholly different direction – hence its influence. Most recently, and too late for this discussion, Elkins (2010) offers an extended critique of Barthes's singular melancholy. Other theories of photography I could describe were not translated into English so readily and have not been so influential – such as Henri Van Lier's *Philosophy of Photography* (2007 [1983]) and Vilém Flusser, *Towards a Philosophy of Photography* (2000 [1983]).

2

Practice/theory exchange

This chapter aims to establish a theoretical foundation for the examples of photography that will be discussed in Part II. It briefly outlines the significance of post-structural theories that have radically adjusted how we understand subjectivity and representation.[1] It focuses on a selection of key thinkers who have influenced the way we think about interpretation and practice: Barthes's attitude towards subjectivity, Foucault's attitude to knowledge and discourse, Derrida's rhetorical structures and Kristeva's attitude to the developing subject. Each of these has an interdisciplinary approach that has included discussion of visual work. Many post-structural texts parallel a chronology in the development of ideas in art practice. For example, Derrida's *Speech and Phenomena* (1973 [1967]) and Kosuth's *One and Three Chairs* (1965) are both concerned with the differentiation, definition and context for understanding meaning, and both embody changes in attitudes to critical thinking and representation, marking a significant point of transition.

Rhetorical display

Arsen Savadov's work is typical of an increasingly rhetorical display evident in photographic work of the 1980s and 1990s. Savadov was born in the Ukraine in 1962, and his theatrical tableaux bring together incongruous references – romance, high culture and industrialisation – to depict a collapsed Soviet ideology. As part of the series *Collective Red Part I* (1998), *Bloody Merry* juxtaposes reference to the 1917 Russian revolution with the interior of a slaughterhouse (Figure 4). *Bloody Merry* refers back to earlier styles of painting in its combination of intellectual and idealistic content with artificial and bizarre visual qualities. It is reminiscent of neo-classical paintings that used mythical themes to speak of morality or religion, such as the grandiose formalism of Jacques-Louis David's *The Death of Socrates* (1787) or the later Romanticism of the nineteenth century such as Eugène Delacroix's *Liberty Leading the People* (1830), which is politically motivated and full of symbolism. *Bloody Merry* does not depict a real scene but an ideological fantasy, which speaks simultaneously of tragedy and humour:

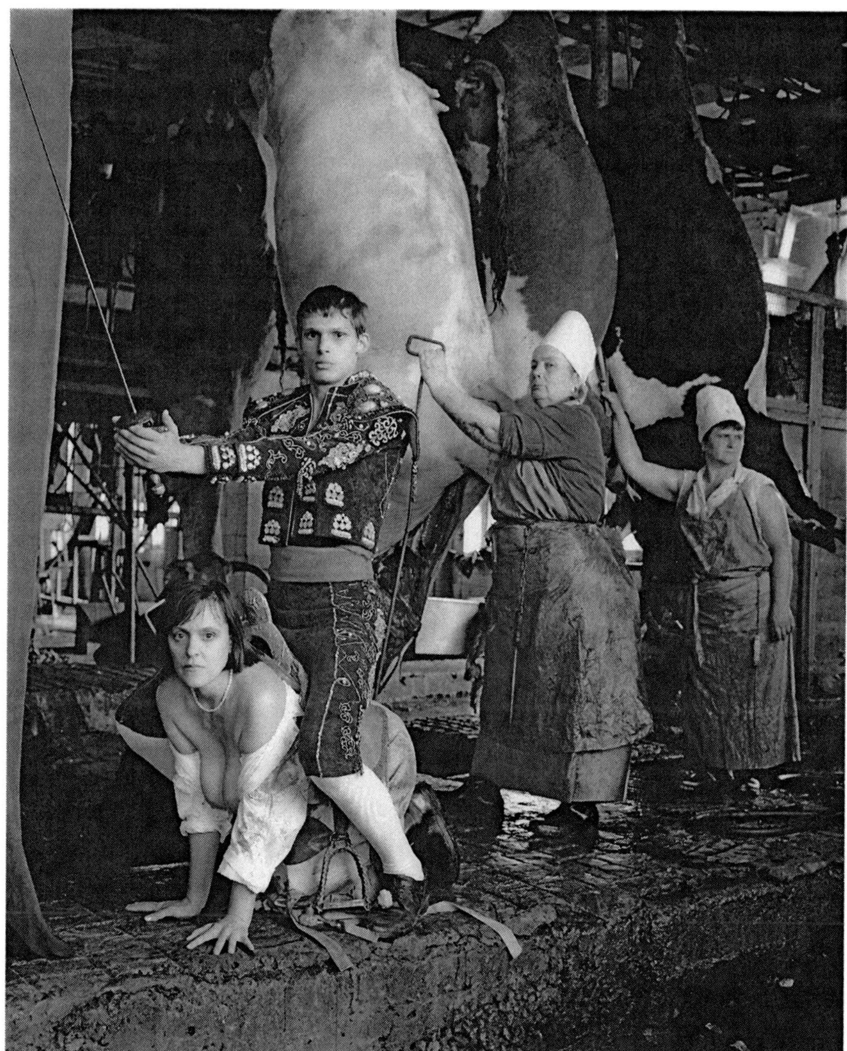

Figure 4 Arsen Savadov, *Bloody Merry,* Collective Red I series, 1998.

The characters wear nineteenth-century costume that references class divisions and the military. They are not positioned naturalistically but are organised geometrically and in an artificial manner that displays what I suppose are the hierarchical relationships between them. The woman posed on all fours is 'mounted' by the young man wielding a sword. This pose, suggestive of sexuality, is exaggerated by the fact that the photograph is most obviously staged and stylised, as the two characters in the foreground look defiantly, unconcernedly, at the camera. The extraordinary political event of bloody revolution contrasts with the ordinary but inevitably unpleasant consequence of meat consumption; the hidden horrors of the slaughterhouse associate with the hidden and suppressed horrors of Soviet rule; the ideological social advance of revolution contrasts with the harsh realities of the communist state; bloody contrasts with bloodless revolution. Blood is used as a repetitive referent; there is blood on the white sleeve of the woman on the floor, on the aprons of the two standing women, the carcasses of meat and implicitly in the red jacket of the young man. Savadov's work demonstrates a network of meaning, made more complex by its staging. It indicates a number of characteristic features that have become commonplace: it is demonstratively expressive in an artificially mannered way; it displays layers of contradictory meaning; its numerous references include concrete objects, historical events and ideological concepts; it is implicitly reliant on our knowledge of history and context for it to make sense; because it is a constructed tableau and thereby not real, it relinquishes what is rationally believable and approaches the absurd and nonsensical; it treats history and memory as if they were forms of reality. Bloody Merry is a visual rhetorical display that critiques the absurdity and ironies that exist in such histories by drawing parallels and pointing out contradictions. The relevance of Derrida's work in this regard lies fundamentally with his rhetorical display of meaning that incorporates his argument in the manner of his writing. He uses a play of words to draw parallels and point out contradictions.

Play of difference

The importance of Derrida's work for a post-structural reading of photographs starts with his procedure of questioning assumptions at every level of representation, which has influenced how we understand the construction of meaning. He consistently disturbs what are considered to be normal procedures and our reliance on logical and structural forms of analysis. For example, he questions Peirce and Saussure's analytical models, and demonstrates that linguistic representation is not straightforwardly transparent. He extends Saussure's emphasis that meaning is constructed by the play of differences and similarities between one word and another, and which distinguish one concept or thing from another. He highlights the capacity of a sign to constantly generate further meaning in an ongoing process of association and interpretation (Derrida 1973: 140). So, for example, the words 'pose', 'expose', 'position', 'supposition' reverberate around the similarities between them, their nuances of meaning, their different etymological origins, and the differences in their meaning in different contexts. Similarly, photographic landscapes have the concept 'landscape' and 'photograph' in common and will always resemble, and differ from, an Ansel Adams photographic landscape. Derrida states: 'every concept is necessarily and essentially inscribed in a chain or a system, within which it refers to ... other concepts' (1973: 133). He describes this process of differential construction as 'assemblage' that allows 'different lines of sense' to interweave and separate again. It is particularly pertinent for the way that we understand visual ideas, which may have several 'lines of sense' working simultaneously. In the network of concepts in *Bloody Merry*, a military uniform leads us to think of war, blood and dead meat, and the presence of blood in a photograph will always make death present as a possibility.

Philosophy's traditional starting premise searches for pure essential meaning that exists independently from the signifier (word or image) and asks: what is its one meaning? So, when looking at photographs, we expect a degree of transparency in being able to name what is represented; we logically start with the subject matter and ask: What is this? Whereas an inter-dependent chain or system of meaning, which prompts many definitions, puts into question what is considered to be 'fact', 'truth' or 'reality' (1973: 139). His oft-quoted statement 'there never was any "perception", in simple terms, rejects the possibility of our perception being pure or unaffected by existing knowledge (1973: 103).[2] This attitude, echoed in texts by Barthes and Foucault, questions idealised abstractions of meaning and insists that experience and representation must be influenced by context and interpretation. In consequence, the particularity of context becomes a positive characteristic of post-structural debate and practice. Derrida introduces an interest in what is beyond, below or besides what is articulated or visible, by constantly exploiting what is only very slightly implied in his use of language – in what is absent. An important aspect in responding to photographs is that we can look for what is implied by both what is present *and* what is absent, so that we ask: What is not visible? What is implicit or *besides* the subject depicted? What is provoked? What meanings are constructed around the object?

The dispersal of meaning

Derrida's written neologism *différance* provides a model that embodies a change in attitude toward the desire to establish fixed meaning. I will use it here to illustrate the shift of emphasis in understanding representation in general. *Différance* plays on the grammatical differences between noun (indicating concept or object), adjective (indicating property) and verb (indicating action). *Différance* derives from the French verb *différer*, which bears two meanings – one refers to spatiality like the English verb 'to differ', to be dissimilar, distinct, discernable as different. The other meaning refers to temporality like the English verb 'to defer', to delay or postpone (1973: 129–30). The principles of difference and delay associated with *différance* are pertinent to a consideration of the photograph's framing of space and the transience of a moment in time and will be seen as recurring themes throughout discussion in later chapters. *Différance*, as it combines difference (the spatial) and deferral (the temporal), encourages the play of many different meanings, which are sometimes contradictory and resist logical progression towards synthesis. Derrida distinguishes what he refers to as 'dissemination' (which *disperses* meaning), from 'polysemia' (having multiple meanings), which he describes as representing the desire to anchor and organise multiple meanings by finding one that is 'unitary', original or shared (Derrida 1982a: 45). In the context of writing, dissemination undermines two basic principles – the logical sequencing down the page of one point following another and the logic of something definitely being either this *or* that. Applying the principle of dissemination to photographs undermines dependence on the defining characteristics of photographic depiction. Modernist photography traditionally aspires to finding universal significance in the subject. And because a photograph depicts objects caught momentarily, we tend to focus on the concrete substance of objects, rather than what is in the process of happening or might happen. Derrida's approach shifts attention away from literal subject-matter. Acceptance of the inevitable dispersal of meaning challenges modernist aspirations to find essential meaning, or the authority of photographic definition that expects 'objectivity', or the expectation of an expression of truth behind appearance. Dissemination introduces what *might* be and what is not literal, so that the Russian uniform in *Bloody Merry* provokes an assemblage of different possibilities that may or may not be so, and defers the possibility of finding unitary meaning. This adjustment to thinking about representation signals a move toward an avoidance of the universal symbolic purpose found, for example, in Cameron's *Whisper of the Muse* (1865). Dissemination suggests that we can relinquish what is rational and enjoy absurdity.[3]

Derrida's writing makes use of two elements, besides reference to objects or concepts, to demonstrate figurative meaning in verbal representation. First, the performance in the way that something is uttered in speech and, second, the very visibility of the written form that shows us additional differences, which are not distinguishable in speech. Speech expresses in ways that writing cannot – by its intonation, stress, rhythm, emotion. Writing can do things speech cannot such as make visual connections – *différance* needs its visibility in written form to show the full play of its significance. By exploiting visuality and the manner of performance, Derrida's theoretical position is inseparable from the way it is expressed. The rhetorical display embedded in the term *différance* demonstrates that expression cannot be separated from form. In a photograph, the logical reference to objects can be seen superficially as visual evidence of reality – here is a picture of *x* – simple. On another level, there is all manner of complexity that the referent signifies. Structural analysis attempted to distinguish separate constituents of the photograph: the photograph's formal aspects such as depth of field, the photograph's literal reference to objects, and the photographic rhetoric – that is, the mode of expression and style used. Derrida's attitude to representation insists that the referent is simultaneously influenced by the manner of expression, in the selection and framing of the image, in the context in which it is shown, in the position of those contained in the image and so on. Derrida's gesture of visual signification signals an important change that gives emphasis to *how* something is expressed in addition to *what* is expressed. An emphasis that does not separate logic from expression can be seen in the demonstrative methods used by photographers, such as Savadov, who deliberately exploit style and mannerism. In placing emphasis on the manner of expression, Savadov switches focus from what is literally depicted to its context and to what is implied, assumed and absent. *Bloody Merry*'s structure demonstrates a contrived formality that presents elements of both sense and nonsense. The mode of expression is inseparable from literal reference to factual information and from the more elusive and absent aspects such as the implicit presence of violence and death, which accompanies blood.

Derrida's writing reminds us that a logical conception of the world is not necessarily 'common sense'. Trust in logical truths and certainty depends on the notion of an entity that is separated from history and thought, and that has an essential nature that does not change. The status of the photograph, with regards to its representation of reality, remains at a point of conflicting interpretations. On one level it is popularly considered as mirroring the world of reality. On a post-structural level, this is seen to be misguided and contrary to the fictional properties of a photograph such as *Bloody Merry*. An understanding, *post* post-structuralism, considers that signs, reference and sense cannot be kept separate from received ideas and the agency that affect representation and expression.

Knowledge, history and representation

Foucault's work has contributed an additional perspective to Derrida's examination of representation. His writings have influenced the way we think about the world, signalling implications for practice and interpretation. His approach forces the reader to challenge assumptions about the construction of ourselves as subjects, our relationship to history and representation, and how we have established knowledge and attitudes about them. Sharon Lockhart's project (1999) in the Amazonian Aripuanã River region in Brazil, points to the significance of Foucault's influence with regard to our attitude to difference, the specificity of locality and culture and to the relationship of power between individuals and peoples (Figure 5). The photographs vary from a linear series of simple black and white studies taken on a seventeen-day trip along a river, which are very much in the tradition of Evans's documentary style, to a more concentrated series of coloured portraits.

Lockhart attempts a snapshot of life in the region that crosses a range of different aspects and includes alternative views and stories. Her focus is on specific lives rather than constructing a general and simplified impression for the spectator. As much as possible, her methods avoid the photographer's selection process that frames and fabricates situations. Instead, she collates a range of detailed perspectives from the family's material surroundings. Aware that the artificiality of the documentation process itself can isolate subjects from their context, she includes images of the vacated interview locations and the contrasting background incidentals, such as possessions of personal value and the walls covered in collected newspapers and magazine clippings that advertise glamorous lifestyles. The ironies of regional politics are evident in the contrast between the realities of living in this region and the material desires and political motivations evident in the selection of wallpaper.

Lockhart's collection of photographs is described as 'episodic and discursive' (Martin 1999: 13) because of the varied methods used and the attitude of the author to the different people and their histories encountered in different locales. The series

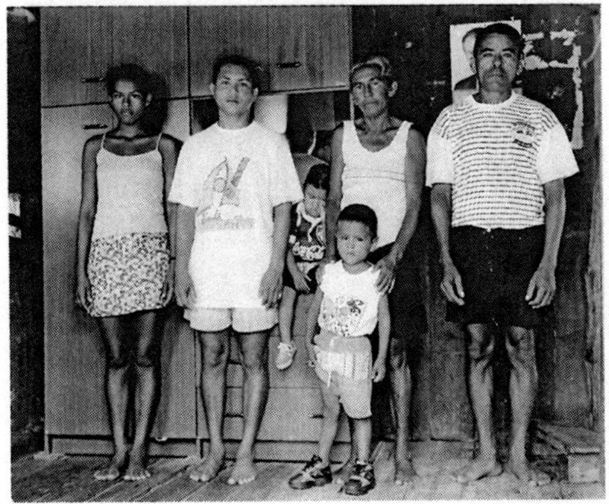

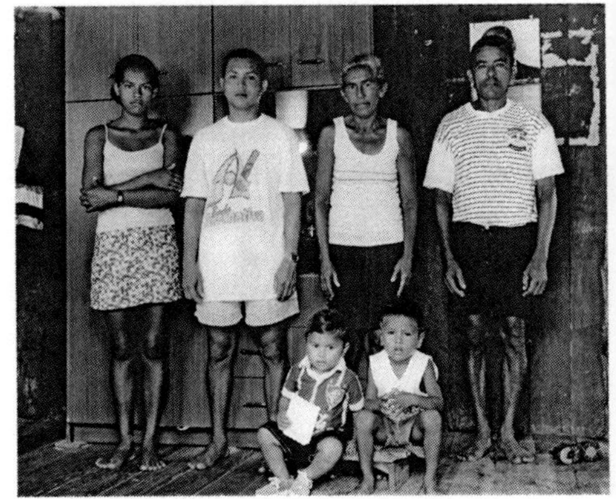

provides a document in which different stories are told from a number of specific perspectives. Many of Foucault's writings have taken the form of interdisciplinary histories, which examine our representations of specific fields of concern, such as illness, crime and sexuality. He explores the significance of differences between what something is, its material effects and how it is represented. He demonstrates also that, rather than being stable, meaning is dependent on our use of words or images to situate and describe everything. In his introduction to *The Order of Things: An Archaeology of the Human Sciences* [1966], Foucault states his intention to demonstrate that 'the knowledge of living beings' (2003: x) is dependent on current ideology, culture and its location, and proceeds to critique modernity's habitual procedures of thought, which I described briefly in Chapter One. He strives to respect the differences between areas of knowledge, rather than treating them all in the same way or trying to find some common feature in order to arrive at a point of resolution. He leads us to more actively acknowledge the significance of difference, specific kinds of knowledge, situation and experience, rather than trying to synthesise ideas and find universal principles by making them fit our familiar conceptions. Significantly different from Sartre's concern, Foucault rejects 'the phenomenological approach which gives absolute priority to the observing subject ... which places its own point of view at the origin of all historicity' (Foucault 2003: xv). He switches focus, therefore, from analysis that is determined by 'the knowing subject' to 'a theory of discursive practice' that places debate as central.

Discourse and authorship

Foucault approaches the analysis of debate (discourse) from the perspective of scrutinising the rules that operate within it. 'Discourse' is a term that refers to the arena within which a particular group and its language exists, such as photography and photographic discourse. He asserts that any 'discursive practice' regulates itself in the process of its own making so that rules and traditions emerge in the

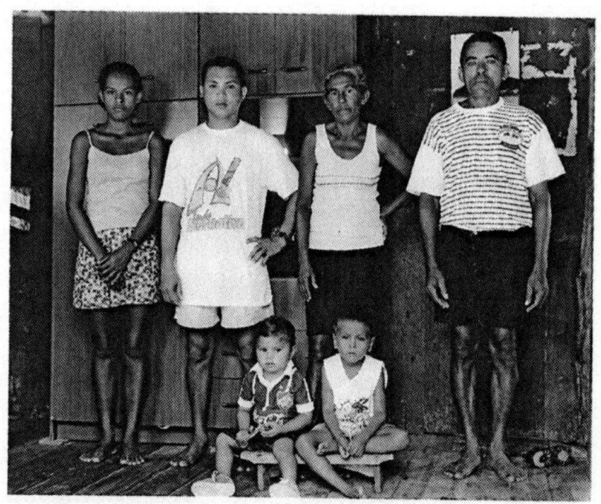

Figure 5 Sharon Lockhart, *Apeú-Salvador: Families* / The Oliveira Family / Naíze Barbosa Ferreira, Mário Ferreira, Nadilson Barbosa Tavares, Maria José Ferreira de Oliveira, José Barbosa de Oliveira, Danielson Barbosa Ferreira / Apeú-Salvador, Pará, Brazil / Survey of Kinship / Relations in a Fishing Community / Anthropologist: Isabel Soares de Souza, 1999. Three framed gelatin silver prints. 17⅞ × 22¾ inches each (26⅞ × 31¾ inches each framed).

way that any history is written, or any practice is described and continues to be described in the light of present ideologies and preoccupations. A discursive practice does not have an essential character, but is always in process; its significance changes and, in the process of change, it becomes a way of thinking. In this way, photographic practice establishes its own history, rules and characteristics in reaction to other practices, so that one practice is written upon another; photography's history is written upon art history and vice versa. It follows then that any model of photographic practice inherits conventions underwritten by all previous forms and derives as much from the discourse about it as from the work itself. Our understanding of photographs will be dependent on the manner of previous descriptions. And as Barthes states (1982: 12–13), any current genre will dictate emphasis, purpose and expectation, which will be defined in turn by that genre. Each explanation of a photograph, genre or artist's work becomes part of our perception in subsequent encounters and thereby constrains our response. As we explain the characteristics of a photograph within the context in which we define it, the description justifies previous descriptions and the process becomes self-perpetuating, so that the debates relating to realism can be self-referential and sometimes tautological. What appears to reside in any particular work is confirmed by the concepts attached to it, so that it is difficult to distinguish between what we think we see and the knowledge we have of it. Douglas Nickel (2001) identifies that the history of photographic art has persistently confirmed values that are dependent on the equivalence of its physical properties with authenticity and the photographer's integrity, as evident in Beaumont Newhall's *History of Photography*, 1949. Nickel describes the way in which commentators have followed each other's conceptions of photography without question so that the assumed necessity to define 'photography's essence' and subsequent reconfigurations of 'essences' has been constructed by previously stated ideologies. For example, Newhall (1993: 45), reappraising his own earlier history, admits his bias towards 'realism' and failure to discuss 'pictorialism'. In so doing, he identifies photography's persistent battle that requires *either* 'realism' *or* 'pictorialism', a division that continues to remain significant for the development of meaning. As a result, Nickel suggests that photographic discourse is practised in discussing essentialness relating to its ontology, but unpractised in terms of discussing its content or ideas. It is, as Strand predicted (1980: 141–2), that the reliance on photography's physical properties, its 'absolute objectivity', is both its strength and its constraint, and at the root of the difficulty in conceiving different aesthetic criteria for photography. Part II will explore photography's preoccupation with the ideas associated with realism and pictorialism throughout the period.

Photographer as author

Foucault's essay 'What is an Author?' (1998 [1969]) and some key texts by Barthes ('The Death of the Author' [1968] 'From Work to Text' [1971]; in Barthes 1977) have contributed to the breakdown of what we understand to be 'knowledge' and the traditional assumptions about the primacy of the author's intention, which the reader is compelled to track down as the one true meaning or original vision. Whilst the author's position will always contribute, it is no longer seen to be central. Instead, it initiates or adds to a discourse. The reader, now an active participator, also contributes to that ongoing discourse (what Barthes refers to as 'text'). Any 'work' that generates meaning (a piece of writing, an artefact, a film, a photograph, an object, a performance, a space) provokes its extension in subsequent attitude and discussion. Foucault's essay discusses the importance of recognising how we frame a work (visual, written, oral) and questions assumptions about our conception of it and its contexts: What constitutes the work? What makes an author? And, if the author is no longer the prime source of meaning, how does the author's name function? He distinguishes between the author, the 'author function' and the discourse that arises from any work. The author (photographer) is defined by reputation, biography or what the work stands for. The establishment of a known 'author' does more than name the individual; it represents what is characteristic about an author's work. Foucault suggests that the notion of 'author' is a projection – a coherent construction that focuses on biography and examples of the same style. The author then is a function of discourse, which is variable and not historically constant or universal across cultures. Patterns of discourse are subject to the 'telling' of a history, which can silence some aspects of practice at the expense of others. In terms of photography, the visible work can become secondary to what it characterises, so that the work of Walker Evans is equivalent to the attributes with which his works are most associated. His work for the Farm Security Administration in 1936 is adopted as characteristic of Evans and typical of photographic modernism (epitomised by *Allie Mae Burroughs*, 1936). It is contradicted by his much later Polaroid portraits (1973–75), which could be described as more characteristically 'postmodern' and are largely omitted from his historiography. The work and influence of 'Walker Evans' establishes a discourse beyond the work itself by its subsequent contribution to the 'rules' of the photographic discourse.

Power structures

Lockhart is mindful of the power structures involved in going to a foreign land and taking photographs of the people who live there. The methods by which Lockhart engages with her subjects attempt to avoid the hierarchies and judgements usually imposed by the author. Working with anthropologists in the region, she used the procedures of ethnographic research, which assumes the premise of ethical mindfulness and responsibility. As 'author' her procedures were not predetermined, but opportunistic in that the conditions of the situation, and the response of the people to her, dictate the specific manner of construction. Foucault's analyses avoid oversimplifying or assigning fixed meaning to any particular history, and concentrate instead on describing how histories, contexts and meanings change in different locations and time. Thereby the conception of any area of knowledge evolves, requiring us to ask: What attitude and perspective shapes this knowledge? How does one account for this position? What are the laws governing this particular discourse? What validates these ideas? (Foucault 1998: 314) It is a process that attempts to set aside bias and assumptions by insisting that knowledge is something besides that of a physical fact and that it must consider its context and agency. In the essay 'The Subject and Power' (1982a), Foucault examines what power is and where it comes from. He indicates the implicit presence of power relations in any communication or institution, which can be subtle and are very often indirect, so that it is not always a simple relationship in which one individual exerts power over another, but that power relations are a 'complex interplay' of actions that act upon, and which modify, other actions (Foucault 1982a: 788–90). He introduces a wholly different perspective to the relationship between subjects, and from which to look at the world, by pointing out different attitudes to subjectivity betrayed by two questions: 'Who am I?' assumes a static, individual subject 'I', who is a 'unique but universal and unhistorical subject' and who is also 'everyone, anywhere at any moment' – this is a concept of subjectivity as being at the centre of knowledge. On the other hand, we can ask: 'What are we? What's happening to us?' – at this precise moment in history, and in this precise context – this is a concept of subjectivity influenced by changing contexts and is therefore different at each and every moment (Foucault 1982a: 785).

Nothing is fixedly this or that; there is no essential meaning to things, to the subject or to history. Power is the dynamic that moves between individuals and groups and as such power relations are embedded within social structures. And social structures and discourses develop the 'order of things', which dictate our normative way of thinking. Foucault's argument in 'The Subject and Power' forefronts two significant issues for the reading of photographs – the implicit underlying agenda, which often goes unrecognised, and the changing condition of the subject, both photograph*er* and photograph*ed*. The significance that very specific knowledge or experience makes a difference, establishes a-historical or generalised reductions of subjects, practices or events as problematic. Discussion of the subtleties of subject-to-subject relations is extended in *Dialogical Realism*.

Writing in the 1980s, John Tagg applies Foucault's consideration of power to the context of the examination of photographs. In general terms, he describes how photographs, conceived as evidence, are used by agencies and institutions or contribute to the writing of history. By giving examples of photographs used as a means of surveillance, as historic record and as provocation for reform, he questions photography as a record of reality at all and exposes their use as instruments of power and influence. Recall the Farm Security Administration project of the 1930s, which aimed to provide photographic evidence to justify government policy and spending. However, as Berger points out (Berger and Mohr 1995 [1982]), no photograph can be a simple record and Tagg explores this in an extensive discussion of a number of historic case studies. Tagg establishes that photographs not only have been used as evidence but are claimed to have the status of knowledge. A photograph of an event constitutes knowledge of that event, so that 'evidence' is assigned to photography as another metaphor (Donald 1999: 37). Tagg's argument is that photographs are not merely passive instruments for contemplation but can be actively used to evoke emotive and political change. Tagg applies Foucault's questioning of motivations to scrutinise why photographs are taken: 'By whom? Under what conditions? For what purposes? Who is pictured? And how were the pictures used? To whom were they meaningful? And what were the consequences of accepting them as meaningful, truthful or real?' (Tagg 1988: 119) Any use of photographs necessitates consideration of cultural attitudes to photographs and their use. Tagg is talking about 'documentary' photography in its simplest sense – as opposed to fine art photography, which has had to consider its attitude to 'documentary' in order to establish its position as an art form. Savadov's work challenges the traditional notion of 'photography-as-truth' and presents a different order of truth and knowledge by presenting combinations of fantasy, memory and history. Lockhart's project attempts to avoid generalisation and to present a document that considers what is happening, in one specific location, at one particular time.

Subject in process

Julia Kristeva's writings about the processes of meaning are useful because they combine structural analysis with theories derived from psychoanalysis. Her work provides a background to the impact of psychoanalytic theory on photographic-art, and her readings (1984 [1974], 2000 [1980]) of Sigmund Freud and Jacques Lacan serve as a filter here for theories concerning the construction of subjectivity. They introduce some basic principles that adjust the way we think about the development of the individual subject and which are best explained in terms of our relationships with others. And the photographic portrait manifests these abstract terms in a real, physical context. In the 1970s, portrait photography began to move away from prescriptive traditions towards an informality in which the subject is often photographed in the process of doing something else. Formal, definitive statements were giving way to more interactive portrayals. Nan Goldin's work, for example, holds a significant place in the story of 'realism' and, in particular, the development of a vernacular aesthetic that resembles the casual snapshot. Her diaristic approach started in the early 1970s with *The Cookie Portfolio*, and images from *The Ballad of Sexual Dependency* (1979–86) were first shown as slideshows with music in the 1980s. Her work, known for its uncensored documentation of friends, actively addresses the intimate relationship she has with her subjects, rather than what they might look like. She has said that whilst the pictures are specific, the concerns are universal, and whilst others may not *look* like the particular individuals photographed, they are about 'others': 'it's about the nature of relationships' (Goldin 1996–97). She talks about people being strangers to each other, of their desire to make relationships however destructive they might be, of different emotional realities, which cause disruption in relationships. Goldin's photographs, which result from her direct involvement with others, describe this interaction on both bodily and psychical levels.

Kristeva's writing challenges the idea of a static subject – a unified whole – and emphasises a subject that is unpredictable, contradictory, *un*-unified and in a constant process of change. Foucault's examination establishes that the subject operates within the bounds of constructed ideologies, and Kristeva's approach accentuates the subject as a '*process* of becoming' (Kristeva 1984: 37). As with Foucault and Derrida, Kristeva points to the limitations of phenomenology because of its reliance on the idea of a unified and self-contained subject. Phenomenology explains the 'object' and 'others' (in this context the photographic-subject) as given identity by a judging subject, which does not allow for the contradictory forces that complicate relations with others. In contrast to Sartre's cerebral existential encounter described in Chapter One, Kristeva identifies the derivation of 'subject' as being grounded in the materiality of the body and in the unpredictable mobility of particular circumstance. She refines the notion of being constituted by another and makes it a *process* that responds to psychic drives, emotional clutter and the singularity of daily life (1984: 25–7). Kristeva's is a psychoanalytic stance, which understands the identifiable subject as constantly unstable. Kristeva's notion of the subject as a mobile *process* lends a different perspective to a system that prefers definition and which can be seen in the traditional portrait.

Goldin's intimate approach to photographing people demonstrates key features that parallel the participatory process of psychoanalysis: first, the process demonstrates the difficulty in establishing authentic identity, which is confused by the opacity of our unconscious. Second, photographs in series, rather than one self-sufficient image, demonstrate an attitude in which the individual subject does not remain static but changes in the course of continuing relationships that emerge within and between images; it is a *process* of signification. Third, psychoanalytic theories challenge the oppositional relationship between subjects, and Goldin's method photographs the *experience*, which is being shared by both photographer and photographic-subject; the emphasis is different. The power structures of conventional portraiture are broken down along with the relationship of the viewer to interpretation. Descriptions of just one of Goldin's subjects (Siobhan, Figure 6), shown at different times and in different psychological states, visually demonstrate the sort of instability and process to which Kristeva refers. We can see in the *Siobhan* series how appearance can be different on each occasion and how the particularity of a number of different contexts builds a picture *in process*.[4]

Jacques Lacan's psychoanalytic theories have had an enormous influence on post-structural ideas and on photography theory specifically via, for example, Laura Mulvey (1989 [1975]), Victor Burgin (1982) and, later, Kaja Silverman (1996). Lacan's notion that the unconscious is structured like language recognises the influence of structural theories that stressed the impact of culture on the development of subjectivity, and linguistic theories, such as Saussure's, which identified the process of signification. Applied to the context of a subject's development, and using Lacan's terms (1977 [1966]), the construction of the ego moves from the pre-symbolic order (before language and equivalent to nature) to the symbolic order, which is defined by culture and language. The pivotal stage in the development of a sense of self is the point of self-perception, which is metaphorically illustrated by the child seeing her image in the mirror (the mirror stage). This initiates a process of self-identification that is sometimes illusory and, at least in part, imaginary. Kristeva's writing (1984 [1974], 2000 [1980]) repositions the relationship between biology and culture in the construction of subjectivity. She gives emphasis to the double meaning of a subject 'in process', which is an active material and psychical process whilst, at the same time,

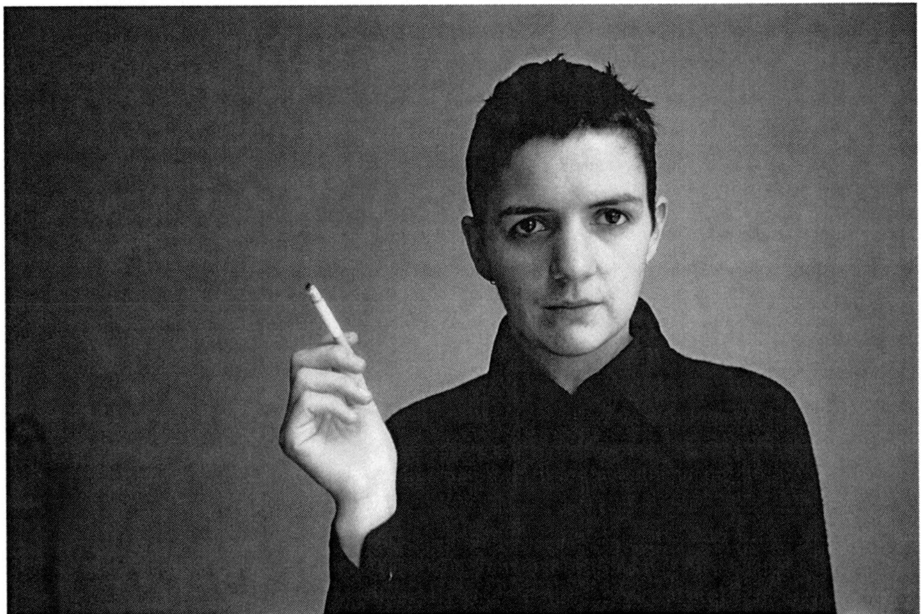

Figure 6 Nan Goldin, *Siobhan with a Cigarette, Berlin*, 1994.

produced also by the process of cultural influence (Kristeva 1984: 37). In psychoanalytic terms, the notion of a fixed identity is an illusion (Kristeva 1996: 132–3). In the context of photography, the portrait can be seen as a kind of fiction or a metaphor for a revelatory event that reveals essential character, in the same way that Lacan's 'mirror phase' represents the development of the individual psyche.

Like many photographers, Goldin's portraits are prone to accusations of objectification and even victimisation of the subject (Buchloh 1998: 161). However, they display a struggle that invites a reciprocal confrontation, which produces a form of equality in the relationship between Goldin and her subjects. She wants them to actively confront her, resulting in images that betray a shared vulnerability (Goldin 1986: 6). She strives to view from the inside looking out, as opposed to the outside looking in, as she says documentary does. She wants her 'subjects' to 'stare back'. Kristeva's notion of the subject-in-process emphasises an ethical relationship between identity and difference, self and other, citizen and foreigner. Her use of the term *process* incorporates 'the sense of a legal proceeding where the subject is committed to trial', because our subjectivity 'is constantly called into question' (Kristeva 1996: 132–3). In the encounter between photographer and photographic-subject, both subjects are metaphorically on trial, and the instant that the photograph is taken provides a symbolic confrontation, as if it were a mirror, which reflects the 'other' back on ourselves. The encounter with others calls into question what we stand for, and provokes feelings to the surface that are normally repressed. These 'others', usually taken for granted, are here paused and highlighted. So that the photographic encounter, rather than focusing on the 'subject' of the photograph on a personal level, or 'artistic' or 'ideological' level, can become a trial for the photographer instead.

Feminist thinkers such as Luce Irigaray extend many of the ideas that have contributed to the shift in thinking about subjectivity, which are represented here by Kristeva's work – particularly with regard to the role of corporeality as being crucial to psychical existence. Later developments in feminist theory have reinvigorated understanding of subjectivity: for example, Judith Butler's expansion of the 'performative' subject considers subjectivity as constructed by a 'script' (1990); Rosi Braidotti's *Nomadic Subjects* (1994) considers the intersection between identity, subjectivity and the issues of power deriving from sexual difference; Donna Haraway's hybrid subjectivity, *cyborg* (1991), rethinks the blurring distinctions between body and machine, nature and culture; Elizabeth Grosz (1995) considers the body in relation to philosophy, knowledge and desire. They each propose interactive models that incorporate the physical, psychological and the social. Kristeva's emphasis is on the backwards-and-forwards exchange of subject and productive process, as opposed to a system that prefers definition and which represses the *process* of signification. Kristeva sidesteps the existential position evident in the Western philosophical tradition exemplified by Sartre's fear of the 'other' and offers something more positive. Her themes signal what can be seen as a recurring dynamic throughout late twentieth-century photographic portraits, of the oscillation between individuation (establishing oneself as separate from others) and identification (establishing an identity for oneself) (1996: 132–3). Her thinking disturbs our conception of the constitution of the subject as being existentially and visually played out in the photographic encounter between photographer and photographic-subject and in the photographic pose, which assigns all the power to the photographer. Kristeva's emphasis has introduced the critical dynamic of interactive process in the making and reading of photographs and heralded a portrait depiction that is less dramatic, more incidental and participatory. Two important consequences of her work are, first, the insistence of a material and bodily dimension to interpretation that is very different from more abstract metaphysical notions of transcendence and which moves towards an emphasis on response instead, and second, an approach that asserts process rather than product as being central. Her ideas will be explored further in Chapters Three and Five.

Transitional aesthetics: towards a post-structural photography

Kristeva's application of the theoretical and psychoanalytical to creative texts has contributed to the inclusion of other disciplinary perspectives in the consideration of art practice, and which many photographers have actively employed. As the divisions between criticism, history and practice have become less rigid, *post* post-structuralism, so the relationship and exchange between them has shifted in the development of what is termed 'visual culture'. Practitioners do not function in a wholly separate realm from the more general cultural framework and, with the interdisciplinarity of visual culture, the remit of artistic content has been extended. The insertion of cultural theories such as psychoanalysis to the discussion of aesthetics changes the parameters by challenging its boundaries. It moves the consideration of art practice from the more abstract aspects of theoretical aesthetics and resituates it in relation to a wider debate. The study of art potentially becomes another means to understand the role that ideologies play in history. More fundamentally, the conjunction of aesthetic, cultural and political concerns are able to be part of a visual discourse and contribute to changes in understanding.

In the light of these shifting perspectives, I return to photography's developing history of practice and theory. The influence of post-structural thought emerged in Victor Burgin's influential *Thinking Photography* (1982), which introduced a change in thinking about photography and how it operates. It established, first, that the photograph can no longer be taken at face value in the light of, for example, Foucault's or psychoanalytic theories and, second, confirmed the influence of structural semiotics in what has become known as 'photography theory'. As an example, Burgin's essay 'Photography, Phantasy, Function' traces a psychological perspective to 'looking', with reference to Freud and Lacan, and demonstrates a rethinking of photography with regard to the unconscious. Burgin speaks of the 'intricate psychic network of our knowledge' and the 'psychic interruptions to rational thinking', which prevent the possibility of disinterested response originating in Immanuel Kant's critique [1790]. According to Kant, aesthetic judgement should not be concerned with the object's function or the subjective 'interest' of the viewer (Kant 1952: 43–4). But it is an attitude that persists as a goal in traditional approaches and underpins the recurring theme of the photographer's objectivity/subjectivity (Burgin 1982: 195, 206). Burgin's later book (1986), in discussing Barthes's *Camera Lucida*, introduces more subjective perspectives as being valid and, with regard to postmodernism, considers art practice in relation to wider cultural theory, rather than the more isolated territory of art history. Writers such as Burgin, Tagg and Rosalind Krauss (1986) developed photography's legitimacy as an art form by assimilating the values of conceptual art and by promoting alternatives to modernist photography. The critical awareness that interpretations of Foucault brought to the development of a critical history of the photographic image contributed to the perception of 'photography theory' as being central to postmodern criticism (Burgin 1986, Tagg 1988). In the 1970s and 1980s, much photographic analysis, such as Tagg's, focused on photography as a cultural subject rather than on its aesthetic merit.[5] During this period, photographic practices and 'photography theory' established an influential, if contentious, position in relation to art practices more generally because of their critical stance. As a result, photography's history is influenced by a suspicion of theoretical interpretations that are perceived as prioritising critique over aesthetic values. In effect, this perception contributes to the continuing debate, which considers photography either as art or as cultural phenomenon. Divided attitudes to photographic practice have persisted on two counts: in its relation to theory and wider cultural discourses, and with regard to the use of its changing technology and subsequent adjustment to how photographs are made. By 2000, the assumption of photography into mainstream art practice had only in some respects displaced a modernist philosophy that prioritises authorship and authorial expression, with one that forefronts 'idea' over expression. It is likely that tension will remain between the more traditional photographic community and those of fine art or other cultural discourses.[6] The exploration of 'realism' here aims to celebrate the post-structural ideas and a presentation of theory as having made a positive contribution to practice.

What is valued or considered to be aesthetic continues as a developing discourse that can swing between very different positions. Photographic practice, like any practice, recreates meanings in reaction and counter-reaction to the presiding ideology. What is significant for its history is the process in which truth-values become embedded in a critical framework. Certain artistic heroes gather acclaim, confirming the mood and desires of the time, and providing a focus for a point of historical significance. An individual body of work will come to permanently signify a prevalent aesthetic trend, as with, for example, Walker Evans of modernism,[7] or Sherrie Levine of postmodernism.[8] Evans provides an example of the construction of artistic value, formed from a series of biographies that emphasise heroic qualities and the evolution of an aesthetic, articulated in his own writing on photographic 'quality' (Evans 1994b). Exhibitions can also contribute to the establishment of photographic value. Significantly, the practice of adopting metaphoric umbrella themes in order to give more coherence to a collection of very different practices contributes to the fixing of attitudes and traditions. In 1955, *Family of Man* (curated by Edward Steichen) defined a modernist humanism by presenting the idea of a global human community as a 'family' and confirming the assumed existence of an underlying common essence, irrespective of culture. Subsequently critiqued by Barthes as exemplary of generalised assumptions, it later contributed to the disassembly of such attitudes (Barthes 1993a: 100). In a similar way, *The Photographer's Eye* (curated by John Szarkowski, 1964) celebrated modernism and the exhibition *Pictures* (curated by Douglas Crimp, 1977) helped to define the central role of photographic practices in the formation of 'postmodern art'. The exhibition *Cruel and Tender* (Tate Modern, 2003) provided validation of what was perceived to be respectable photographic practice in the last decades of the century. The title *Cruel and Tender*, deriving from a description of Evans's work by Lincoln Kirstein, refers to the contradictory possibilities of the photographer's distance or intimacy, and of objectivity and subjectivity. *Cruel and Tender* created a coherent overview of the state of play by collating works in thematic groupings, such as 'On the road' and 'Exploring vulnerability'. It presented the dominant aspects of photographic vision that underline 'realist' traditions and the 'masters' of twentieth-century Western photography. It reiterated aspects of the 'everyday' and perpetuated the central photographic purpose of revealing the hitherto unseen, in works ranging from the Bechers' dispassionate catalogues to Boris Mikhailov's confrontational theatricality. Like *Pictures* and *The Photographer's Eye* before it, *Cruel and Tender* signposted a point in photographic history. As the first photography exhibition held at the Tate, it at least heralded the arrival of photography as an accepted form of art, whilst maintaining a position of separation by the implicit need to name 'photography' in order for it to be legitimised.

Postmodernism

Many of the attributes identified by post-structuralism are articulated in different terminology as 'postmodern'. Since the inception of conceptual art, photography has facilitated, and to a large degree defined, many of the familiar aspects of what is commonly termed 'postmodern art' more generally. The history of postmodern art-photography can be traced back to a series of essays: by Douglas Crimp, 'Pictures' (1979) and 'The Photographic Activity of Postmodernism' (1980); Craig Owens 'The Allegorical Impulse' (1980); Hal Foster, 'Re: Post' (1982) and his volume *The Anti-Aesthetic* (1983); Abigail Solomon-Godeau, 'Playing in the Fields of the Image' (1982) and 'Photography after Art Photography'(1984); Victor Burgin, *The End of Art Theory* (1986); Steve Edwards, 'The Snapshooters of History' (1989). This last example reviews the influences of post-structuralism on photography and its demonstration that the possibility of stable meaning is an illusion. Collectively, the many reviews in the 1980s constituted, and reiterated, what have become recognised as the characteristic features of postmodern art: appropriation, irony, seriality, simulation, with repeated reference to works by Cindy Sherman, Barbara Kruger, Sherrie Levine and Richard Prince.

The postmodern condition, in Jean-Francois Lyotard's terms (1984 [1979]), is defined as a fractured experience of the world. With regard to culture, it is conceived as a transitional state that interrupts tradition, which provokes a recurring cycle of tradition and anti-tradition, and which precedes the acceptance of different ideas within an established discourse, such as 'art'. In these terms, postmodernism is not an era, but a dynamic that tests the rules of existing aesthetic practice, and provokes a series of successive 'anti-aesthetics'. This process of discontinuity in the evolution of a discourse is interrupted itself by the will to fix processes and trends – such that 'postmodern' art practice is labelled as characterised by irony and appropriation from popular culture and historical traditions, and thereby all uses of irony or appropriation are postmodern. Whilst labels such as 'postmodern' serve as a convenient mechanism to stabilise discourse, there is no essential postmodern art practice. What is recognised as postmodernism's reaction to modernity's pursuit of universality and 'grand narrative' has been reduced to but a few features (Lyotard 1984: xxiii). This then amounts to an over simplification of the term 'postmodern' itself, which has become unfashionable and contested. As an all-encompassing term, different commentators have interpreted the 'postmodern' differently, and the negative 'anti' connotations and their relationship to modernism have tended to dominate its definition. Jürgen Habermas (1985 [1981]) interprets modernity as a project that is not yet fully realised and is suspicious of postmodernism because of its impulse to negate positive and utopian aspects of modernism. He clarifies distinctions between anti-modernists, who reject all that modernity stands for, from those who regret the decline of reason and distinct disciplinary enquiries, and from those who welcome contemporary developments, which problematise reason, or changes in attitude such as the assertion of difference over the pursuit of universal meaning. Explaining postmodernism as 'late capitalism', Fredric Jameson (2009 [1991]) attempts to classify these divisions in attitude by distinguishing between a postmodernism that is essentially anti-modern, and a modernism that is anti-postmodern, which depend not on an historic break but on ideological differences (Jameson 2009: 58–9).

Photography since the 1980s is often characterised as 'postmodern photography', and thereby persists in attracting commentary that betrays a prejudice against anything labelled by 'postmodernism'. For example, ridicule is implicit in this Independent review of the V&A's exhibition *Signs of a Struggle: Photography in the Wake of Postmodernism*:

> There are lots of 'ofs' in Postmodernism. So we have a photo of an advertisement by Richard Prince, a photo of a model of an apple by James Casebere and a photo of a mock staging of the aftermath of a party by Anne Hardy. (Ward 2011)

In describing the story of photography, I distance this discussion from those prejudices because, whilst parody and appropriation – not perceived as serious attributes – were common themes in the 1980s, practice displays many more pervasive effects. Photographic practices visibly reflect changes in attitude that centre around a number of premises that are recognisably post-structural, which suggests a more appropriate term than 'postmodern' might be 'post-structural photography' or a post-structural aesthetic. This is manifested in the way that photographers use strategies to challenge theoretical hierarchies. For example, just as Foucault examines power structures or Barthes introduces subjectivity to analysis, photographic practices offer alternatives (as seen in Goldin's work) to the modernist desire for objectivity. An awareness of the conditions of power is evident in the choice of subject-matter and the way it is photographed (as seen in Lockhart's *Apeú-Salvador: Families*, Figure 5). Photographic themes echo a range of post-structural concerns, such as disseminated meaning, or a suspicion of universal certainties, and assume methods of seriality / singularity / avoidance / obliqueness / blandness / artificiality / contradiction. More deep-seated adjustments to the conceptual framework of photographic practice are evident than the literal translations of reference, characterised in appropriation, or an exhibition such as *Cruel and Tender* suggest.

Chapter One outlined debate regarding the ontology of photography, which the impact of digital technologies forces us to rethink. However, the special condition of photography's nature – originating in darkness, light and chemical process – and the metaphors it acquires are difficult to relinquish, particularly when it comes to what is valued as aesthetic – truth, reality and so on. Camera-less photography presents an example of practice that confronts what is meant by 'ontological' and I could argue that direct uses of light in the works of Garry Fabian Miller, Adam Fuss and Susan Derges, for example, come nearer to the origins of photographic ontology than representational uses.[9] What is interesting about Miller is his postmodern reworking of one of photography's earliest applications such as the photogram (see Hippolyte Bayard's *Arrangement of Specimens* c. 1842) – which knowingly assumes the metaphorical possibilities of light. It is this *knowingness* that becomes an important theme in post-structural practice. Work such as this introduces a discussion also of 'abstract' applications of photography in the manner of painting, *post* abstract expressionism, which echoes previous debates about art-photography and whether it should emulate 'art' (e.g. Edward Steichen) or be true to its own form (e.g. Paul Strand and the champions of modernist purity). But more significant for this study of photographic realism are examples of representational photography that function in an almost abstract manner, such as Andreas Gursky's. I emphasise 'representational realism' as needing further discussion, rather than abstract constructions, because photographic realism presents the appearance of reality, with the knowledge that neither the photographer nor the viewer's response is without agency. It is a subtle, but profound and far-reaching, distinction.

Section Two aims to reconfigure issues of theory in relation to photographic practice, by reviewing recurrent themes and strategies, and by identifying developments in reaction to established photographic traditions. The following chapters will give emphasis to photography that accesses ideas, besides its preoccupation with its physical origins, to determine its aesthetic. It presents photographic practice as a form of discourse that visualises implicit truth-values, and participates in debate by demonstrating the interface between visual practices, philosophies and interpretations.

Suggested further reading

Burgin, V. (ed.) (1982) *Thinking Photography*, Macmillan, London

Derrida, J. (1982a) *Positions* [1972], trans. Alan Bass. University of Chicago Press, Chicago

Foucault, M. (1998) 'What is an Author?' [1969], in D. Preziosi (ed.), *The Art of Art History: A Critical Anthology*. Oxford University Press, Oxford, 299–314

Johnson, B. (2004) 'Translator's Introduction' in J. Derrida *Dissemination* [1972], trans. B. Johnson [1981], Continuum, London; New York, vii–xxxv

Kristeva, J. (1996) 'A Question of Subjectivity: An Interview' [1986], in P. Rice and P. Waugh (eds), *Modern Literary Theory Today: A Reader*. Arnold, London, 131–7

La Grange, A. (2005) *Basic Critical Theory for Photographers*, Focal Press, Amsterdam; Oxford

Oliver, K. (ed.) (1997) 'Introduction: Kristeva's Revolutions', in *The Portable Kristeva*, Columbia University Press, New York, xi–xxix

Tagg, J. (1988) *The Burden of Representation: Essays on Photographies and Histories*. Palgrave Macmillan, Basingstoke; New York

Notes

1 The term 'post-structuralism' encompasses a lot of ideas associated with the questioning of metaphysical origins of thought that assume the possibility of transcendental certainties. 'Transcendental' refers to an original knowledge or state of being, as with the 'transcendental ego' that assumes one constant identity, or 'transcendental signified' that indicates the possibility of one stable meaning that exists independently from the signifier (word or image). Post-structuralism questions assumptions regarding any form of representation or attempts to systemise its analysis. It establishes meaning as having no fixed reference points such as authorship, history or universal identity, and the development of the subject as similarly unstable and subject to change. In post-structural terms, language, meaning and representation are uncertain and subject to context, locality and difference.

2 See Derrida speaking about the desire for presence: www.youtube.com/watch?v=J1IScOonGMQ, accessed 15 September 2010.

3 In English, the word 'meaning' presents some problems because it relies on context to determine how it is intended. It is a very general term that is impossible to avoid because it covers so much territory. It is exactly this sort of ambivalence to which dissemination refers. The usefulness of this ambiguity is that a photograph can both signify and impart a sensation or impression. More specifically, the term 'signification' indicates the 'concepts' attached to a sign (word or image) and bears no relation to intention – Saussure identifies the connection as arbitrary. In verbal language a word signifies an object or concept; the process depends on the differences and similarities between words in order to distinguish one concept or thing from another – a process known as differential signification (Derrida 1973: 140). Whereas the verb

'to mean' carries an intention – if we mean something, we intend it, which is different from the terms 'signify' and 'signification', which indicate denotation and reference – 'Mean' can be used in the sense of denotation and reference, and it can imply that a sign is more meaningful or more valid in a particular context. 'Sense' equates with the signified content of the sign – its concept. The term sense, as a noun, can also carry the implication of inward feeling or impression because of its alliance with the senses, and as a verb is confused with 'to have a sensation' and to 'sense'. Sense can be confused in translation from the French, and Derrida's use of 'meaning' (*sens* and *vouloir-dire*) incorporates the French sense that literally means 'will to say' and which includes the understanding of purpose and intention (1982a: 14). The French word *sens* is ambiguous and can indicate both, or either, 'meaning' or 'direction', as, for example, the street sign, *sens unique*, a 'one-way street'. In philosophy, a distinction has long since been made between 'sense', as timeless and context free, and 'reference', which is contextually dependent on the relation of a sign to the world. Distinctions are therefore made between sense and reference (Gottlob Frege) or indication and expression (Edmund Husserl), where reference equates with the referent and its sense is the way it is expressed. This distinction assumes that what something means is distinct from what and how they are applied (Garver in Derrida 1973: xv). Both Derrida and Wittgenstein question this is possible.

4 Many photographs of Siobhan can be found online. See for example, http://elenazapata.blogspot.com/2009/03/nan-goldin-photography.html, accessed 9 August 2010.

5 Tutors on the influential BA Film and Photographic Arts at the Polytechnic of Central London in the 1970s included Victor Burgin, Simon Watney and John Tagg.

6 See, for example, *What Happened here? Photography in Britain Since 1968*, conferences held at Derby University and Tate Britain, 2005 (e.g Simon Watney's paper typifies the mood – 'Tunnel Vision' (2006)).

7 See contrasting perspectives of his work in Mora and Hill (1993), and Tormey (2003b).

8 See, for example, the Whitney Museum, http://whitney.org/www/2008biennial/www/?section=artists&page=artist_levine, accessed 24 August 2012.

9 See, for example, www.vam.ac.uk/collections/photography/past_exhns/miller/index.html, accessed 24 August 2012.

Part II

Introduction

Photography's realism demands an ongoing relationship with the questions of authenticity and representation. In 1896, Robinson's essay 'Idealism, Realism, Expressionism' (Robinson 1980) was concerned with the potential of photography to be used and read in different ways, as is the central theme of *this* book. However, this discussion is nuanced by photography's contradictory relationship with reality. Chapters in Part II explore how, as a result of shifting conceptions of representation, photographs construct different kinds of reality. Chapters will demonstrate how post-structural ideas contribute a number of perspectives from which to understand and respond to photography, and how practice, in turn, contributes to an interdisciplinary discourse. The following chapters will review some mechanisms of meaning, with the aim not to define but to recognise what photographs might contribute to ideas and our approach to interpretation. They will explore how photographs do more than merely illustrate verbal discourse, and how they work *through* their reference to real things in order to consider what questions they ask. I will focus on those functions that contribute to the power of the photograph, which challenge the distinction between 'form' and meaning, between visual and verbal text, and will consider how these elements are conjoined. In asserting the photograph's contribution to discourse, I deliberately avoid the habitual division between verbal discourse and visual exemplification, and avoid the displacement of one hierarchy with another – in which the image becomes superior to the text – pure visuality and thereby mysterious again.

Uses of photography have confused all manner of category, genre and function and borrowed from different disciplinary frameworks. I emphasise that, whilst photographers may have appropriated different modes of practice, discussion here is restricted to the function of 'art-photography'. Comparison across genres – for example, the work of Allan Sekula with that of Robert Capa, or David LaChapelle with Jeff Wall – without mention of the different motivations and traditions is problematic. What these comparisons share is the fact that they use photographic media – and that is all. I emphasise also that the use of photography in the context of fine art must assume the history of the language of fine art, which distinguishes it from the possibility of unmediated connection with reality. Since fine art's function is, to some degree, an autonomous construction and just as other forms of art practice have assimilated, for example, the heritage of the 'readymade', the unconscious and expression, so too has photography. Art-photography encompasses both the history of art that has subsumed the use of photography and, by default, the history of photography that has aspired to be 'art'. Each chapter discusses a dimension that incorporates the inheritance of conceptual and performative art practices and the self-conscious re-adjustment *post* 'photography theory'.

3

Dialogical realism

This chapter discusses ideas that have influenced the relationship between the photographer, the photographed subject and the viewer. First, it makes use of a post-structural renaissance in portrait photography to consider photographers' strategies that 'play' with conventions and formality. It makes reference to Emmanuel Levinas's discussion of 'face' and Jean Baudrillard's encounter with photography. Second, it focuses on alternative processes for reading photographs with reference to Kristeva's discussion of *dialogism* and Derrida's *perquisition*. This chapter extends the perspective of 'realism' by factoring in the psychology of participants and incorporating subjective response. It indicates the power of the photograph to assert influence and an adjustment to the production of meaning from an emphasis on the author to one that is multi-dimensional. An important development is signalled for the appraisal of photographs: one that encourages a self-reflexive approach that is uninhibited by formalism and asks first: what is it that I see? And what does that provoke?

The portrait encounter: subject-to-subject

The photographic portrait, traditionally a visual statement of judgement, can be seen as a metaphor for the power relations that exist between two subjects: the photographer-subject and the photographic-subject. It serves to illustrate the legacy of our existential relationship with others, described in Chapter One, where traditionally the convention of portraiture establishes a distance between the photographer-as-director and the subject-as-performer, who is 'directed'. This oppositional subject-to-subject process has been described as a game in which the photographic-subjects must reveal themselves to the viewer (Kozloff 1987: 144–53), and is demonstrated, in its extreme form, by portraits of celebrities portrayed as signs for themselves. For example, Yousuf Karsh's *Einstein* (1948) presents Albert Einstein as 'man-as-genius'.[1] Portraits in this mode create defining statements about the photographic-subject by accentuating and 'capturing' their character (Kozloff 1994: 76–89). In order to reveal the subject's character, the photographer-as-author must have some 'idea' about the subject in order to construct an objectifying comment for the viewer that glamorises, symbolises or mythologises.[2] Photographic representation of people easily lends itself to the fabrication of stereotypes and can present individuals as motifs, so that their condition or attribute overrides their individual subjectivity. For example, Evans's image *Allie Mae Burroughs* (1936) can be seen as an immortalised motif, which no longer describes an individual, but an idea of a particular type of individual, in this instance objectified in a 'representation-as-poverty'. Photographs can reduce their subjects to a generalisation, marking an authorial style, or eventually becoming sentimental cliché. Karsh's portraits, which are considered to be either classic examples or caricatures of 'portraiture', have been presented with accompanying texts extolling the subject's virtues with interesting anecdote, so that the 'portraits' become illustrations of the myth that they amplify and confirm. Karsh (1976: 9) claimed that 'the mask we present to others ... may lift for only a second to reveal the power in the unconscious gesture, a raised eyebrow, a surprised response, a moment of repose. This is the moment to record'. Whereas, Walker Evans [1971] denied that there was any 'reality' to be found in the deliberate posing of portraiture or the very mannered pretensions of Karsh's claim to catch the psychological power centre of his famous subjects; his grandiose 'search for greatness' (Evans 1994d: 37–8).[3] In contrast, Evans repeatedly struggled and played with the dilemma of wanting to 'keep it simpler' (Katz 1981: 368). However, whilst Evans despised approaches such as this that spell out interpretation for the viewer, he articulates the tension between intimacy and distance when photographing people. Talking about the detachment required, Evans [1971] says: 'Well, its like a surgeon. It's psychologically determined. A surgeon has to be detached from the human pain when he's going to cut into somebody or detached from gore and its effect on him' (Evans 1994c: 19).

The impact of psychoanalysis and post-structuralism on ideas about representation and objectivity is evident in changing attitudes to the portrait genre and in the development of a different dynamic between photographer and the photographic-subject. The event of the portrait serves a more complex function than that of finding essential character and, having moved away from prescriptive configurations, it is no longer constrained by an insistence on authorial distance. It introduces new classifications (e.g. documentary-style-portrait, snapshot-style-portrait) and, as it evolves more subtle strategies, it is more difficult to determine the location of power in the relationship between the photographer and the photographic-subject. For example, photographs by Tina Barney (*Theatre of Manners*, 1997), which depict individuals-as-aspects-of-society, are difficult to categorise because by using members of her own family and involving them in making fictional reconstructions of past scenes, she inserts the subjective complication of poignancy and irony.[4] Whilst Larry Sultan's personal involvement with his subjects is an increasingly common strategy in the 1980s and 1990s, his aim to search for the essential identity of his parents is a traditional one that identifies a number of issues. His description of the project *Pictures from Home* (1992) reveals the conflicts involved in representation: between authorial intention and what is imagined to be psychological reality.[5] It relates conflict on a number of levels: the relationship between his mother and father; the difference of perspective between himself and his parents, who do not understand what he is trying to achieve and yet try to do their best for him; different notions of what a picture should or should not describe; and an account that describes the letting go of 'trying to make pictures' (Sultan 1992: 16). His attempt to contrive a reality for himself, reflected in the life of his parents, highlights the distance between what the same activity might mean for the photographer and for the photographic-subject. He tries to find some sort of position – what his parents are like *for him* – but he is so busy constructing images that they become something else. Ultimately, the possibility of communication between them is the central focus, which directs the resulting photographs. Sultan's projection makes it difficult to discriminate his parents' story from that of his own: 'I look at the pictures I've made and I don't know whom I was photographing. It looks like my father but it feels like me' (Sultan 1986: 32–4). This reversal suggests that, in responding to others, photographers inevitably reveal different aspects of themselves. Each time 'subject' confronts 'subject', another side of each is revealed. Each invents the other; they run in parallel. Sultan's parents relate the experience of constituting themselves in the manner of their son's imagination and memory. Sultan endeavours to maintain his own position as author in the face of his parents' struggle to assert something else. In seeking intimacy or interaction, he arrives at himself – and ultimately his emotional distance from them. Portraits in the 1980s and 1990s begin to accentuate either intimacy, with the intrusion of subjectivity and emotion, or distance, with the active avoidance of expression or contact.

Release from the necessity of formal portrayal has resulted in constructions that make deliberate use of this relationship between intimacy and distance. Thomas Struth, Rineke Dijkstra and Thomas Ruff have each appropriated the formality of the portrait genre as a 'style', which makes the location of photographic expression difficult to define. With different degrees of complicity, they each use a version of the deliberately staged formal pose, which requires the photographic-subject to participate in the event. In *The Languages of Art*, Goodman explains that when we look at photographs of people we look through the individual toward a categorisation (genre) that is familiar, which usefully directs how we respond to a photograph (1969: 26–30). He clarifies a common confusion where we might say that a picture 'expresses' a feeling when strictly speaking the photograph presents a metaphor that alludes to a feeling, as with Stieglitz's *Equivalent* (1969: 46–50). In the context of a photographic portrait, certain gestures and expression can be recognised as signifying a feeling such as 'thoughtfulness' or 'integrity', as with Karsh's Einstein. Ruff's series of portraits from 1981[6] (e.g. *Portrait*, 2001 – Figure 7) exploit this distinction between different kinds of denotation – the 'representation' of objects and the 'expression' of feelings:

This appears to be a simple portrait of a young girl, but I am confused because it denies my expectations; there is no visible contextual setting and she is expressionless. Positioned squarely and symmetrically within the frame and in relation to me, she looks straight at me. The predominant colours are shades of red – her cheeks, her lips, her T-shirt – and black – her hair, her eyes, her choker. Her gaze and stance penetrate: big black pupils, carefully arched eyebrows, scraped-back hair. Beyond that there are no clues offered me. Unlike Allie Mae Burroughs, *this portrait doesn't present even individual stance in a turn or tilt of the head. There is no way I can penetrate that inscrutable look because it is so formal. I cannot define any element of character because there is no expression. She doesn't present expressive qualities and neither does she appear to allude to a feeling. It is almost as though her face is not real.*

Like Karsh, Ruff makes use of the simplicity of the 'portrait' genre, but in a dispassionate, contrived way that relinquishes expressive pretensions. His authenticity lies with the primacy of the image rather than the character of the subject. He

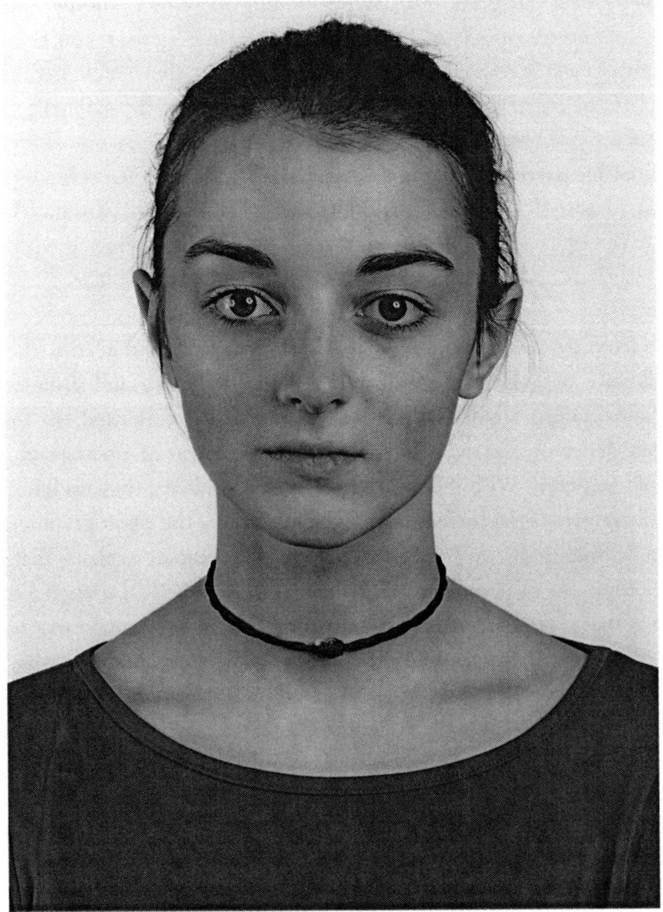

Figure 7 Thomas Ruff, *Portrait (A. Roters)*, 2001.

does not pretend to represent truth about his subjects and constructs his image in total artifice, replacing representation with a kind of fiction. He makes use of the face as motif so that the extremely sparse form, devoid of expression, appears to deny obvious meaning. Ruff's realism is descriptively clear, but facial expression is abstracted from reality to present something abstract in quality, and is unclear as a result. The control and consistency in Ruff's presentations – the pose, the size, the regular background, the proportion within the frame – reduces individuality to abstraction, so that everything in the image assumes enormous significance. In this absence of psychological narrative, we are bound to read meaning into the smallest clue (a choker, a red T-shirt) and the smallest detail becomes potentially significant in our endeavour to understand the girl's individuality. We seek prescriptions for response in expression, character, narrative and Ruff denies us them all. Ruff presents a face with as little indication of the other's personality as possible and gives us image and surface only. Ruff's statement 'photographs aren't depictions they're just images' emphasises the difference between 'depiction', which refers back to the person depicted and the possibility of describing them, and 'image', which refers us to the representation in front of us (Ruff, quoted in Wulffen 1993: 66). Ruff's logic insists that the whole affair must be pared down to its minimum, thus avoiding symbolic description of the kind sought by Karsh. His belief that one cannot portray an individual leads us to another consideration that the portrait, as a likeness of a real person, somehow incorporates the desire to 'know' the other.

'Face': confrontation with the other

Looking at someone's face presents contradictory positions: the compulsive search for what is recognisable and familiar in something that is strangely different from us and ultimately unknowable, and the possibility of possessing power or vulnerability. We cannot easily comprehend something that is both the same as us and yet strange. Emmanuel Levinas introduces physicality into philosophical discussions of our encounter with others, which tend usually to remain abstract and ambiguous. Very like Ruff's bald presentation of 'face', Levinas uses the word 'face' to name our confrontation with the other. Levinas's (and Ruff's) 'face' functions as a metaphor for what is different from us and what we cannot know; it is both abstract idea and material reference to someone specific (Levinas 1988: 171–4). Levinas introduced a perspective that is between individual psychology and object, between real person and abstract concept, between familiar and strange. As with Derrida, Foucault and Kristeva, he challenged the fundamental givens of philosophical thought – the centrality of the subject – by attempting to avoid comparative and judgemental processes of thinking. Levinas's ethical consideration of others challenges the more obvious connotations of an actual face-to-face encounter – the habitual existential position between two people – that assumes alienated distance and positions the other as an object (Levinas 1986: 19). Significantly for the photograph, in Levinas's version of encounter, the possession of power moves back and forth between the two protagonists. He describes 'the action of the face' as demanding: as unknowable and yet compelling, vulnerable and yet authoritative, unpredictable and yet potent (Levinas 1988: 168–9). Rather than aiming to establish comfortable familiarity, he seeks an encounter that maintains this strangeness and which does not involve dominance by one or the other (Levinas 1969: 43). He sees others as so completely alien that they cannot be incorporated into the same familiar territory as our own. If we apply this sort of non-oppositional attitude to the photographic relationship, it suggests a photographic-subject who is defiant, elusive and ambivalent, certainly not submissive, and not easily revealing their psychology. Levinas's philosophy establishes recognition of the other's difference that neither reverses nor submits to power, does not generalise strangeness, but allows the possibility for what is same *and* strange, rather than reducing the subject to a vehicle for a photographer's idea.

Levinas's insistence on maintaining the strangeness of alterity requires that in some way we must distance ourselves from our self-obsession sufficiently to 'receive' the other. In the context of the photograph, the possibility of non-oppositional encounter realigns the supposed power of the subject-photographer over the other – the photographic-subject. Such realignment balances out the 'I' and the 'you' to something more ambivalent, less arrogant and less certain, suggesting an attitude more of exchange. Portrayal of people frequently adopts a participatory strategy, rather than a distanced objectivity. Non-oppositional approaches to subject can be seen where the relationship of subject-to-object is visible, or in which the photographer participates. Goldin's *Siobhan* series would be good example of this, as she states: 'I'm usually engaged in activities that I'm photographing' (Goldin 1996–97). In contrast, Boris Mikhailov's *Case History* (1999) provides a provocative example of portrayal that maintains the strangeness of the other and realigns the power balance – very subtly.[7] This series documents aspects of poverty and social disintegration following the collapse of the Soviet Union, specifically the life of the homeless (*bomzhes*). Mikhailov dispenses with pretensions of expressing the dignity of vulnerability or disadvantage. Instead he exposes disadvantage by portraying the awfulness of an unspeakable situation. Somehow, the omission of critical comment, or disapproval or apology for his intrusion, amplifies an argument wholly rhetorically. For example:

Three figures nearly fill the frame. The room is bare and neglected; nothing hanging from a clothes rail; doubtful looking electrics; faded wallpaper. Two women are supporting a third naked woman. They seem barely able to hold her, as she seems to slip obliquely between them. The woman on the left inclines her head toward the other two and looks at me with resignation, whist the one on the right concentrates on keeping her grip. But it is the central figure who holds my attention and looks unashamedly straight at me. She disarms me, denies me any certain position in relation to her. I am made ineffectual, hopeless and wholly irrelevant in the face of this display. I feel accused, responsible somehow.

Mikhailov's work has consistently challenged ideologies by using controversial subject-matter and irony. *Case History*, being particularly confrontational, reverses the humanist position of compassionate, but generalised, presentation by confronting the viewer's assumption of power, which is present in patronage and in looking at images of people. This series affronts our condition of comfortable privilege that recognises those more vulnerable than ourselves. Mikhailov's theatricality amplifies the strangeness of these 'others'. This strangeness depends on the specific histories of Stalinist Russia: the politically manufactured stigma attached to unemployment and the subsequent lack of sympathy for the unemployed and homeless at the time. Instead of bringing them nearer to us, by pointing out aspects of common humanity and making them effectively the same, Mikhailov keeps them and the experience separate – strange, and very difficult to look at.

'Disappearance': avoidance of the encounter

Allied to Levinas's attitude to alterity, Jean Baudrillard discusses signification and the relation between subject and object in the context of taking photographs.[8] Baudrillard's involvement with photography provides a figurative narration of his more general critique of culture and the contemporary condition. For example, his essays in *Photographies* (1999b) circulate around the foundational themes for photographic practice: reality, truth, originality, fictionality. The photograph, photographers and the photographed become a visual syntax for appearance, truth and the human subject. And the portrait, as metaphor for a mirror of consciousness, is suitably positioned to visually demonstrate the nature of objectification and/or authorship and what he calls 'the emptiness and fragility of exchange' with others (Baudrillard 1999a). Speaking as photographer, Baudrillard's provocative rhetoric, some of which I have reconfigured below, searches for ways to achieve a 'true photograph' (Baudrillard 1999b: 146), suggesting the need for a sort of innocence:

I must empty my mind, hold my breath, immerse myself; disappear as a subject and enjoy my own absence; do not attempt to represent reality; abandon the instinct to interpret; defy all resemblance and look elsewhere; suspend my judgement, my gaze, my vision; do not seek an image; struggle to assert myself, yet lose control.

Echoing Barthes's description of posing for a photograph (1993b: 11), Baudrillard describes the photographic act as a duel: a reciprocal 'dare', but one in which the photographer-subject might potentially disappear and be defined by the other – the photographic-subject. This 'mutual disappearance' challenges the oppositional tradition of the power of the photographer-subject on the one hand, and the objectified photographic-subject on the other. And, in contrast to Karsh, Baudrillard suggests that what is interesting is the photographic-subject's superficial appearance, their 'secret alterity'. Because we cannot lift the mask, the photographer should not seek the identity beneath the mask, but the mask beneath the identity – 'the face that haunts us and deflects us from our identity' (Baudrillard 1999b: 137). His attitude to photography recalls Barthes's critique of Western humanism that assumes its values to be universal (demonstrated by *The Family of Man* exhibition, 1955). Describing photographers as predators, plundering that which doesn't concern them, Baudrillard looks for something besides socially concerned documentary, or aesthetic idealisation of the sort characterised by the work of Karsh. He despises what he calls 'realist' photography that documents 'real situations' in the 'pursuit of naturalness'. He also suggests that photography with purposeful intention loses its potential for potent quality, and photography that is 'aestheticised, calculated and composed' is not interesting (Zurbrugg 1997: 35). Like Ruff, he contends it is impossible to describe the 'essential' nature of an individual and challenges the expectation that photography should be either definitive or transcend words (Baudrillard 1999b: 136–7). In asserting the object's influence over the subject, he suggests a reversal, or at least an equality, of power relations.

> Annelies Strba: 'When I push the shutter release. I close my eyes' (Strba 1997: 326)
> Luc Delahaye: 'I hold my breath and let the shutter go' (quoted in Baudrillard 1999a)

Reminiscent of Baudrillard's attempt to 'disappear' as subject, these two statements demonstrate two contrasting means of relinquishing power and authorship by allowing the *physicality* of the camera operation to dictate the photographic event: Delahaye, by secretly concealing the camera, controlling the shutter from his pocket and not looking through a viewfinder and Strba, by shutting her eyes. In taking no part in active image construction other than the decision to press the shutter, they each manufacture *disappearance*. Delahaye's position is one of anonymity and Strba's of intimacy (*Shades of Time*, 1977–97).[9] Following a tradition introduced by Strand and Evans, Delahaye's series of people seated in the *Metro* (1999) shows individuals staring, focus-less, with no apparent awareness of being looked at, and separated from us. Baudrillard describes them as 'divested of identity' and, for the moment of the photograph, 'absent from their lives' (1999a). Delahaye relinquishes responsibility as he cannot ultimately 'see' what he is looking at. Having to hide in order to take the photograph, he too is absenting himself from the confrontation and, in a sense, becomes object. As Strba shuts her eyes, her authorial voice disappears and her 'absence' denies the intentional 'photographic eye'. Strba presents a detailed portrayal of her family over a twenty-year period, with particular focus on her two daughters – as children and as parents – carrying out ordinary activities. It is a wholly subjective and digressive series that does not conform to any sequential logic explaining behaviour, location or story. Because the subject-matter is so commonplace, it presents the extreme eventlessness of domestic life. Her subjects are diffused by the insistent inclusion of incidental detail and disarray of bedding, cats, pots and pans, clothing. There can be no objectivity, because both roles, of photographer and photographic-subject, are confused and blurred by their shared intimacy, and ultimately it is this intimacy that determines the results (Tormey 2003). Series such as this – or Richard Billingham's *Ray's a Laugh*, 1996 or Tierney Gearon's *I Am a Camera*, 2001 – are examples of a vernacular realism that uses careless unpreparedness as a method (Batchen 2000: 262–71). They appear indistinguishable from family snapshots and celebrate increasingly crude versions of the 'everyday' and the 'natural' in their presentation of very ordinary situations. Realising Robinson's 'glorification of the Unessential' and the 'bare, bald, and ugly' of 1896, raw and unbeautiful realism persists as a metaphor for truth. Thought to be more genuine and direct than self-conscious art-photography, the qualities of the snapshot have become signs of authenticity. Baudrillard's rethinking of the primacy of the subject suggests for photography an avoidance of the active fabrication of meaning. He suggests that 'poetic order requires that the event should not exactly take place' and that there should be a 'fracture in this excessively well-crafted machinery of presentation' (Baudrillard 1999b: 150, 133). The methods that these photographers adopt diminish the possibility of 'calculated and composed' images. What Baudrillard proposed in theory and what their work performs is that, in the lack of control or search for intentional meaning, the photographic-subject and meaning emerge independently without anything having been done.

Ulf Lundin's *Pictures of a Family* (1996) presents a contradictory take on anonymity and intimacy in which the photographer negotiates permission to photograph an old school friend's family life, on the condition that Lundin's presence remains hidden

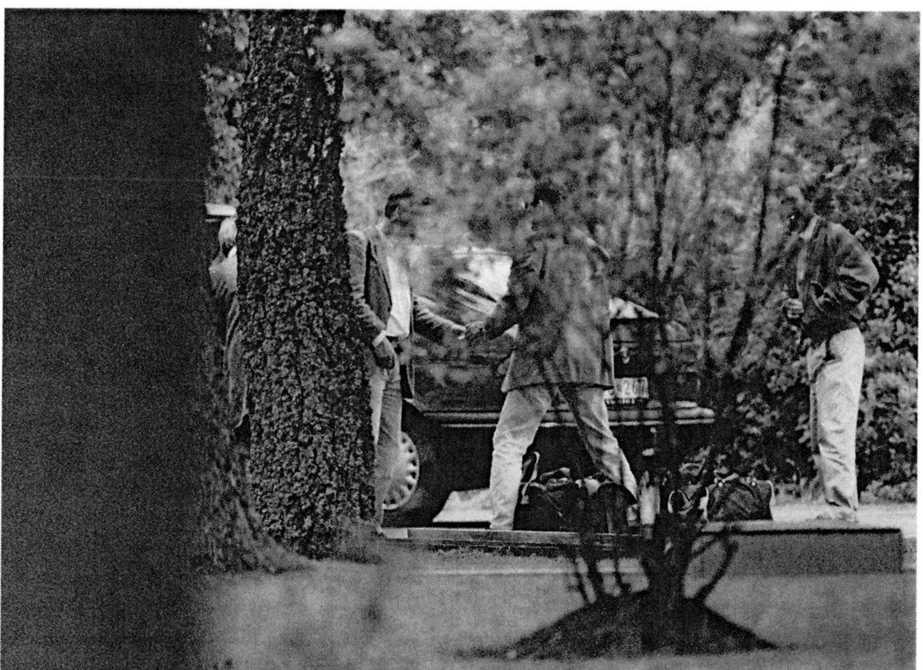

Figure 8 Ulf Lundin, *Pictures of a Family*, 1996.

(Figure 8). It is intimate in the scrutiny of the behaviour, relationships and peculiarities of a man who had been Lundin's friend in childhood, and anonymous in that we don't know who this man is or where he is and he doesn't know when Lundin is observing him. The series is founded on a complicit contract of voyeuristic indulgence, which satisfies the desire to observe others without censure. It is an example that exploits the norm of subject supremacy and of objectification, which Baudrillard was concerned to expose. Baudrillard's desire for alternative models of representation to humanist universality or moral documentation is paralleled in numerous examples that seem to test the tension between the respective positions of photographer-subject and photographic-subject. Shizuka Yokomizo fabricates a situation whereby, having sent her subjects a letter inviting them to be photographed at a prearranged time, she photographs them looking out from an illuminated window, anonymously (*Stranger* series 1998–2000). She never meets her subjects 'face-to-face'. Marjaana Kella has photographed people from the back (*Reversed Portraits*, 1996–97) and under hypnosis.[10] Bettina von Zwehl adopts elaborate methods to control the appearance of her subjects and to limit the variability of expression or mannerism; in one series they are told to hold their breath and in others are presented in a highly prescribed and artificial manner.[11] Each artist adopts a bald portrait methodology as a frame, which entirely contradicts their appearance as 'portraits'. Yokomizo and Kella display an anxiety to present subjectivity untouched by directorial control and to tackle the encounter in a way that circumvents confrontation; they thus avoid being accused of objectifying their subjects. They are implicitly intent on demonstrating the *difference* in others not reduced to a reflection of themselves and thereby the same. Each instance is indicative of deliberate strategy – an ironic game of self-conscious 'knowingness' – that swings between control and lack of control and explains the photographic-event as being fundamentally an invention – fictional.

The matrix of looking

Focusing on our response to photographs, this section extends discussion of the relationship between the photographer-subject and photographic-subject to include the viewing-subject. Foucault's essay 'Las Meninas' (2003 [1966]) demonstrates the interpretation of images as being initiated by a matrix of looking. He discusses Diego Velázquez's painting *Las Meninas* (1656), which depicts the painter looking towards the viewer and the subject he is painting, which we cannot see.[12] What the painting points to ultimately is the absence of the subjects being painted – the king and queen, whom we only see reflected in the mirror facing us. *Las Meninas* self-consciously displays the mesh of looking: the painter looking at his model whilst appearing to look at us the spectators; the subjects within the painting looking at each other; the *Infanta*, surrounded by looks, looking at us. In describing the physical geometrical intersections of a painting, Foucault roams round the picture, considering each protagonist, the role they might play and the possible relationships between them, speculating on motivation and on past and future event. Like Derrida's encounter with writing, Foucault's engagement with the image and looking points to a network of exchanges and meanings. This web of relational gazes and positionings becomes more complex as his contemplation includes what is *not* represented within the space of the painting. Like Derrida, he also gives attention to what is absent, by describing the space and movement that can be imagined, between what we see and what we don't, and what may happen next. Foucault points to the many different realities presented by the picture, which are realised in our reflection of it: the reality of the painter, the material figures in the painting looking at the painter and us, the reflection in the mirror. Foucault ponders the exchange between the subject and the object in this encounter, in which we are both subject looking at a painting and object being looked at by Velasquez, in which 'the spectator and the model, reverse their roles to infinity' (Foucault 2003: 5). Looking at *Bloody Merry* (Figure 4), I find myself caught in a similar, but less resolved, web of looks and it is in this exchange of looking that I can imagine the scene as part of an ongoing linear narrative:

This infinite movement of looking actively involves me, as spectator; it requires me to complete the process by looking back and searching for explanation. The two figures in the foreground look back at me in a seemingly passive yet confrontational way. I look back at them and wonder why; I can imagine what went before and what might happen next; I can anticipate that they are about to act in some way and can imagine what those actions might be; I can imagine their attitude toward the photographer or to me. The central figure's gaze is ambiguous; is she looking at me, or at the couple in front of her? The woman at the back does not engage with this fantasy at all. She looks away to her left towards some other place.

Dialogical matrix: subject-to-subject-to-subject

The painting *Las Meninas* draws us into a dialogue with the author (painter) by visually incorporating the painter in the painting. Kristeva's exploration of narrative and novel (1980 [1969]) suggests that we (the spectators) will always be drawn into dialogue with the author and protagonists – at least figuratively. In exploring ways in which to consider texts other than by formal analysis, Kristeva discusses the ideas of Mikhail Bakhtin. Her application of Bakhtin's work is significant for the reading of photographs in two respects: first, with regard to the process of *intertextuality*, which confirms that simple sign systems are inadequate in the face of the interminable exchange of looking, and, second, by suggesting a breakdown of the fixed oppositions of author/reader and signifier/signified. Kristeva introduces the term *intertextuality* whilst exploring Bakhtin's idea of the 'intersection' between the writer, the reader, context and history (Kristeva 1980: 65–6). Using Bakhtin's terms, the photograph can be defined *horizontally* by the photographer and the reader (e.g. I see *Bloody Merry* as amusing and repellent), and *vertically* in its relation to other photographs –

historically and contemporarily (*Bloody Merry*'s reference to historical tableau paintings and to other examples, of current theatrical staging, such as Jeff Wall's). Rather than having any fixed meaning, a photograph, as with any text, can be described as a 'mosaic of quotations' and as an 'absorption' of past and present practices. This is a process that occurs besides artistic intention; it is not the same as the intentional quotation used by Sherrie Levine in *After Walker Evans* (1979) or *After Edward Weston ca. 1925* (1980).[13] Bakhtin's term *dialogism* describes the method of identifying different voices in a literary text, so that responding to texts that are understood as a matrix of interactions between author, reader and character described in the work encourages the inter-penetration of actual and imaginary, virtual worlds. Kristeva explains narration as a dialogue between the author, the reader and the characters in the text (1980: 74–6). Transporting this idea to the context of photography, all of the protagonists in the event of the photographic portrait are subjects who relate to each other: the photographer is subject, the viewer is subject and the characters/objects depicted in the photograph assume the status of subjects. Each assumes multiple roles. In Ruff's *Portrait* (2001):

The photographer (Ruff) is absent and not visible in the photograph, but is included in the narrative matrix, represented by the photographic-subject (the girl), who is visible. The photographer becomes a split subject: as active subject, he fabricates the photographic-subject and positions me as viewer-subject. Ruff is represented within his own photograph, disguised and manifested as the girl. He is also defined by the image because I, as viewer-subject, name him as 'author'. The girl becomes object, fabricated by Ruff and named and interpreted by me. She is also active subject because she represents the photographer. She is therefore both representative of the photographer and represented as object by the photographer. My process as viewer-subject is twofold: I actively interpret the photograph and, as passive subject, I am defined by Ruff, who has fabricated the photographic-subject for me. Both Ruff and I are disguised within the photograph and form part of a 'dialogical matrix' (following Kristeva 1980: 76).

Dialogism inserts psychological aspects implicit in even the most literal depiction, as a series of internal dialogues. With regard to the photograph, it presents us with an alternative process of meaning to the assumptions that I itemised as 'real' in Chapter One. Kristeva's psychoanalytic approach to understanding the dynamics of the creative process and 'poetic language', explored in *Desire in Language* (1980 [1979]), assumes the value of the psychoanalytical process and provides a useful perspective from which to look at photographs. Psychoanalysis is a structured encounter between analyst and analysand that aims to explore an individual's subjectivity and the patterns of relationship with others. The psychoanalytical process encourages the exploration of displaced meaning, which lurks behind any articulation of experience. Language (visual and verbal) reveals clues that point to our unconscious motivations. In this sense, psychoanalysis in practice demonstrates what Derrida seeks to expose in written representations, by scrutinising and playing with texts. And the psychotherapeutic process provides an alternative model for 'interpreting art'. This is an approach to reading photographs that breaks down the strict roles of exchange by way of identification and transference; an approach that does not aim to achieve any one ultimate goal or discover one essential truth, but sets out to trouble the photograph. This is a conception of meaning that does not seek to find any *one* hidden or stable meaning behind appearance. In this process everything that is presented is useful; there is no privileged meaning and all details and gestures are equally fruitful and meaningful; there is no-thing that is meaningless. We can identify significance in any number of ways that are equally and simultaneously valid, and each one meaning can implicate as much as another. As in the process of psychoanalysis, Kristeva's concept of subjectivity suggests an artistic process that is willing to put itself into question, to face what is unfamiliar or uncomfortable. From this perspective, both the photograph and the subject reading the photograph, are in *process*.

Kristeva's exploration of *dialogism* serves to unify discussion of authorship and the relationship between all protagonists in the photographic event and invites a more complex interrelationship than that of simply subject and object. I use the term *dialogical* to indicate a form of interpretation that can be understood as a dialogue, which is not one of linear narrative where only the author is active. It presents an alternative conception of analysis to one that seeks objectivity or a universal voice. The dialogical process forces alternatives to the stable predictability of what Bakhtin calls the *monological*, which follows familiar linear structures, and aims to establish a static transcendental signified (Kristeva 1980: 74). In contrast, *dialogism* presupposes an intervention by the reader/viewer within the narrative, which moves back and forth between subject and subject, between photographer and reader (1980: 67). *Dialogical* methods in photographic practice adopt a dialogical involvement with character and force alternatives to narrations that follow the familiar hierarchical structure of authorial voice (1980: 78). Series such as Strba's *Shades of Time* presuppose an intervention by the photographic-subject, focus more on the relationship between the photographer and photographic-subject, and break down the fixed positions of author / subject / reader. The strategy of photographic seriality, rather than sequentiality, offers the simultaneous presentation of a range of experiences, traversing chronology and psychological dimensions. Series such as these depend on the relationships between different elements within the structure and set up a dialogue between photographs and between photographer, photographic-subject and ultimately the viewer (1980: 71). *Dialogism* parallels descriptions of the dual roles assumed by photographers and their respective 'subjects', where not only the photographed-subject is actor but also the photographer. Larry Sultan's *Pictures from Home* is an example in which the author appears as the subject, represented by the portrayal of his parents: Larry is substituted by his father Irv, and his mother Jean. Alternatively, the narrator (photographer) is figuratively inserted alongside the subject, as in Goldin's work, and, in its extreme form, narration can be barely indistinguishable from the characters depicted. For example, Nikki S. Lee's *Projects* (1997–2001) are self-portraits that conflate the photographer-subject and photographic-subject – they are the same. She photographs herself, having adopted an appropriate persona and 'having become' one with her subjects by infiltrating an identifiable community, gaining their trust and adapting her looks, mannerisms and behaviour accordingly. Her working process takes parody to a living extreme, in an extended performance. Lee immerses herself in that other culture for a number of months, incorporating the cultural codes of each group. As her subjectivity is always false, it is difficult to differentiate reality from performance:

It is remarkable how she achieves the appearance of different identities through dress, stance and expression: compare the joyful engagement with friends in the 'Hispanic project' with the hard, defiantly serious and almost aggressive stance in the 'Hip Hop project'. In each of these series, Lee looks at the camera knowingly, enticing me to separate her from the group; she seems at ease within the group and yet identifies herself by the centrality of the pose; her disguise is, in some cases, minimal and yet convincing (e.g. Punk, 1997; Yuppie, 1998; Hispanic, 1998; Hip Hop, 2001).[14]

'The photograph is a machine for making talk'

Lee's projects are exaggerated and visual manifestations of Derrida's consideration of the daily predicament of coming to terms with others. In his lecture *What Is Called Not Thinking* (2001), Derrida examines the process of internal thought by giving a self-reflexive account of a face-to-face encounter with someone.[15] He describes his thinking as it proceeds throughout the course of a conversation, questioning his interaction with his own thoughts, and with what the other is saying. The other person makes a difference to what he thinks and says, as he follows what is said to him, as he is interrupted, as he lets himself be surprised or persuaded. He describes the process as a sort of meta-narrative, because as he follows his own speech his thinking changes, his intentions change, his feelings change – he is at each moment something different to both himself and to others. His thinking has 'intrinsic multiplicity' as he continually reinvents himself; he is at once narrator / character / author / reader / writer / written about – all interchangeable – following each other. Derrida's description of encounter with being-different introduces a 'radically discontinuous' and divided subject, whose thought is in disarray and influenced day-by-day simply by speaking with other people.

Derrida's demonstration of the discontinuous nature of thought echoes Kristeva's *dialogical matrix*. And 'Right of Inspection' (1989) ['Droit de regard', 1985] recounts a response to photographs that similarly follows a multi-layered sequence of thought that is recognisably *dialogical*. Derrida's title – the *right* of inspection – plays with our assumption that photographs give us the right to looks at others (as I described in Chapter One, looking at *Allie Mae Burroughs*). His immersive reading of Marie-Françoise Plissart's photographic sequence is a speculation that deliberately avoids a definitive account or obvious interpretation. He adopts an *active* procedure that takes the form of a dialogue between the photograph and the viewer-subject, which allows every detail in the photograph to have significance and each participant in the process to have a voice. Derrida's *perquisition* (a combination of pursuit, inquisition, search, inquiry) allows him to speak about the photograph from different points of view. In a typical, rhetorical performance, he demonstrates the mediation of perception, via thinking and association, as inseparable from the imaginary and symbolic (Derrida 1973: 103). The following passage is a condensed appropriation following the first few pages of 'Right of Inspection':

It is assumed that a photograph presents something that can be recognised and a plot begins to unravel. It fascinates and seduces us by ciphering all sorts of diagonals. It is the story of a secret that may or may not exist. It is the opposite of construction – a back-to-front construction of reality, somewhat in the way one speaks of constructions of psychoanalysis – that puts oneself in question, that is not fixed. This then will be the rule; I'll refrain from confessing to you all the stories. Of course these stories are not infinite in number but they remain practically innumerable. And with the denial, the desire for stories becomes all the more intense. So tell a story, a large number of possible and unspoken stories ... not to recount, enumerate – not to totalise ... I would rather call it a photographic search (perquisition), a pursuit of photographic acts or experiences, photographic histories. The photograph is a machine for making talk – inexhaustibly – that has an altogether different relation to any spoken word ... The photographic event has another structure.

Whilst they are not systematic methods as such, Derrida uses two active procedures which characterise this dialogical approach. The first is the use of words (*photogrammar*) that split and contradict themselves throughout the text and make use of photographic terminology as meta-metaphor for meaning. For example, the use of the word 'develop', the physical process of making a photograph, works as metaphor for the process of understanding and finding meaning. *Photogrammar* functions as a dynamic destabiliser in the text, which keeps the meaning mobile and ambivalent in the very structure and expression of the writing. The play with words incorporates both noun and verb functions, so that qualities can be static (pose, *n.* = a posture that is assumed) or can actively disturb and influence (pose, *v.* = propose a problem): *The photographer presents a position (artistic) by instructing the photographic-subject to assume a position (attitude) and a position (location) within the photograph.* The playing together of different senses beside each other establish a sense that lies *between* the activity of a verb and the passivity of a noun. Referring to visual works as 'mute tableaux', Derrida makes use of the contextual mutability of words and their meaning.

The second procedure is Derrida's dialogical structure, which subverts the opposition of viewer-subject and photographer-subject, of outside and inside. He tests interpretation with an internal 'drama' that can be read in many directions (Derrida 1989: 18–23). He speaks about the photograph from a number of different points of view: looking at the photograph from outside its frame, and from a number of imagined points of view (as protagonists) inside the frame of the photograph, so that each position takes its turn as nominating subject (1989: 25). Like Kristeva's *dialogical matrix*, this play-function allows him to speak from the position either of reader or of one of those depicted in the photograph, and to move between them. The one who is subject may be... I, you, he, she, we, you, they, in turn. In such a way he uses multi-subjectivity and the displacement of words to contradict himself and to change his view (opinion and/or viewing position). The series of interconnected associations hypothesise, repeat and extend meaning, generating a process of understanding between text and reader. Derrida's rhetorical performance provides a conceptual framework for any number of qualities simultaneously. Here, in looking at Jeff Wall's *Insomnia* (1994, Figure 9), I adopt Derrida's process of internal dialogue, his conception of the photograph as 'a machine for making talk' and as a 'photographic event' (1989: 25) as I speak from the point of view of the photographic-subject and speculate as follows:

I am lying on the floor. I am under the table. Somehow I feel better here – the table covers my body and yet I have a clear view to the door between the fridge and the table. The floor is cold. I have felt the surface of the floor – I have moved my palm across and around the surface – it is smooth, it is cold. I have noted the imperfections. I have removed the clock from the wall; I have no wish to know the time. There is no time outside of this room. The fridge in front of me is cold. I have explored what is under the fridge already and I wish that I hadn't looked. If I shift my body and view, I have plenty more options yet to explore this other world of underneath. Underneath the sink, underneath the cooker. I have exhausted my looking in cupboards – I understand what defines my world by what is in my cupboards. The experience disappoints. Particularly the long thin cupboard, which promises so much. And the brown paper bag – I had forgotten what was in it. And I climbed on the chair and looked right at the back of the top shelves and climbed on the table and felt across some of the ceiling. I understand now the stretch of the room – the walls, the ceiling and now I am understanding the floor. I didn't put the butter away or wash the pan; I didn't do anything practical – that is for the daytime. I have a clear view now to the door. And I have made myself comfortable; I have a pillow at least, so I can really look and understand the view through the door.

Responding to a photograph can be seen as a matter of reflection that moves through history – an event that happens when it is looked at, rather than a record of something past. In this kind of description, a photograph is active in generating thoughts and in supporting contradictory interpretations. This manner of speaking to photographs does not distinguish between what is seen and what is imagined. Meaning is allowed to emerge, invoked by dialogue, in what is absent and in imagination. Derrida's influence can be seen applied more generally in the context of visual semiotics and art history. For example, Mieke Bal's image analysis acknowledges three aspects of Derrida's work most pertinent to art history: his concern with intertextuality, polysemy and the shifting location of meaning (2001: 67). Bal focuses on *who* is looking and *how* they are looking, necessitating reference to historical, social

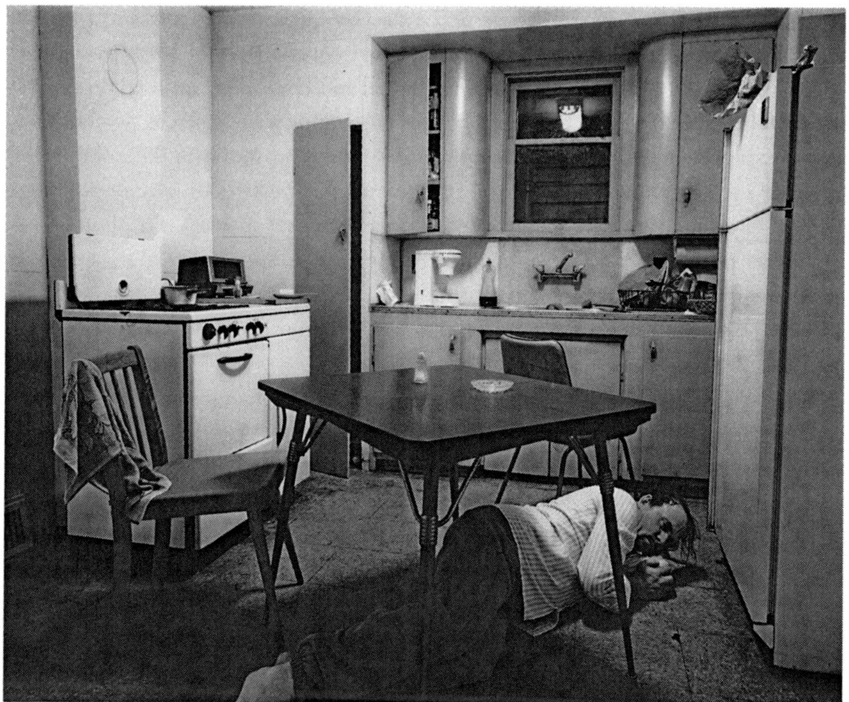

Figure 9 Jeff Wall, *Insomnia*, 1994.

and subjective contexts rather than the traditional aim of 'disinterested' analysis. Her readings, which start with the margins of detail rather than general overview, approach a reading that uses visual and discursive elements (Bal 2001: 78). However, Bal's distinction between 'pure visuality' and 'meaning' (Bal 2001: 69) perpetuates the interpretation of meaning as primarily verbal, and assumes that the image cannot speak sufficiently without its translation into narrative, whereas Derrida's process of *perquisition* promotes thinking within the text in a way that plays with subjectivity and realities, and counters the development of narrative.

I have adopted Derrida's procedure of multi-positional dialogue intermittently throughout this book, where I may appropriate or paraphrase texts either by reapplying them in a photographic context or in an entirely subjective way in order to demonstrate the simultaneity of visual meaning and to amplify the potential exchange between different discourses. In assuming different roles in a dialogue with an image, I can be more reflexive in my consideration. I can consider what differences these positions make and what my commentary is telling me about my assumptions – whether they are psychoanalytical, representational or political. I can ask what the concepts are that are presented by the photograph: what is the discourse? A reflexive approach recognises the inevitable subjectivity in my thinking and, in acknowledging that subjectivity as being central, I can utilise it. A subjective position demands an active viewing and an active questioning. However, I do not suggest that when reading photographs we must enter a state of inner psychology but, in recognising the mismatch between verbal and visual description, I do suggest the usefulness of strategies that maintain 'intrinsic multiplicity'. Just as psychotherapeutic exploration roves around different viewpoints and speaks in different voices, as object and subject, it is possible to keep a roving perspective, which enjoys a range of meanings found in the course of the process. On first looking at a photograph, we can try not to be constrained by predetermined assumptions. Visual meaning can be encouraged to reverberate and to *avoid* verbal explanation of the visual – at least initially. This requires response on several levels: semiotic, emotional, conceptual, political.

This chapter establishes the photographic portrait as a manifestation of exchange dependent on *process* and dialogue. It identifies alternative positions for photographer, subject and reader to objectification or didactic authorship. The degree of complicity in the relationship between protagonists determines the particular mode of exchange. The portrait illustrates the perpetual struggle with two notions: the existence of an essential individual and the possibility of objective representation. Attempts made to mirror reality in as crude a realism as possible, as with the adoption of a snapshot appearance, may be a subversion of tradition but it is one that perpetuates dependence on a belief that there can be an essential reality to be found – ultimately in visual appearance. The search for truth persists even if, on a rational level, we may have absorbed the post-structural adjustment that there is no truth outside representation, that we do not experience the world and others in a simple process, unaffected by the structure of the world in which we exist. Whilst the goal of speaking to a unified subject or of finding a conclusion is established as problematic, it remains our desire and Derrida would not advocate that we should not attempt to satisfy it. Whilst the post-structural theories described in this book counter the classic modernist view, I do not mean to assert them as superior – but different.

Kristeva and Derrida demonstrate meaning as inseparable from the inter-relationship of thought, imagination and perception that asserts a discursive *process*. Both assert a dialogical engagement with texts or images, which begins to articulate an internal conceptual procedure for responding to photographs. A photograph can move us quickly from the referent to our own interpretative conceptual framework and towards metaphoric expansion, which will be examined in the next chapter. Following Derrida's *perquisition*, the photograph can be understood as being a place *of* and *for* dialogue – literally a spoken discourse, a place of exchange. Thought of in these terms, rather than its alliance with the faculty of reason, discourse can incorporate different theoretical or subjective positions so that I can speak *to* and *with* the image/object in different voices and from different perspectives, as spectator, as participator, as narrator. Derrida's multi-faceted description of thought demonstrates the susceptibility of self to the whims of chance, circumstance and the idiosyncrasies of encounter. This condition underlines the nearness of any presentation, however self-present, to fiction. What I have termed *dialogical realism* offers the possibility of an expansive photographic event and one in which the viewer is invited to interact with the photograph, which provokes a kind of dialogue. I am asserting the dialogical process as a positive adventure and a significant feature that liberates the photograph from the moment in which is taken and that requires a durational response.

Suggested further reading

Bal, M. (2001) *Looking In: The Art of Viewing*, G+B Arts International, Amsterdam

Barthes, R. (1993b) *Camera Lucida* [1980], trans. R. Howard [1981], Vintage, London

Colebrooke, C. (2005) *Philosophy and Poststructuralist Theory: From Kant to Deleuze*. Edinburgh University Press, Edinburgh

Derrida, J. (1989) 'Right of Inspection' ['Droit de Regard', 1985] with Marie-Françoise Plissart, trans. D. Wills, *Art & Text* 32, 19–97

Foucault, M. (2003) 'Las Meninas', in *The Order of Things* [1966], [English translation 1970], Routledge, London; New York

Kozloff, M. (1994) *Lone Visions, Crowded Frames*, University of Mexico Press, Albuquerque

Levinas, E. (1988) 'The Paradox of Morality: An Interview with Emmanuel Levinas', in R. Bernasconi and D. Wood (eds), *The Provocation of Levinas: Rethinking the Other*, Routledge, London; New York

Oliver, K. (ed.) (1997) *The Portable Kristeva*, Columbia University Press, New York

Zurbrugg, N. (ed.) (1997) *Jean Baudrillard: Art & Artefact*, Sage, London

Notes

1 Karsh wrote of his own work in *Karsh Portfolio* (1968), 'Within every man and woman a secret is hidden, and as a photographer it is my task to reveal it if I can. The revelation, if it comes at all, will come in a small fraction of a second with an unconscious gesture, a gleam of the eye, a brief lifting of the mask that all humans wear to conceal their innermost selves from the world. In that fleeting interval of opportunity the photographer must act or lose his prize.'

2 Barthes [1957] describes the way that myths are created and formed by images that have become cliché and ideologically loaded (published in Barthes 1993a).

3 'I really disapprove of photographing celebrities... the worst of it is something like Karsh' (Evans 1994d: 37–8).

4 Search online collections for Tina Barney: Museum of Contemporary Photography, Chicato (www.mocp.org) or The Art Institute of Chicaco (www.artic.edu).

5 Search online collections for *Pictures from Home*: Museum of Contemporary Photography, Chicato (www.mocp.org) or The Art Institute of Chicaco (www.artic.edu). See Sultan (1992).

6 Search online for images on 'Thomas Ruff portraits'.

7 www.saatchi-gallery.co.uk/artists/artpages/boris_mikhailov_285.htm, accessed 8 August 2010. See also Mikhailov (1999).

8 Baudrillard's ideas can be interpreted literally and as a result are frequently associated with the shallower aspects of postmodernism, whereas his manner of writing is figurative and his perspective a form of idealism. I do not suggest therefore that Baudrillard intends a literal assumption by photographers of what appears to be a manual of instruction. Nor do I suggest

that photographers attempt to respond to Baudrillard's challenge, but that this practice offers an alternative perspective from which to view the same issues.

9 Strba presents a detailed portrayal of her family over a twenty-year period. Started as a private document, the work represents the boundaries of the private broken by its later public display.

10 See for example *Reversed Portrait* series – *Woman In a Patterned Chemise* (1997/2002) and *Grey-haired Man* (1997/98), www.shanelavalette.com/journal/2007/02/22/marjaana-kella-reversed-portraits, accessed 7 August 2010.

11 See for example, *Untitled II* and *Untitled III* (1998 and 1999), www.steidlville.com/books/441-Bettina-von-Zwehl.html, accessed 7 August 2010.

12 Diego Velázquez, *Las Meninas* (1656): http://paulcorio.blogspot.com/2007/02/paintings-i-like-pt-2.html, accessed 24 August 2012.

13 Search the Metropolitan Museum, New York, www.metmuseum.org/toah/works-of-art/1995.266.2 and www.afterwalkerevans.com, accessed 24 August 2012.

14 Search online for *Hip Hop Project*: Spencer Museum of Art, University of Kansas Collection (www.spencerart.ku.edu/collection) and Museum of Contemporary Photography, Chicago collection (www.mocp.org). See also the Creator's Project video at http://thecreatorsproject.com/en-uk.creators/nikki-s-lee, accessed 10 September 2012.

15 Derrida's *What Is Called Not Thinking* refers to Martin Heidegger's lectures, *What Is Called Thinking?* [1951–52] (Heidegger 1968).

4

Poetic realism

This chapter uses the two models – of poem and space – to discuss aspects in a photograph besides the literal reference to appearances in the real world. It is concerned with how the photograph accesses what is besides the referent, and how we move between two spaces – the physical space of the photograph and the mental space of our projection. In so doing, it focuses on two pivotal and dichotomous relationships: the verbal/non-verbal and absence/presence. The artist Gabriel Orozco likens the photograph to a *space*, rather than the familiar 'window' to the world (Orozco 2009: 21). What he calls *space* indicates a conceptual space in which a number of ideas coexist or, in Derrida's terms, an assemblage of inter-dependent meanings interweave. Orozco's work demands that we engage our intelligence in response, because it does not rely on revealing the hidden beauty or peculiarity of objects; it does not provide all the answers for us. His references focus on slight but profound differences within a space, which are dependent on qualities of object, material and surface or on particular contexts. References can be subtle or obscure and can require sustained contemplation in order to recognise the full range of significance available. Orozco's photographs frequently make use of objects to describe a conflation of ideas – metaphorically:

Empty Shoebox (Figure 10) presents an empty white shoebox incongruously placed on snow. I assume it is empty because it sits in its lid, open, and I see nothing inside its brown interior; it presents a void. There is very little else: no contrast of form, colour or content. Its extreme minimalism prompts questions. How can I find any meaning other than its simply stating the concept of 'shoebox'? I may ask – whose shoes were once stored in here, and where are they now, and where is this snow? I speculate on the photographer's intention: is it perhaps to present the essential shoebox? I then resort to my knowledge: I recall the perfect minimalism of Donald Judd's boxes – but this shoebox is not perfect and references function. I know that it was exhibited at the Venice Biennale (1993). And the white box is a slab, a bare container almost a cube and surely makes reference to the debates that emerge from the dispersal of the art object and its reliance on the gallery, symbolised by the white cube.[1] The incongruity, the contrast of reference, comments on the emptiness of institutions and the inflated aesthetics of

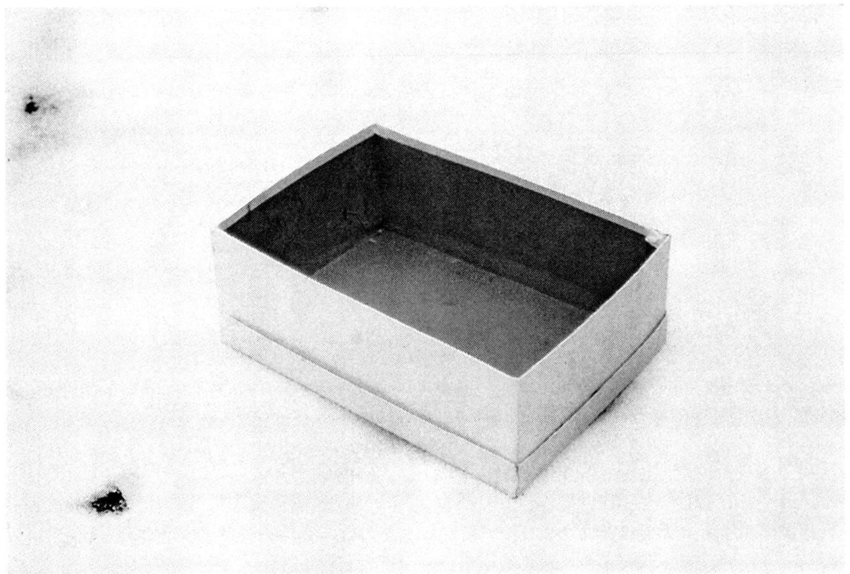

Figure 10 Gabriel Orozco, *Empty Shoe Box*, 1993.

art history. Jean Fisher (2003: 115) describes Orozco's work as reticent and 'closer to the workings of a dream than rational thought', suggesting a similarity with how one might describe poetry or Surrealist thought. Poetry constructs figurative meaning by using words in ways that encourage imagery to collide and meaning to reverberate. It is expected that poetry can dispense with rational logic and incorporate reference to real, psychological and imaginative worlds – simultaneously. Fisher alludes to a chimerical quality in Orozco's work that is neither one thing nor the other – in between fabricated and found, order and chaos. She likens it to a 'slippage into incoherence', like a sideways slip of the tongue – as if one says 'white' instead of 'wide' – much in the same way literary metaphor forces a reassessment of meaning by displacing context. Orozco's use of photographs plays with the rules of logic in crossing contextual domains and draws the analogy with satori (a sudden illuminating change of perspective, central to Zen practice):

> Question: 'What is the sound of one hand clapping?' or: Question: 'What is Buddha?' Answer: 'Three pounds of linen'. (Fineman 2004: 24)

Verbal/conceptual slippage like this is exemplified also in the Japanese poetic form of haiku, which, in very few syllables (17) constructs language in order to provoke an image in the viewer's mind. The play of visual and verbal imagery in haiku introduces the kind of poetic discourse that Orozco's work induces. His work requires an understanding of literal/present reference and figurative/absent meaning. This sort of disarming and often nonsensical logic bears a sense of its own:

At the ancient pond
a frog plunges into
the sound of water (Basho 1644–94)

The task in this chapter is to consider how these slippages in logic occur visually. They can be illustrated in a literal way by the displacement and juxtaposition of image fragments found in the Surrealist photography of, for example, Maurice Tabard or Man Ray.[2] Rosalind Krauss suggests that these forms of spatial dispersal, which use the 'anti-realist' effects of doubling, mirroring and cropping, rid the photograph of the literal reference that aspires to a form of photographic purity defined by 'the unitary condition of the moment' (Krauss 1986: 109–10). Photographic montage escapes this realism by literally cutting and pasting disparate elements or interrupting temporal sequence. The photograph's reality – 'that-which-was-present-at-one-time' – is thereby disturbed by distortions of time and space that disrupt the association of vision with what is considered to be an immediate and pure apprehension of experience (Krauss 1986: 104–7). But, being physically displaced, these methods deprive the photograph of its illusory reference. And non-literal photography need not be interpreted in this physical way.[3] My focus here is 'realism', and how photographs work *through* their indexical reference to express ideas. I focus therefore on the photograph's capacity to operate figuratively without resort to fragmentation, photogram or distortion. Photographs present a complex interaction of perception, language and image, and can draw us away from what is pictorially there by indicating what is absent. Because, besides referencing the presence of objects, they evoke immaterial concept – by means of metonym, metaphor and allegory, as with Orozco's *Empty Shoebox*.

Absence and presence[4]

Chapter One referred to the photograph as confronting the phenomenological activity of looking and naming things. The notion of photographic transparency assumes that because an object is 'named', by virtue of its visual resemblance, it will reveal its meaning transparently. At the same time, art-photography expects a dimension of meaning that is inexpressible in words and which cannot be named. This chapter, and the next, explores some of the mechanisms that explain how these inexpressible elements occur and how they are un-nameable. The un-nameable (ineffable) condition, or more simply elusive quality, lends a photograph something besides what is literally there. Its existence, seen as certain but undefined in structure, provokes an array of terminology, for example: *undecidable* (Derrida), *figure* (Lyotard), *pure meaning* (Barthes); its location is variously described as *punctum* (Barthes), *parergon* (Derrida); its function as *integrational*, *metonym*, *metaphor*; and its motivation driven by *desire* (Sigmund Freud) or the *semiotic* (Kristeva). Each term contributes a means to explain the whereabouts of resonant quality that evades definition, and each concerns the aspect in visual imagery that is *not* transparent to meaning. A photograph such as Evans's *Allie Mae Burroughs* (1936) might qualify as an example where words fail to adequately express its quality because it possesses something that *is* depicted and yet is indescribable. In this respect it is necessary to distinguish between those photographs that display unspeakable objects or places, such as the sublime landscapes explored by Anselm Adams, or horrific events such as 9/11/2001 (Joel Meyerowitz, *Aftermath* 2002), and photographs that either *amplify* or *construct* such qualities. A photograph of a person, for example, presents a conflation of this difference, in subtle characteristics displayed by the subject themselves *and* in the photograph *of* that subject, so that elusive qualities in the person become elusive qualities in the photograph also.

Consideration of the indescribable element inevitably involves the boundaries between the verbal and non-verbal and between the *literal* and *figural* as key concerns. In simple terms, the indescribable element cannot be wholly expressed linguistically. However, I do not suggest that, because photographs possess 'indescribable' qualities, we should not attempt to describe them. Neither do I suggest some mysterious, unattainable meaning that cannot be accessed or is only, for example, available to the author. Nor can we exclude the elusive aspect from our discourse by simply declaring it to be ineffable or transcendent. But I do emphasise that photographs visualise attitudes implicitly and contribute a different understanding from one that is only verbalised. Photography presents ideas using its own representational structures, which can *add* to our understanding and can amplify qualities that are difficult to describe. By discussing in some detail the mechanisms of association, I will be exploring how photographs provoke meaning and how photographic ideas might be expressed in words. I focus, in this chapter, on the mechanisms of metaphor and the meaning that the photograph can *provoke*, and, in Chapter Five, on the potent qualities *evoked* by the dynamics of detail. Both *provocation* and *evocation* require an understanding of the photograph as possessing *literal* and *figural* content. These I use as key terms throughout the following chapters. Both depend on the ontological dual properties of the photograph – presence and absence, named and the un-nameable. From here on, when I use the term *literal*, I mean what is denoted and can be located in the photograph. When I use the term *figural*, I mean those elements, qualities, implications that cannot be located.

Discussion of the photograph is framed within the relation between object and concept, and between the photograph 'naming' an object and intending a concept (Derrida in Glendinning 2001: 62). A photograph refers to what things look like, but simply 'naming' objects that we recognise is not how we respond to a photograph; this is a more complex process of seeing, thinking and collating. Photographs display the referent, whilst simultaneously referring to what is not there – the *additional* (supplementary) elements in the real world besides the object photographed, which are without specific location or absent entirely. It is a contradictory process. How supplementation operates in the photograph can be compared to the structure of substitution in the linguistic system, in which verbal reference is sufficient to indicate concept or absent object. A basic premise of language depends on our ability to imagine the existence of something that is not there. Our understanding *assumes* absence, and we expect further dimensions to meaning that exist besides the reference to an object, which may not be present. Linguistic expressions are full of supplementary meanings that are present by implication (metonym) or similarity (metaphor). The function of supplementation is intrinsic to the substitution process, which attaches additional levels of meaning to the sense of that object; supplementation therefore introduces elements that are not straightforward and are not fixed or certain. Photographs, like words, operate as substitutes for objects – a photograph of a shoe refers to the concept 'shoe' and in this respect is the visual equivalent of the word 'shoe'. Despite photographs lacking the same level of regularity as a linguistic 'system of denotation' (Goodman 1969: 26–30), this principle of substitution exists in our reading of photographs as literal statements of the things depicted, and is evident in the belief of photographs as transparent so that, in speaking of a photograph of someone, we commonly speak of *that person*, as if they were there, *not* merely represented in an image of them. However, unlike words, in a photograph, every referent can be seen, which contradicts the fact of its absence. This contradiction, between visual illusion and physical absence, confuses the apprehension of supplementary meaning added by implication or similarity.

A word attempts to identify a meaning or thing, whereas a photograph circumvents meaning and things. Pictures cannot be 'read' in the same definitional way that words can be, so that the term 'mean' is problematic because a photograph can express and indicate, but will not 'mean' any one thing. What could be more appropriate and effective than 'what does this photograph mean?' would be to ask 'what concepts does this photograph provoke?' And if we could avoid using the word 'meaning', we could release photography from the subsequent assumption that meaning = truth. With the photograph's capacity, through metaphor and metonym, to reference what is absent as well as what is present, concepts and meaning can *depend* on oppositional relations between referents and our response to them. Photographs can play with this riddle of absence and can provoke contradictions between what is there and what is implied. For example, the full impact of *Bloody Merry* depends not on the referents themselves, but on our knowledge of Russia's history and our understanding of the incongruity of references. Photographic meaning relies as much on what is absent as is present. And much of what is interesting in photographic representation is physically absent or not easy to locate.

Space of projection: what, how and who?

Derrida's lecture and essay 'Restitutions' traces attitudes to representation and the question of what can or cannot be named (Derrida 1987: 255–382). A recurring debate, which originates in Martin Heidegger's discussion (2000 [first presented in lectures in 1935/36]) of what constitutes the truth of things and the artistic nature of paintings, refers to the meaning inherent in Van Gogh's painting of shoes (1888). The debate is extended by Meyer Schapiro (1998 [1968]), and subsequently Derrida, whose lecture describes the malleability of meaning in representations of any 'thing', which becomes much more than that 'thing' as we construct meaning around it. Heidegger's concern is that a work of art should disclose what he terms the 'truth' of a 'thing'. His speculation is concerned to locate its essential nature, as determined by the manner in which it is made. He tries to bypass the prevailing thought and knowledge about that 'thing' (the 'thing-concept') because he considers this obstructs access to the 'thingly character of a thing', which constitutes its artistic nature. He tries to see the 'thingly element' as it essentially *is* (Heidegger 2000: 88). In contrast, Derrida's concern is to chase the way in which its meaning is constructed, rather than the notion of truth, and exposes the contradictions in Heidegger's attempt to explain what a work of art *is* and the whereabouts of the 'essential thing'. Derrida points to the habitual fixation with subject-matter and questions the distinction between *matter* (what is there) and the form it takes in *expressing* what is there. In looking for 'truth', discussion focuses on *what* it is, where it has come from, *what* it represents. In describing the nature of the 'thing', Heidegger reveals that his intention is to transcend its representation by speaking of what is absent and *not* there, what is held metonymically in the shoes:

> From the dark opening of the worn inside of the shoes the toilsome tread of the workers stares forth. In the stiffly rugged heaviness of the shoes there is the accumulated tenacity of her slow trudge through the far-spreading and ever-uniform furrows of the field swept by the raw wind... (Heidegger 2000: 87)

Here Heidegger projects onto the shoes all kinds of imaginings that are provoked by them, such as what kind of person (absent in the image) might have worn these shoes. He opens a space of projection, which demonstrates that a very simple image of a very simple object allows all manner of issues and symbols to emerge. When looking at any picture we start with subject-matter: 'what is it?' Then curiosity drives us to conjecture what is not there and what we can only imagine and, given the clues in the image, we ask: 'what does it mean?' Heidegger and Schapiro both ask: Whose shoes are they? Whom do they represent? Thus they project onto the inanimate shoes animated qualities found in who might have inhabited them. Krauss (1986 [1980]) gives an account of Derrida's lecture 'Restitutions', in which he demonstrates the significance of who it is that might be asking the question, and from what standpoint (e.g. psychological, cultural, historical). To illustrate this literally, he uses his voice in a deliberate and performative way to continually interrupt the flow of his own more formal, philosophical discourse. This voice appears to be that of a woman who repeatedly interrupts his measured tone to question the discussion's assumptions. Slightly hysterical, exasperated, and insistent and short, 'she' says: 'What pair?' and 'Who said they were a *pair* of shoes?' (Krauss 1986: 292). Derrida's concern is to expose implicit assumptions and ask: What is there besides the visible subject? What is *not* the 'thing'? What is provoked? How is meaning constructed around the object? Who is asking the question? Like Foucault, he questions our insistence on subject-matter, or on what the image is 'about', and proceeds to explore the perspective from which the questions are asked.

Space of projection: metaphor

It is the verbal description of objects in a photograph that can prevent us from 'seeing' the metaphoric meaning that accompanies reference to those objects. Our presumption tends to look for what a 'thing' possesses in substance and fact, rather than what it lacks or what is not physically there. But photographs evade meaning and Derrida speaks of the struggle to find a language that adequately describes visual conditions, which are not only linear and logical but can include the spaces between particular elements of content to which they refer. He experiments with this in the *Right of Inspection*. This approach requires us to move away from the hierarchy of subject-matter and 'what is' present. My playful speculation below responds to a number of points in contemplation of the photographic space: Heidegger's questions (2000: 87), Derrida's rhetorical expression, and the potential for metaphor and metonym in the photograph. I use an example of work by Philip-Lorca diCorcia (*Mario* 1978 – Figure 11) that follows the photographic tradition of depicting ordinary, everyday things.[5] The passage describes *Mario*'s contemplation of a fridge and

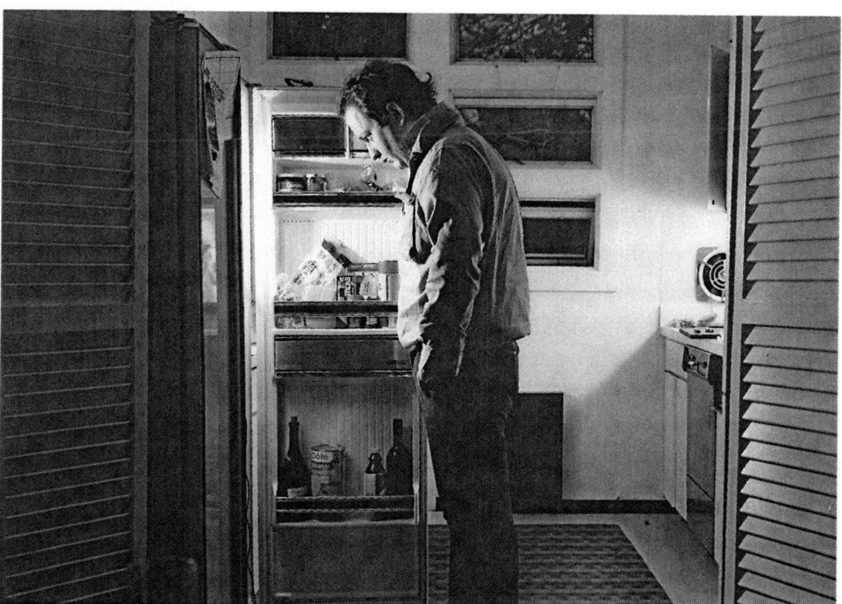

Figure 11 Philip-Lorca diCorcia, *Mario*, 1978.

demonstrates the difficulty in articulating the content of any photograph in words as I attempt to explore the range of conceptual association available, without prioritising any in particular. This description is a linear, verbal approximation of a non-linear conceptual speculation, but it is linear only out of necessity. And I could continue in this way and never arrive at any definition because photographs can be described in different ways, with different agendas and be influenced by different traditions. The sequential structure of words and sentences attempts to relate the simultaneous event of looking. This is thought derived from visual reverie, bordering on fiction – the void of the space, the back and forth of association:

'From the dark opening of' the cluttered insides of the fridge, light shines forth. Within the shelves of the door, jars sit next to wine, next to beer; pasta piles on cheese. The fridge promises food and domesticity and the prospect of cooking and care. It promises more than nourishment: comfort, nurture, sustenance and certainty. Mario stands as if chilled by the cooling preservative powers of the fridge. He stares fixedly into the interior of the fridge, which I am unable to see. He can see the layers of shelves, one upon another, the provisions placed and piled, ordered or disordered within, by whoever successively replenishes and uses its content, a testament to taste, priority and housekeeping. The manner of placement in the fridge door is the one visible trace of human uncertainty in a room of clean lines and decisive surfaces. It is dark outside, but light inside the fridge. It is as if Mario feeds off the light, the source of sustenance. He is expectant; he is submissive before its power, its electric energy, its light. When he shuts the door, the light will go and, whilst it is open, he absorbs its strength. The illuminated space is surrounded by edges, framing the interior and the light that emanates from it. Mario is now frozen and detached from reaching into the fridge and taking out what he wants, what he needs, what he desires. What nourishment does he seek? Is he forlorn because what he expected is not there or is he focused, not on the content, but on the light – of the future, or of the past? Is it the future that he sees, as if in full cine-colour, illuminated and moving before him? The fridge, full of light, promises much; food, nourishment, time travel, the mystery of the universe. The opening of the door is absolute. My view cuts me off from the view inside the fridge; cuts me off from the meaning that is within. The fridge defers; it is accessible and inaccessible; it is neither full nor empty, neither giving nor taking. It is not a fridge; it is a cave of sustenance, a nourishing light, the end and the beginning of the world, the rebirth of Mario.'

The linguistic metaphoric process provides a model for understanding how photographs bring together unrelated, incongruous elements. In applying the term 'metaphor' to the analysis of photographs, many of the properties described in literary analysis are familiar – such as resemblance, substitution and supplementation. Metaphor's main feature – resemblance – is shared with the photograph. Metaphor is a process of substitution, where meaning from one context (domain) shifts to another, where it speaks of (sees) one thing in terms of another and enables the possibility of seeing an object in a wholly different way. This process of analogy leads us to make connections – the fridge is *like* a time machine or even an 'abyss' (Indiana 1993) – so that we arrive at interpretation via a number of conceptual leaps

– light > emission > utterance > speech – light is *like* speech – *like* knowledge – *like* oracle. This procedure of making connections relates to the capacity of the brain to process thought, language and concepts. The condition of *aphasia*, evidenced in patients following a stroke, demonstrates how the brain operates when the links between thought and language are disrupted. The condition demonstrates verbal slippage – they often make words up or substitute a semantically related, but incorrect, word. Linguistic metaphor similarly disrupts the rules of sense and depends on the three basic functions of substitution, comparison and interaction. In simple terms, a metaphor is divided into two parts, the literal and figurative: the primary subject or the literal frame (*tenor*) = the fridge – and the metaphoric secondary subject, the figurative concept (*vehicle*) = nourishment or enlightenment (Ortony 1993: 3). Different theories have emphasised different aspects of the properties of metaphor, but all of them point to the change in the relationship of associations, by bringing previously unconnected things together, forging contradictions between terms and forcing tensions between relationships. Max Black (1993) describes the process as an interactive system of relationships (reminiscent of Derrida's interweaving), where the metaphoric *vehicle* projects associations onto the literal reference, and the reader assigns properties to both primary and secondary subjects, just as Heidegger does with the shoes. Importantly for the reading of photographs, *tenor* and *vehicle* reverberate back and forth, suggesting a continuous process, more complex than mere comparison. Black uses the term 'resonance' to describe the degree of implication that determines the potency of a metaphor: the more complex the association, the stronger the resonance. Other theories suggest that it is the distance between domains connecting the literal (domestic fridge) and the figurative (enlightenment) that makes for strong metaphor. Visual resonance is dependent on both the degree of implication and the interaction between all the elements. In this way *Mario*'s fridge is complex and can be associated with the functions of the kitchen and cooking, and simultaneously access the mystery of the unknown. It becomes a system of reverberating ideas rather than 'things'.

Space of projection: thought and concept

Placing an empty shoebox in a strange context, on snow-covered ground, demands a different response from the norm. In order to reappraise its significance we have to recall both similarities and differences from all previous encounters with shoeboxes. George Miller's theory of metaphor proposes that in reading a text we use 'memory images' to gather information and make sense of it. The process is first *constructive*, setting a context for understanding, and then *selective*, becoming more abstract in understanding concepts. We then use a set of alternative possibilities (what he calls *semantic models*) that can be applied to the text. This is a process that allows alternative and different ideas to coexist. *Semantic models* allow ideas to change, fluctuate and contradict, so that ideas can contain, for example, the possibility of a shoebox with shoes, and without shoes, simultaneously. If we apply this theory to the looking at photographs, it explains the recurrent opposition of absence/presence in a logical way, so that when we see a photograph of an empty box we also understand that the box could be full in numerous possible ways. And we understand an empty shoebox as significant, because the very fact that there *could* be something there adds more meaning to the fact that there is not. Similarly, it may be seen as both a *particular* shoebox and, ideationally, as the function of a shoebox as a useful container; the abstract concept of 'shoebox' encompasses all the possible functions for which a shoebox can be used.

George Lakoff's 'contemporary theory' of metaphor focuses on the relationship between thought and concept. He questions the traditional literal/figurative distinction and challenges theories that prioritise literal meaning (Lakoff 1993: 148). He proposes that what we call 'metaphor' is embodied in our thinking and is the main mechanism through which we understand abstract concepts (Lakoff 1993: 203). His notion of the metaphoric instinct as being 'fundamentally conceptual not linguistic in nature' and pervading thought (not just language) is seen as controversial because he makes the switch from analysing how metaphor uses language, towards seeing how language is influenced by metaphoric thought. Lakoff proposes that specific things are understood in terms of common abstract concepts via large *generic metaphors* – such as 'time', 'being', 'change', 'causation', 'action', 'purpose'. The mechanism of comprehending the general in terms of the specific is seen here in the representation of the universe, life and death made accessible in the light of the fridge. The photographic space of meaning encompasses both particularity and meta-metaphor, such as 'the meaning of life', 'mortality', 'life after death' or 'life is a journey' (Lakoff 1993: 232). Lakoff explains a tendency in interpretation to personify abstract concepts so that events (like death) are understood in terms of the grim reaper or angel of death (Lakoff 1993: 245). This, as a principle, can be seen to happen with the fridge: the fridge is personified; it is a source of energy that will sustain 'Mario' in some way; the fridge is intelligent and speaks; it is an oracle and if we open the door we may find the answer. In photographs, many such generic schemata occur simultaneously and one schema does not necessarily follow another but generates further images in a continuous process. Lakoff's analysis echoes Derrida's insistence that metaphor is always present in any representation – including thought. Representation is never without a property of resemblance, either one of physicality or one of function. There are two consequences particularly relevant to photography and for this discussion. One is the dependence on what is absent in generating meaning; the other is the deep embeddedness of metaphor within any ideological system (e.g. photographic practice). Derrida's example of the generic metaphor 'sun', which embodies the metaphysics of light and dark, exemplifies both of these. He describes the heliotropic metaphor in the language of philosophy as illustrating meaning that is sensory, and exceeded by knowledge beyond sensory experience: 'the very opposition of appearing and disappearing ... of day and night, of the visible and the invisible, of present and absent – all this possible only under the sun' (Derrida 1982: 251). It reminds us again of the photograph's ontological association with metaphysics – light. In terms of effect, the metaphoric process, and the photograph itself, makes manifest metaphysical oppositional expressions such as light and dark, presence and absence.

Lakoff's view of the cognitive process suggests that as soon as we talk about abstractions and emotions, rather than what is concrete and physical, metaphor facilitates our understanding and contributes to the way we approach a photograph as a conceptual space. He asserts that experience is conceptualised besides (if not before) language. 'Conceptual knowledge' is a primal process shared by both visual and verbal meaning, which is prior to translation into language and works below the level of consciousness, incorporating psychological associations. And the notion of conceptual knowledge, before the interference of verbal articulation, releases the understanding of visual metaphor from the subordination to linguistic structures. There are various theories about the precise nature of conceptualisation and the extent to which it is shaped by linguistic representation: how language is processed, how abstract concepts are conceived and how conceptual knowledge is organised. Views range from the formation of concepts being dependent on language (thinking is linguistic) to the other extreme that separates language and thought and sees absurdity in the idea that thought is the same as language (Nuyts and Pederson 1997: 14). Each of these theories describes a model of categorisation. As a form of categorisation, a 'concept' is a way of establishing a type of entity, condition or event by ordering its features or properties. The term 'concept' is commonly allied to language and words, whereas here the context of 'reading' a photograph is determined by visual apprehension, which accesses 'concepts' via visual figuration. The aim here is to understand a photograph as a conceptual space in which ideas circulate, and to engender a process of active looking, a conceptual grasp of meaning before words are allowed to close down possible implications. Whether conceptualisation is pre-linguistic, as Lakoff implies, or whether it is parallel to language, a concept can be conceived as not necessarily articulated by language and, like disseminated meaning, defers linguistic categorisation. My use of the term 'concept' is akin to Lakoff's 'conceptual knowledge' because I am assuming the concept's reliance on visual play encompasses a dimension besides one that it is determined linguistically. The sort of thinking that a photograph provokes is one that expands, rather than confines, thought. In apprehending photographs we assimilate, condense and shift elements without necessarily naming them; it is a more fluid assemblage of 'multiplicity'. Rather than aligning 'concept' with essential substance, what is important here is its capacity to 'hold' several possibilities simultaneously. The mental space of the photograph is conceived as a configuring *process* of accumulating qualities, as yet un-named, and which I call 'conceptual'.

Figural space: the visual/verbal dichotomy

> Neither words nor the visual can be 'reduced to the other's terms: it is in vain that we say what we see; what we see never resides in what we say. And it is in vain that we attempt to show, by the use of images, metaphors, or similes, what we are saying. (Foucault 2003: 10)

Words and pictures are irreconcilably different and it is in the face of this that we attempt to respond to photographs. In outlining the metaphoric process, I emphasise the production of meaning in images as operating differently from words, without suggesting a reversal of hierarchies (e.g. images over words) or the necessity of either the one or the other. Words do some things better; images do other things better. Words can explain and clarify and, once articulated, can also inhibit consideration of other possibilities. What I say in words, in attempting to describe what I see in an image, images do by default. Images do not require the order of linguistic procedure (top left proceeding to the right and down the page) that we have when reading written texts. Images can open up possibility. The two systems can exclude each other – or subordinate each other – either the image illustrates the text or the text merely comments on the image or assumes a contradictory role. More often the text is used to explain the image, which is another form of subordination to the text. The text tends to be a 'linear channel' for the image's simultaneous forms so that the image is dominated by the text. One or the other is always prioritised (Foucault 1982b: 32–3). Foucault (2003 [1966]) introduces the possibility of a radical re-adjustment to the way in which we habitually use language when describing images. He proposes that we should treat the incompatibility of language and vision as a 'starting point for speech instead of as an obstacle to be avoided' (Foucault 2003: 10). By this he indicates that, when describing pictures, even if the words used may not always be adequate to the task, language should not limit the possibilities of interpretation. Foucault signals the possibility that words need *not* lead interpretation, or be reductive, and that the incompatibility between word and image can *initiate* dissemination. In order to 'preserve the infinity of the task', like Derrida, Foucault is advocating the uncertainty of dissemination over the certainty established by structural analysis. Derrida's *perquisition* provides a practical demonstration of how interpretation of the visual need not be limited by language. His rhetoric, which does not separate expression from form, suggests an approach to understanding the potential of photographs and how we speak of them. Most importantly he starts with the visual and, in allowing the photograph to dictate 'talk', he maintains an open and multi-faceted dialogue.

Roni Horn's *Another Water (the River Thames, for example)* (1999) challenges this visual/verbal dichotomy, by demonstrating words and photographs working together (Figure 12). *Another Water*, which represents an interaction of photograph and text, questions the presupposition that ideas must be expressed in language, and that either language or photographs must dominate. This series of photographs was taken from the point of view of someone looking into the water from the riverbank, as we

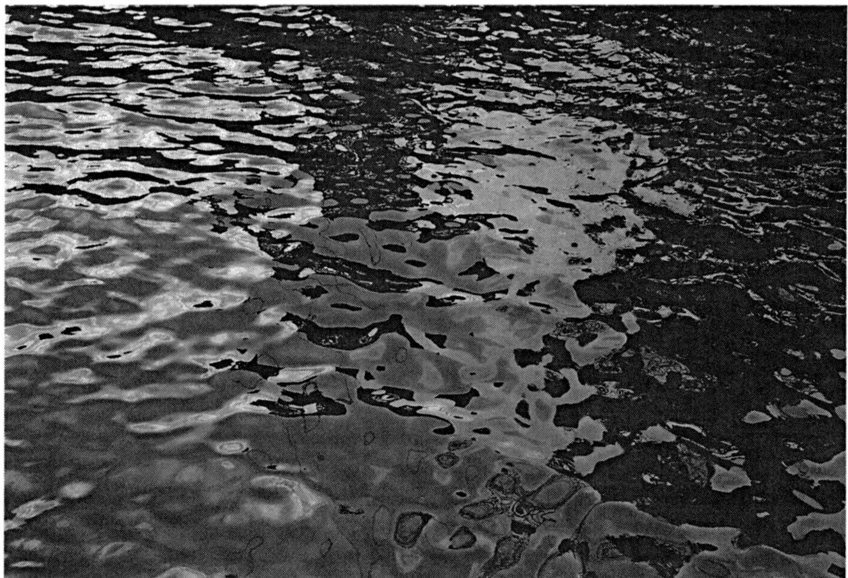

Figure 12 Roni Horn, *Another Water (the River Thames, for example)*, 1999.

are compelled to do when walking alongside any large river. *Another Water* explores water in terms of the many qualities associated with it. Specifically, a big river like the Thames provokes emotional response on a number of levels: its physical force, its depth, its history. The project involved gathering together individual responses to water from a number of interviews with people working on, and living by, the river. Water demands attention – it is powerful and dangerous – and the collection of notes interweave factual, emotional, irrational and spiritual observations. The many different photographs of water, each presented with the same formal configuration, sit above hundreds of numbered entries, which repeat and glide over each other with a slightly different cadence each time. Horn wanted to maintain a sense of the 'infinite range of appearances' that water presents, so that, rather than closing response down, the presentation invites an open-ended relation with water.[6] The photographs operate much like Derrida's *perquisition* as the words skirt around and barely touch the surface of what photographs of water can potentially provoke. The series recounts the physical properties of the river and its appearance, which cannot avoid metaphor:

> 668. You say water is troubled or calm. You say water is rough and restless. You say water is disturbed. You say water is quiet. Water is serene and sometimes clear, it might be pure and then it is brilliant. Water is heavy; that's a fact. Water is often tranquil, even placid. Water is still and then it might be deep as well. Water is cold or hot, chilly or tepid. (Horn 2000)

The descriptions include literary references to Dickens and Conrad, and sequences of imaginative reverie. They proceed for example, from accounts of the fear of water to incorporate a series of newspaper reports of suicide by drowning. Everything to do with water is demonstrated as metaphor, so that *Another Water* brings together two domains: water's materiality and suicide by drowning – one being a consequence of the other:

> 1 In the waiting room of a doctor's office some years ago I overheard a mother talking about how her kids were afraid of it. If they couldn't see into it, they wouldn't go into it. It's like being dismembered. When you wade into this dark fluid, a kind of milk without nurture, you disappear.
>
> 2. Disappearance: that's why suicides are attracted to it. It's also why children fear it. It's a soft entrance to simply not being here. When I imagine the river, it's something I can enter, something that will surround me, take me away from here... (Horn 2000)

Foucault discusses this presupposition that ideas must be expressed in language, and the fact that history has consistently asserted the separation of visual representation (e.g. photography) from linguistic reference and discourse (Foucault 1982b: 43). Foucault's discussion of Magritte's differentiation between *resemblance* and *similitude* suggests there may be different modes of discourse. The property of *resemblance* encourages a habitual process of thinking, which presupposes a primary reference, from which increasingly less faithful copies can be made. However, *similarity* develops in series, in which each similar photograph is different from the other, if only slightly – as in *Another Water*. A series has neither beginning nor end, can be followed in one direction as easily as in another, obeys no hierarchy, but repeatedly propagates small differences. In discussing the nature of representation (1982b) with reference to Magritte's painting *The Treachery of Images* (1928–29), Foucault considers the ambiguity of pictures with regard to the exchange between words and images. He describes the painting of the pipe that declares 'This is not a pipe' as simply *demonstrative* in that it states the obvious – this is not a pipe, but a reference to a pipe. Magritte's painting indicates the concept of pipe just as the word 'pipe' would do. More complicated in many respects, a photograph cannot escape pointing to a particular pipe, or any particular object. Much photographic interpretation is concerned with the beautiful formality of the specific object (e.g. Edward Weston, *Two Shells*, 1927) or with the incongruous placement of the specific object (*Empty Shoebox*). *Another Water* makes the distinction between resemblance to any one definitive and original moment, or one absolute concept of 'water', and a condition that recognises 'an infinite range of appearances'. Horn's *Another Water* brings text and photograph closely together. We can barely detect the numbers hidden in the water, which locate reference to the text below and to what is visually demonstrative. Each image uses numbers and notes to signify linear elements arranged in space – between figure and text – which launch a whole series of inter-dependent meanings. The text, being below the photograph, assumes the function of its title, but is not allowed to dominate. As with Derrida's term *différance*, which requires the intersection between the word and its visual form to demonstrate its meaning, *Another Water* is a demonstrative manifestation of ideas, presented both visually and verbally. It effectively equates the meaning that we glean from looking with the meaning that we glean from reading – it forces word and photograph to play each with the other. The text 'invades' the photograph. Whilst we cannot digest the words simultaneously with the photograph, we immerse ourselves in the water in order to find the reference that correlates with the words. *Another Water* makes use of our durational concentration in locating numbers and in reading the words, because we are forced to enter the photograph in order to read the words. *Another Water* integrates verbal discourse, visual display and figurative reference.

The habitual separation of word and image constrains response to an image. Attempting to upset that dualism, Lyotard's *Discours, figure* [1971] explores the differences between discursive (generally associated with linguistic) signification and the rhetorical nature of *figure*. Lyotard's *discours* refers to representations that are governed by the rational and organised systems associated with communicating unambiguous meaning – transparently. He aligns 'discourse' with a reductive model of signification, which defines identity by its differences: by what something is not. His concept of *figure* interrupts the process of communication, making it opaque and not wholly comprehensible (Readings 1991: 3–12). He refers to three orders of *figure*: *figure-image* is visible in dreams, in pictures and in photographs; *figure-form* is the compositional arrangement of the whole – it is the 'architecture of a painting' or 'the centring of a photograph'; *figure-matrix* is the dynamic force of *figure* that 'violates the discursive order' and recognises elusive qualities that cannot be communicated; *figure* 'harbors the incommunicable' (Lyotard 1983: 333–4). Importantly, Lyotard gives emphasis to the visual rather than the linguistic. He challenges the limits of structural analysis and its assertion that meaning must emerge from language. Language, he says, forms 'the problem of knowledge' because it forces us to desire fulfilled signification (Lyotard 2006: 38). It is this desire to find synthesis that swallows up the possibilities of resonant meaning. He speaks of the violence of language as being divisive and tending to encourage oppositional structures because, in giving verbal articulation to the figural, the full sense is reduced or lost (Readings 1991: 51). Echoing Derrida's argument with Heidegger's emphasis on establishing the essential 'thing', Lyotard's discussion identifies *figure* as a force, rather than a thing, that interrupts the move toward coherence or completion. The figural, like metaphoric displacement, remains outside the grasp of structures – and encompasses the inexpressible. It is a process that negotiates both *figure* and language, not in opposition exactly, but as a compulsive dynamic working within it, which breaks down the distinction between the linguistic and the visual, the plastic and the experiential (Crome and Williams 2006: 15). And, echoing Lakoff's conception of the relationship between thought and language, *figural space* engages both conceptual and psychological domains; it requires an adjustment from the phenomenological focus on pure perception, to one that can encompass the unconscious and desire. The figural exceeds the literary implications of the term 'figurative' and marks the resistance to everything being sayable about an object.

Figural space: visual poem

Modernist photography adopted Heidegger's prevailing concern with essential 'thingness' in a particularly acute manner; it insisted that a photograph depict a 'thing' in a very 'straight' way and yet, simultaneously, that it should reveal some 'truth' about that 'thing' beyond its resemblance. Paul Strand's aspiration for photography was for it to attain poetic form in the simplest of objects. His reference to its capacity for 'subtle feeling' and 'penetration of vision' and its use for the creation of an 'intuitive knowledge' suggests that a pure photography, 'uncontaminated by alien influences', can align itself with poetry (Strand 1980: 143–8). The aspiration to reveal the truth-quality is embedded in the photographic aesthetic concerned to transcend the appearance of the everyday object. Orozco also depicts the everyday but Orozco's awareness of history displays a version of straightness, whilst simultaneously subverting it. *Empty Shoebox* is presented in a straight manner but is deliberately placed in an unfamiliar context. His practice, which depends on acute observation, directly references the tradition of showing us what is ubiquitous and hidden, together with Surrealism's celebration of incongruous elements in collision. Orozco adds another dimension to these modernist traditions by sometimes rearranging what he finds, by throwing pebbles onto a roof (*From Roof to Roof*, 1993) or by riding a bicycle through a puddle (*Extension of Reflection*, 1992). He intervenes and makes use of accident, deliberately confusing documented interventions with those found situations, which he simply records. He avoids a formal operation, which, following Heidegger's 'thingness', focuses on presenting something in its essentialness; he avoids dynamic composition, elegant tonal description or the dramatic moment. Late twentieth-century photography distinguishes itself from the preoccupation with objectivity which treats everything with the same indifferent gaze, and which is typified by Weston. Orozco's methodology reflects the 'liquidity of things' and 'paths of thought' (Orozco, quoted in Birnbaum 1998: 115). His sensibility is not one that seeks essential quality, but follows instead the traditions of conceptual art and the anti-aesthetic practices of Ed Ruscha or Dan Graham. Orozco's *space* can be seen as a container in which supplementary ideas move culturally, geographically, and make use of what occurs or what is absent. His work quietly notices the small differences that are local and idiosyncratic. Rather than waiting for that one moment of reality (Cartier- Bresson), Orozco describes himself as working 'in reality' so that he invents a fictional space (Orozco, quoted in Joselit 2000: 173). His photographs are more akin to mental representations than representation of reality. He suggests the photographer intervenes and interrupts reality and activates response or, in his terms, reactivates time in the eyes of the spectator. Orozco says that the 'poetic 'happens because of the spectator' (2009: 21).

The poetic behaviour of the photograph establishes a different sort of reality. Horn refers to the fact of photography and its *dis*similarity with reality:

> 671. When you photograph water you strip it of its form: its restless liquid reality.
> 672. When you photograph water you give it an image that in essential ways bears no likeness to water.
> 674. As is often said of photographs, this photograph is a frozen moment. But a frozen moment is no moment at all, it's an oxymoron… (Horn 2000)

The underlying assumption in much of the discussion of metaphoric function appears to have been that literal statements are true and metaphorical assertions are not. Lakoff (1993) and Black (1993) suggest that metaphor accesses a truth that is not allied to literal fact necessarily. Paul Ricoeur's analysis of metaphor (1978 [1975]) encompasses Black's 'interaction' and Lakoff's conceptual knowledge, by bridging the emotional and the rational, the imagination and the metaphysical in a 'poetic reality' that suggests a different conception of truth. In advance of Lakoff, and speaking from the disciplinary frame of philosophy, he emphasises expression before its constitution in language (Ricoeur, 1978: 306). He sees metaphor as providing a 'common frontier' between logic and feeling, and between the verbal and the non-verbal (1978: 190, 208). Ricoeur stresses the tension at the intersection between literal and metaphoric interpretations (between the mundanity of life in the kitchen and the transcendence of life after death). Metaphor is a contradictory statement that simultaneously indicates both a resemblance (what *is*), and the incongruity of absurdity and 'unreality' (what *is not*). It requires a different sort of truth-value – a concept of truth that is more concerned with understanding things in terms of actions, processes and events than with the verification of facts, things or places (Ricoeur 1978: 305–8). He identifies the contradiction of 'is / is not', of absence/presence as a powerful space that animates the imaginative force of conceptual thought. This is useful for an understanding of the sort of truth accessible to photographs, which is traditionally associated with documentary evidence and thereby verifiable truth. Ricoeur's discussion gives emphasis to the signification process as a state of activity and the metaphor as a 'condition of possibility' (Ricoeur 1978: 287). So 'what does it mean?' would be more suitably expressed as 'what is happening?'

This chapter has considered the photograph as poetry and as a conceptual space. It has described metaphor and the *figural* as straddling the boundaries between conceptual domains, and between linguistic thought and visual thought, suggesting a perspective of realism in which the photograph can represent thought or possibility, or produce a visual hypothesis. This chapter has introduced approaches that move towards the assertion of poetic ideas rather than poetic things, by highlighting the tension between absent and present references as being central to the photograph's elusive quality. In terms of our response, it has identified the conflict between our compulsion to define the subject ('thing') and our inclination to speculate. Lakoff and

Ricoeur introduce alternative conceptions of truth in a poetic realism that anticipates fiction, so that, instead of constructing an interpretation that conforms to conditions in the actual world, we may construct one that 'project[s] ourselves into a metaphoric world' where anything is believable (Levin 1993: 127). Ricoeur's acceptance of both what *is* and what *is not*, and Derrida's self-divided thought, introduces the possibility of fiction, which is explored further in the next chapter. The notion of a *figural space* provides a fluid framework for the set of concepts provoked by a photograph, so that a 'reading' of a photograph requires a different process from that of definitive verbal articulation – and one that allows the 'reader's experience and imagination. The photograph's mutability is a paradox of possibility that can be this and that at the same time. If the photograph is understood as *provocation* rather than 'meaning' any one thing, it can be seen as an open-ended space that allows room for a number of meanings to coexist.

This chapter has asserted equivalence in apprehending the visual and the use of language, rather than a hierarchy of language over the visual, or vice versa. And rather than resorting to explaining the visual as being impenetrable or transcendent, it proposes a number of approaches to describing what is difficult to articulate in words. Chapter Three asserted dialogue as a place of exchange that does not necessarily prioritise reason. In this chapter, in consideration of the visual/verbal dichotomy, Foucault's discussion has pointed to the significance of a historic tradition that separates visual representation from discourse that is supposedly founded in reason. This division, and the tension between *figure* and discourse, provides a useful frame with which to discuss developments in practice that suggest a visual discourse, to which I shall return in Chapters Seven and Eight.

Suggested further reading

Bal, M. (2002) *Travelling Concepts in the Humanities*, University of Toronto Press, Toronto; Buffalo; London

Heidegger, M. (2000) 'The Origin of the Work of Art', in C. Cazeaux (ed.), *The Continental Aesthetics Reader*, Routledge, London

Krauss, R. (1986) 'The Photographic Conditions of Surrealism' and 'Photography's Discursive Spaces', in *The Originality and the Avant-Garde and Other Modernist Myths*, The MIT Press, Cambridge, MA, 87–118

Lomax, Y. (2000) *Writing the Image*, I. B. Tauris, London

Ortony, A. (ed.) (1993) *Metaphor and Thought*, Cambridge University Press, Cambridge

Readings, B. (1991) *Introducing Lyotard: Art and Politics*, Routledge, London; New York

Rodowick, D. N. (2001) *Reading the Figural, or Philosophy After the New Media*, Duke University Press, Durham, NC; London

Notes

1 For a discussion of this see Groys 2008.

2 See www.metmuseum.org/toah/works-of-art/1987.1100.141 and www.manraytrust.com,

accessed 29 August 2012. This tradition of non-literal photography, which fractures and breaks up the image, continues in the work, for example, of Yve Lomax, John Baldessari and the trend of camera-less techniques used in the abstract works of Miller, Fuss and Tillmans.

3 More relevant to later developments in photography is Surrealism's engagement with realism as a social intervention rather than a disturbance of formal naturalism. John Roberts points out that André Breton's original attack on representation and the transparency of meaning, and the subsequent development of the Surrealist photograph, intends a more direct use of signification using the photograph's 'indexical function' (Roberts 1998: 102). But Krauss's discussion of Surrealist photography introduces an expansion of meaning deriving from George Bataille's concept of the 'unformed' rather than the political aspirations of Breton.

4 The term 'presence' is significant for photographs in two distinct ways – in simple terms, photographs display objects that were once present in a particular place, at some point in the past. When looking at a photograph those same objects, now absent, can assume a poignant significance. With regard to philosophy, Derrida refers to the 'metaphysics of presence' as the desire for pure and immediate perception. He argues that the history of philosophy is founded on the metaphysics of presence and yet it is a desire that cannot be fulfilled. Our desire for truth, reality and being finds focus in our concern for the possibility of essences and original meaning. The history of photography incorporates this desire for universal or essential meaning.

5 This tradition develops significantly in the 1970s in the works, for example, of William Eggleston, Joel Sternfeld and Stephen Shore, and here Philip-Lorca diCorcia.

6 Search for 'Roni Horn water' online at the Tate website (www.tate.org.uk/art) and Art21 (www.art21.org/about-art21).

5

Fictional realism

This chapter has two distinct sections: first it considers how the effect of realism and narrative is constructed, with particular focus on the role of detail and metonymy in evoking meaning. Second, it outlines a photographic space influenced by the human psyche and motivated by our desire for meaning and stories. It establishes the nearness of realism to fiction as a theme and the development of photography that uses its resemblance to the real world as useful for the construction of ideas rather than the revelation of truth.

Sophie Calle's installation *Exquisite Pain* (2003) results from an event that took place in 1984 and the intervening years in which she contemplates its impact. *Exquisite Pain* introduces a mode of photo-fiction by two principle methods: the use of metonymy and the use of psychological resonance (Figure 13[1]). Most significantly it assumes a photographic realism in which fact and fiction are indistinguishable. *Exquisite Pain* presents two accounts in parallel: it narrates the events that lead up to 'the unhappiest moment' in Calle's life, and it presents a series of documents derived from responses to the question 'When did you suffer most?' The series repeatedly recounts her memory of one night fifteen years before, when her lover abruptly ends their relationship by telephone. She spends the rest of that night in a shabby hotel room in New Delhi 'gazing stupidly at the red telephone. It was bright red. In the early morning I photographed it.' Each of the ninety-nine accounts is slightly different and, as time progresses, they become shorter. Visually the panels become increasingly dark and the writing less distinct from the background, as the memory of the pain fades. The same photograph of the red telephone, placed on a bed, punctuates each telling and embodies the memory of that pain. Calle's documentation of other people's pain is obsessively systematic in its presentation of objects and places, which serve as mnemonics for each account of painful experience. She makes use of fragments gleaned from her conversations: an array of seemingly insignificant details, arbitrary situations, traversing different personal domains and chronologies. They seem purposefully unremarkable as images, and are often incidental and banal. This series is presented in a straight factual way without expression, artistic

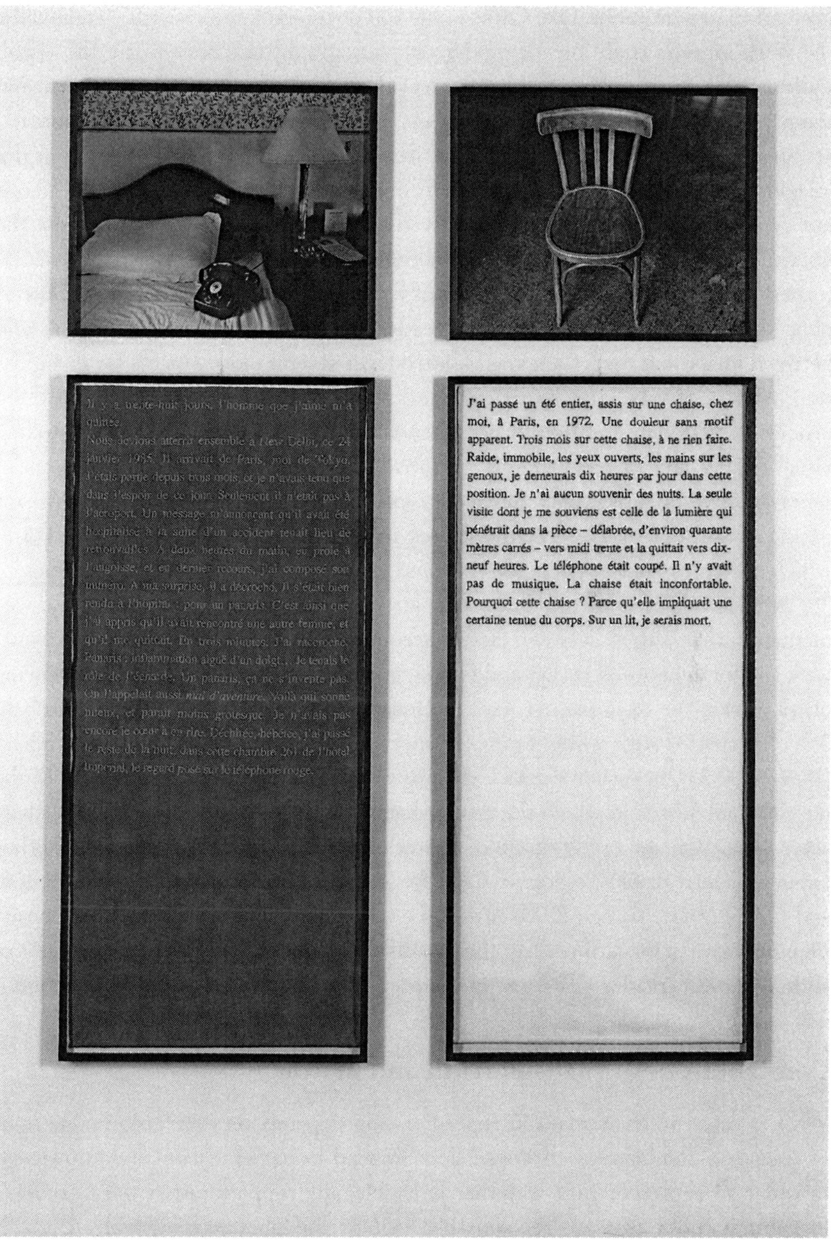

Figure 13 Sophie Calle, from *Exquisite Pain (Day 38)*, 2003.

pretension or sentiment. Like Orozco, she too documents the 'everyday' and, whilst the work inherits traditions of modernist photography that accentuate the visual, Calle constructs a document of living every day, which amplifies the conceptual and the psychological – represented by objects. Her work demonstrates a position and response that hovers between being located in the real world and existing in her imagination. Echoing the *dialogical matrix* discussed in Chapter Three, Calle, who is not depicted directly, emerges as an unseen character within the series because the documentation of other people's pain functions as an exorcism of her own experience.

Besides bringing together a number of features already discussed, such as metaphor, the meeting of author/subject/reader, the interaction between images and between image and text, Calle's work introduces several more aspects for examination: the use of subjective experience and psychological reasoning as content; the process of fictional invention in documentation; the dynamics of detail in evoking visual quality and in constructing narrative; the metonymic power of objects as representative of subjectivity, desire and loss. Paralleling the post-structural reappraisal of authorship, Calle demonstrates an indirect form of author-narration in which she tracks her own experience and reinserts herself into constructions of her own history, by depicting other people's stories. *Exquisite Pain* fabricates a documentation that wavers between factual account and fictional construction, crossing back and forth between reality and fiction. It works intertextually, cross-referencing other works. For example, '38 days to Unhappiness' depicts the trees 'whose bare branches rustled with white scraps of paper', described in a novel by Hervé Guibert (Bois 2004: 33). In earlier works Calle plays a more direct game of fiction with the novelist Paul Auster, in which she models herself in the manner of the fictional character *Maria*. On the credits page of Auster's *Leviathan* (1992) it states: 'The author extends special thanks to Sophie Calle for permission to mingle fact with fiction', and Calle's *Double Game* (2000) makes the same statement with respect to Auster. *Exquisite Pain* is a form of realism that breaks down not only the fixed oppositions of author/subject/reader as we saw in Chapter Three, but also those of fact/fiction.

Constructions of realism: truth and fiction

What is referred to as realistic representation depends on the recognisable signs of realism: a combination of impressions formed from perception and knowledge. In order to represent in a way that is legible, any representation must conform to cultural codes that are recognisable. In film and photography, realism usually coincides with what the world looks like and what appears to us as concrete and substantial, rather than abstract and obscure. We latch onto familiar patterns that make sense – such as narrative, cause and effect – and which reinforce our conception of the world. Therefore, the way that we read film, painting or photography is dependent on conventions. Seeing-film-as-reality immerses the viewing-subject in another world of the imagination, and requires the spectator to participate in the construction of stories (Andrew 1984: 43). Different mechanisms for creating narrative, which are sometimes barely perceptible – long shot, mid-shot, close up – facilitate this illusion; we understand non-real time and look for temporal relationships; we hold scenes together in a sequence of causal events and lock into a narrative which coheres our understanding (Andrew 1984: 44–50). Photographic realism similarly establishes an immersion of a kind, and persuades the viewer to ignore the *process* of signification, which disappears as it becomes accepted as 'natural'. We enter into a particular way of experiencing, which we have learnt from watching other films, seeing other paintings, seeing other photographs (Andrew 1984: 47–51). Each mode of representation requires us to switch to a form of response that relates to the conditions of perception and cognition operating in the everyday life world. This is a response in which we are receptive to the mechanisms of a world that is not real at all, but which presents 'signs' for reality, and which creates a tension between belief and unbelief (Andrew 1984: 42). Each world is a discourse that also defines our response by provoking expectation, memory and projection. And, as we have learnt from Foucault, as conceptions of reality change with history, so conceptions of realism change because they rely on what ideologically influences our idea of reality at any one time. These depend on the representational traditions of art, such as beauty, symbolism or surreal absurdity, and more specifically on the traditions of photography, such as humanist sentiment (*Family of Man*); 'documentary style' (Evans); 'snapshot style' and diaristic record (Strba); intimate psychical exploration (Calle).

Discussion of how we experience photographic work can tend to assume a kind of photographic universalism that crosses genres and contexts and which brands photography in general terms. Photographic realism can be confused with what is understood to be documentary evidence, and in the context of art-photography the term 'document' is problematic. 'Document' has associations with actuality, factual evidence and thereby truth. It is also associated with the completely different context of journalism. Walker Evans's term 'documentary style' is more accurate, because all such works in this context, besides the fact that photographs select only a fraction of what is seen, are to some extent fabrications, which may have the appearance of documentary (Katz 1981: 364). For example, whilst it lacks the intention that distinguishes it as a document, *Exquisite Pain* is a representation in the mode of document. In contrast to the traditional ideal of document-as-truth, art-photography has challenged the possibility of unmediated document. For example: Sherrie Levine demonstrates the promiscuity of photographic representation very precisely by re-presenting an existing representation (*After Walker Evans*, 1981); Calle openly declares her subjectivity and uses it as subject-matter; the large and luminous cinematographic images of Jeff Wall or Andreas Gursky emulate filmic immersion and facilitate our entry into another world; Christian Boltanski, Alfredo Jaar and Calle create installational 'worlds' of experience.

Filmic and photographic realisms reduce our ability to perceive the difference between reality and its representation. And since photography's ontology has been dictated by its description as a 'pencil of nature', expectations persistently refer to values of truth. Even as the premise of veracity is disturbed by a postmodern awareness of the photograph as un-truth, uses of photography are destined to play with ideas of truth in versions of fact and fiction, by distorting or denying the 'fact' of the photograph. Berger (Berger and Mohr 1995: 97) points out that because the photograph only quotes fragments of the real world, its truth can be deceitful. Since its early history, photographers have made use of this contradiction: the artificiality of studio photography; the painted backdrops of classical scenes; the staged mythological tableaux; the idealised spaces of heightened atmosphere and allegory. The inherent fictionality in the photographic process is central to our relationship with the photograph's possibility. And, by playing with fiction, one is by default referring to truth. The peculiar condition of the photograph simultaneously presents the opposition of truth and falsehood, as it invites both literal (due to its indexical nature) and figurative interpretations (due to the power of metonymy and metaphor). Jeff Wall refers [1995] to the two reigning myths of photography – the one that claims that photographs are true and the one that claims they are not, both of which are shown to be grounded in the same principles (Wall 2003: 37). Wall's practice has contributed to a fundamental re-evaluation of what constitutes legitimate photographic practice and ultimately to an acceptance of staged (wholly fictional) photography. The starting premise of fiction marks a break with the photograph's equivalence with evidential truth. Wall's mode of realism presents a version of reality that amounts to fiction, which incorporates his psychology and feeling, together with intellectual commentary and his knowledge and use of photographic histories (Wall 1998: 17). He argues that there is no longer the necessity for equivalence between photographic depiction and what is pictured; the photograph exists independently from the real world. He reminds us that we *assume* that the photograph's reality depends on visual resemblance, and that we *assume* also that the referent has precedence over the photographic picture (Wall 1998: 14). He states that there is no referent in his pictures because they do not refer to any 'condition or moment that needs to have existed, historically or socially' (Wall 1998: 17). Instead, he reconfigures his world, no longer as objective documentary touched with subjective expression (as Walker Evans advocates), no longer subjectivity at a distance, masked and un-stated, but constituted wholly subjectively, so that his photographs are as much part of his own psychology as they are a mirror of the world. Since the mid-nineteenth century, paintings have been free to explore ideas rather than resemblance, whereas photography, because of its historic ontological dependence, has been constrained by its properties of resemblance. Wall proposes that photographic representation has no need to visually *resemble* anything, because what he distinguishes as 'depiction' is an act of construction (Wall 1998: 14). Wall continues many of the traditions of realism, whilst disturbing many of the myths. He puts aside the concern for purity or truth and celebrates a form of fictional pictorialism.

Dynamics of detail: essential and non-essential

Chapter Four outlined Derrida's argument with the idea that aesthetic quality depends on definition of the 'essential object'. This chapter returns to Derrida's examination of how non-essential elements in a work contribute to aesthetic quality. His essay 'Parergon' (1987: 37–82) scrutinises Immanuel Kant's *Critique of Judgement* [1790]; this is concerned with the intrinsic value in a work of art, which is inherently self-sufficient, and not dependent on extrinsic factors such as the literal elements in classical paintings like drape, column or frame or what is of extrinsic value such as function or monetary worth. Derrida adopts *parergon* ('frame', 'edge') as a metaphor, not only to question the appraisal of intrinsic factors specifically, but also for a more fundamental critique of aesthetics generally, which persistently returns to a Kantian view. Kant, referencing what is at the edge or 'merely' ornamentation, dismissed *parergon*, because it is superfluous to aesthetic quality, and assumed that there is a more centred, 'essential' part to the image. Thus his premise for aesthetic quality depended on our determining what is central and intrinsic, and what is extrinsic and superfluous (Kant 1952: 43–4). Derrida questions whether this is relevant and pulls apart this dominant premise for aesthetic judgement, by agitating the literal meaning of *parergon* – that which is in addition to, or beside (*para*), the work (*ergon*). The *parergon* occupies contradictory positions: it is not central to the representation or the empirical 'sense' of the object but belongs to it extrinsically 'as a surplus, an addition, an adjunct, a supplement'. Derrida argues that, whilst occupying a supplementary or detachable position, an apparently insignificant element may not be

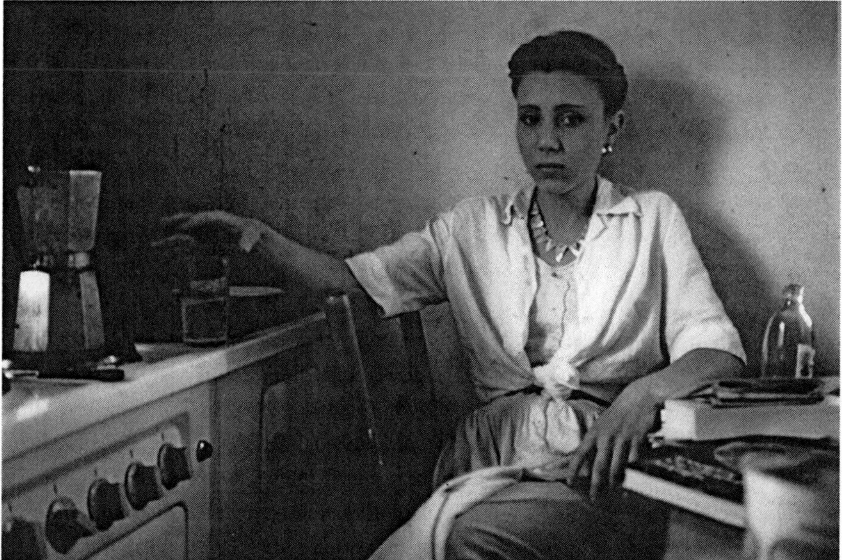

Figure 14 Annelies Strba, *Sonja with a Glass*, 1991, from *Shades of Time* series.

incidental and may operate as an intrinsic component. What seems peripheral may be necessary to the whole, and that it is just such supplementary elements which hold the structure together and give a work resonance.

Derrida's question 'Where does *parergon* begin and end?' points to the literal aspect of essential and non-essential, inside and outside, and ultimately aesthetic judgement itself, which assumes that we can distinguish between what is *extrinsic* (not essential) and what is *intrinsic* to an image (Derrida 1987: 63). His questioning is particularly relevant for photography, which has traditionally celebrated its capacity to reveal what we have not noticed – and what may have appeared previously to be insignificant. The following passage picks up Derrida's example of questioning the hierarchy of what is important in an image, and asks what is precisely intrinsic in Strba's *Sonja with a Glass*, 1991 (Figure 14):

How do formal aspects like the composition of the photograph help in clarifying what is its intrinsic quality? In this photograph the formal aspects do not tell us much at all, are underplayed and hardly seem to be what is important. The image appears to be deliberately unconsidered, approaching the accidental. With the dismissal of 'formal' considerations, the integrity of accident and the use of a deliberate anti-form becomes the 'formal aspect' that contributes to its aesthetic quality. And can I distinguish the detail that seems superfluous from that which is necessary? What is detachable, non-essential? Do such details as Sonja's earring, an item of adornment and unessential in Kant's terms, detract or add poignancy in its glitzy contrast with the drab kitchen? Does it provoke associations, which are dependent on specific cultural knowledge, such as Barthes's discussion of the incisive significance of the necklace in Camera Lucida (Barthes 1993[b]: 53), or the history and appraisal of Jan Vermeer's painting (1665) and its extension in The Girl with a Pearl Earring (Tracy Chevalier 1999, Peter Webber 2003). If a detail is not to be merely ornamental, must it acquire such attributes? And how universally recognisable must it be before it becomes too familiar for it to be meaningful? Alternatively, do the number of knobs on the cooker remain merely insignificant? Clearly the potency of the object does not stop at the recognition of what an object is, but at the status or quality of that object – for example as a marked, scratched glass and not a superior cut glass. What is extrinsic to the glass of water? – its reference to what is outside the photograph or its association? What part of the glass of water is necessary? – the glass, the transparency of the glass, the size of the glass, the dinginess of the glass, or the water in the glass? If I were to substitute different details, it would doubtless make a difference. For example, if it were milk in the glass? Is the glass of water too central a focus to be supplementary? If I consider Sonja's stare to be the focus of the photograph, then what is the glass of water? Is it the inseparability of these two features in terms of dominant focus that contributes to the meaning of the photograph overall? Or is the central feature the dynamic of her gesture? Is the content of the photograph inextricable from the meaning implied by the imminent gesture of her right hand and its possibility? Is it this possibility of directionless movement and uncertainty that is the focus and essentially intrinsic? (Derrida 1989: 40)

Dynamics of detail: absence, metonym and metaphor

Chapter Four described how photographs as metaphors can raise the question 'what is happening?' This section considers how small elements within the photograph can construct the effect of realism and narrative. In an early essay [1968], Barthes discusses the contribution that insignificant details make to context and effect (Barthes 1982: 12). As with Derrida, Barthes also asserts the significance of absence over the certainty of any one visual element so that, where there is no obvious denotative meaning available, it is the insignificant details that make the photograph real for us. He suggests that what is absent becomes 'the true signifier[s] of realism' (Barthes 1982: 16). The 'reality effect' in photography suggests that the 'reality', which we 'see' transparently, obstructs our appreciation of photographic content, which is in addition to resemblance. Writing about the structure of literary narrative [1966], Barthes indicates that details, which can seem inconsequential, can contribute to action by provoking anticipation (1977: 79–124). He contends that even the smallest, apparently insignificant, element contributes to the bigger picture by implying action or character, or by adding to the qualitative value of the scene (Barthes 1977: 89). There are those details that make reference symbolically, by having cultural significance (such as the particular style of cooker, fridge or coffee pot in *Sonja with Glass*), and there are those which are more idiosyncratic (such as Calle's red telephone in *Exquisite Pain*) and have the potential for subjective memory and poignancy. What Barthes calls *integrational* elements are diffuse, psychological or atmospheric, whereas *distributional* elements indicate the possibilities of their anticipated use and help to construct the effect of linear narrative. In *Sonja with Glass*, for example, it is the ambivalent gesture that suggests the glass of water is being picked up and/or being put down:

> *Sonja is about to pick the glass up or she has just placed the glass down on the surface beside her. Her right arm works as if independently and separately from the intensity of her look, which is serious and concentrated. The normal activity of the arm contrasts with the event, which is isolated and special. She sits in a very relaxed way, sat sideways on a kitchen chair, her left forearm resting on the table, her hand dropping down over the edge. Her right hand hovers, holds, looms over the glass of water.*

Barthes aligns metonymic elements as possessing the active function (*distributional*) – the hand hovering over the glass – and metaphoric elements (*integrational*) as having the function of 'being', so that the glass of water reverberates between associations in our contemplation of them (Barthes 1977: 93). *Integrational* features animate the overall quality of what I call resonant meaning, so that the shabbiness of the scene in *Sonja with Glass*, indicated by a mark on the wall, can imbue a value of 'homeliness'. Objects in a photograph will relate to both functions, so that the glass of water is metonymic in the anticipation of it being picked up and the water being drunk, and metaphoric with respect to the enormous implications of the concept 'water', or the implications of the glass being transparent and half full (or empty), or the implications of the hand nearly touching the glass. Clearly there are layers of reference in *Sonja with Glass* that are inseparable: the reality effect of the object depicted and its metonymic reference, which is absent. Removal of the cooker would place Sonja somewhere else, not in a kitchen. Replacement of the glass for a cup would alter the overall effect and metonymic possibility, not the central content, which is Sonja. We can thus verbally describe the possibility of two similar images, as 'Sonja is sitting in the kitchen with her arm outstretched, touching a *glass* of water' or 'Sonja is sitting in the kitchen with her arm outstretched, touching a *cup* of water'. It would appear to make little difference verbally until we behold that implication visually. In *Exquisite Pain*, despite the deliberate use of a kind of narrative, Calle relies on what is conjured up by the spaces between the objects photographed and the descriptions of their significance. The documentation of numerous stories in parallel, and the repetitive significance of the red telephone, is not *distributional* and does not encourage a conclusive direction, but a metaphoric one. The photographic property of absence brings together the dynamic of *parergon* and, as with *différance*, sense, reference and expression. Expression and meaning are apprehended simultaneously within action, and the prime function of detail operates rhetorically.

Dynamics of detail: subjectivity

The supplementary element *parergon* has another dimension: that of subjectivity. Barthes's term *punctum* characterises the condensation of meaning to be found in details. Barthes's 'sensitive' or sharp little point is to be found in chance elements of detail that are provoked by incongruity, irony or repellence, or which invoke a sense of place or 'a kind of tenderness' (Barthes 1993: 43). Fundamentally, *punctum* can be an entirely personal recognition, provoked by a wholly singular response to an apparently insignificant detail, which affects each of us differently. As Barthes defines it, *punctum* arrives by accident, not artistry, and is unlikely to be a result of the photographer's intention. Its characteristics are not part of the photograph that is culturally coded or recognisable, and which he names *studium*. Derrida (1988) sees *punctum* as confirming the impossibility of essential meaning, and as emphasising the significance of absence and metonymic power. He describes it as a 'metonymic force' that drives the latent subjective potentiality resident in the surprisingly incidental (Derrida 1988: 288–90). Derrida uses the analogy of music in his attempt to describe the peculiar cadence of the *punctum*: the *punctum* gives rhythm to the *studium* and resembles 'forms of counterpoint and polyphony and fugue' (Derrida 1988: 269). His resort to this analogy indicates a dimension to the photograph that 'no longer speaks of light or photography or anything to be seen' and which invokes other senses besides sight instead. One cannot identify it precisely and say 'look at this!' It cannot be pointed to as an object or substance. In Derridean fashion, the term *punctum* is contradictory because its name implies purpose (point) but often emerges in what appears point*less*. *Punctum* is pointed in three senses: it is a focal *point* of significance, which elides its *point* of location and thereby becomes the purposeful *point* of the photograph it inhabits (Derrida 1987: 304). The *punctum* has double resonance; it amplifies the possibility of metonymy with its reference to unique subjective significance.

Narrative and counter-narrative

The fiction provoked by photographic detail can be framed either as initiating narrative or, in contrast, as the elusive quality that evades narrative. And whether the photograph provokes narrative or not locates an interesting paradox for its interpretation. Narrative satisfies the desire for completion; we can imagine a beginning, a middle and an end, and the elements we enjoy are enhanced by this satisfaction. Calle's work locks into this desire; if we did not know her story, we would still invent a rational narrative to make sense of the red telephone on the bed. Derrida's discussion of *parergon* represents a shift of emphasis towards possibilities invited by simultaneous and contradictory elements within the photograph and its resonant purposelessness, which is not inclined to resolve itself in a structure, such as linear narrative. *Punctum* shares with *parergon* its marginal reference that is more to do with quality than the narrative progression of time and place. Mieke Bal's interpretation of visual meaning demonstrates her desire to make something happen, and so speaks of *parergon* as the element in an image that, despite its stillness, activates narrative and which makes 'the surface ... no longer still but tell[s] a story' (Bal 2001: 77). However, neither thought nor metaphor occurs in sequence and, whilst they may interrelate, elements within a photograph are not sequential and need not necessarily result in narrative. Being anxious to 'make something happen' can tend to diminish the photograph's capacity to demonstrate a number of possible directions for interpretation simultaneously. The desire for narrative can reduce the photograph's dynamic, so that it is constrained by the directional implication that it must go forward, or go back or must be either/or, this or that. A photograph offers the opportunity to sustain the simultaneity of different interpretations; of this, and this, and this, and so on. The photograph can refer back and forward simultaneously. Recall Miller's 'semantic models' that allow us to imagine several possibilities simultaneously: what is happening *and* not happening at any moment. And consider Derrida's exploration of meanings besides those of narrative in *Right of Inspection*, which remain fragmented, multiple and dispersed.

In his discussion of photographic potency, Barthes focuses also on its quality of 'having-been-there' and its stillness. And photographic modernism has given emphasis to the stillness of a moment of time that is 'frozen'. In Barthes's terms, it is the uniqueness of its having-been-there that lends poignancy to the object's absence. His approach relies on the notion that the photograph is 'haunted' by the referent, which follows the image and reverberates, whereas Wall's dismissal of the need for resemblance to any referent contradicts the reliance on 'having-been-there' for meaningful significance. He establishes a different principle that depends on invention, which constructs a possible what-is-there-now. Wall's fictions do not lead us to any historic narrative but utilise the smallest elements to signify a huge range of possibilities. And, as with Orozco and Calle, he inherits the genre form of the 'everyday' but emphasises idea over a 'found' aesthetic and focuses on social interactions, such as conversation, confrontation, argument, as a source of subject-matter. If there is narrative in Wall's fictional constructions, it is enmeshed in a complex web of psychologies.

There are then alternative dynamics to those that construct narrative fiction. Post-structural theories repeatedly insist on vibration or indeterminate possibility as being as valid a process as resolution. The power of *punctum* is one of subjective projection that accesses a metonymic reality (Derrida 1988: 293; Barthes 1993: 45). It contributes to a sort of reality, not in terms of truth or falsehood, but in poignant contrasts, such as Sonja's earring or the general ambience of a scene, that resist exact location, and which we grasp conceptually. The 'reality' of the photograph is this very metonymic content, rather than what one can imagine about the specific time and place belonging to its referents. Traditionally, in photography, it is the *distributional* function that has been valued, because it requires the 'photographic eye' to capture a significant (decisive) point of feeling, or to anticipate moments of action, whereas *integrational* elements may not contribute to a wholly explicable sense, but instead provide tension for what Barthes calls the 'discursive function', which 'accelerates, delays [...] and sometimes even leads astray'. The dynamics of detail are key in obstructing (deferring) narrative and, in consequence, contributing to the potency of the photograph *because* they do *not* determine anything in particular and come close to meaninglessness. All elements in a photograph can be seen as either central or 'dilatory', in the sense that that they do not move anything forward but function to insert tension (Barthes 1977: 95). Dilatory elements produce the perpetual deferral of resolved meaning and the ongoing possibility of recognising yet another element of minute difference:

The particular quality of the grubby walls in Sonja's kitchen; the position of the solitary pillow on Calle's bed, which appears to gesture away from the lamp and the telephone; the apparent indifference and separation of the woman standing at the back in Bloody Merry.

The perpetual deferral of signification is echoed in the psychological construction of subjectivity, which is constantly in process and never complete, and which Calle visually demonstrates in her many accounts of emotional pain. In a desire to find reasons, logic invites us to establish causal narrative interpretation at the expense of Barthes's 'discursive function', which encourages delay, reflection and interaction. He reminds us that in the Middle Ages, description was not necessarily dependent on plausible reality, but addressed prevalent ideas of the time: 'nobody was bothered when lions or olive trees were placed in a northern landscape'. What was important was the purpose of the 'discourse genre', whether it be politically motivated, ideologically persuasive, pleasingly aesthetic or for sensational effect (Barthes 1982: 13).

Photography integrates its purposive function within the illusion of realism. For example, Savadov's visually compelling dramas quietly exhibit the ironies of history. Add the psychological dimensions of our desire and dreams to the ideological possibilities of display and we have something like the very complex rhetorical structures described here in the works of Wall and Calle.

Psychical fiction: illogical reality

Fictional photography incorporates elements of the imagination in combination with visual accounts of the real world and everyday life. Calle's work assumes that a subjective account of psychological experience is valid subject-matter. The rest of this chapter considers the fictional photograph as a form of psychical space, and describes a psychological origin for what motivates our desire for meaning and stories. Since the influence of Freud (e.g. *The Psychopathology of Everyday Life* [1901] in Freud 2002)) and the recognition of the unconscious, interpretations of reality have encompassed the individual psyche and the unconscious drives of desire. André Breton's Surrealist manifesto [1924] promotes the reality that is present in dreams as being as valid a reality as that of everyday life. His observation suggests the absurdity of how we become accustomed to a particular way of seeing as normal. He remarks that the 'reign of logic', which ignores an *illogical* reality, can itself be nonsensical. For example, the perception of a cropped photographic image that cuts a man in two with a window appears normal to us (Breton 2005: 451). Because we are familiar with this visual shorthand, we complete the picture and 'see' a whole man passing behind a window. Concerned to reconsider thought and its relationship to the unconscious, Breton was interested in the way in which thoughts occur haphazardly and without explanation. Raising an internal reality to this new level of significance suggests that we should appreciate objective reality as being permeated by the irrational. Just as the materiality of the dream has its origins in everyday life, the Surrealists acknowledged the parallel activity of unconscious thought during waking. In their terms, we should allow everyday life to be permeated by dreams, which speak to us in a different but equivalent way:

> A considerable portion of psychic activity (since at least from man's birth until his death, thought offers no solution of continuity, the sum of the moments of dream, from the point of view of time, and taking into consideration only the time of pure dreaming, that it is the dreams of sleep, is not inferior to the sum of the moments of reality, or to be more precisely limiting, the moments of waking) has still today been so grossly neglected. I have always been amazed at the way an ordinary observer lends so much credence and attaches so much more importance to waking events than to those occurring in dreams. (Breton 2005: 448–9)

Surrealism searches for a reality that acknowledges the unconscious. One mechanism used to emulate the illogic of dreams was automatism, which strived for a fidelity to the voice of the unconscious and a response to an internal reality unmediated by the rational. Luis Buñuel's description of making the film *Un Chien Andalou* (1928) with Salvador Dalí shows their aversion to artistic fabrication and their attempt to avoid all conscious deliberation or any logic that initiated narrative.[2] Their intention was to '[open] all doors to the irrational and [keep] only those images that surprised us without explaining why' (Buñuel 2000: 4). The film is initiated by the encounter of two dreams the night before: Buñuel's featured a 'long tapering cloud [slicing] the moon in half like a razor slicing though an eye' and Dalí's, a hand crawling with ants. The plot results from a conscious psychic automatism, which does not attempt to reproduce the dreams in a literal way, but to emulate the way analogy occurs in dreams:

> It should be noted that when an image or idea appeared the collaborators discarded it immediately if it was derived from remembrance, or from their cultural pattern or if, simply it had a conscious association with another earlier idea. They accepted only those representations as valid, which, though they moved them profoundly, had no possible explanation ... *Nothing* in the film symbolises *anything*. (Buñuel 2000: 10)

The film aims to provoke in the spectator reactions of attraction and of repulsion, and positions itself on the level of poetry and desire, rather than resolved narrative. It celebrates the wayward insignificant element and its alliance with the unconscious, which encourages nonsense. Concerned with the playfulness of mind and irrational humour, Buñuel and Dalí attempt to avoid cultural significance, temporal progression

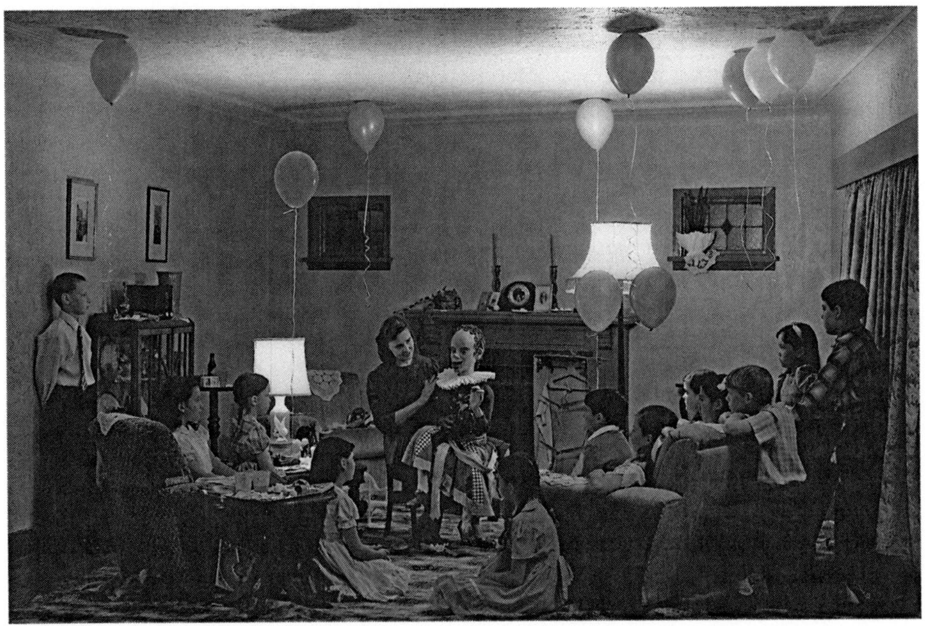

Figure 15 Jeff Wall, *A Ventriloquist at a Birthday Party in October 1947*, 1990.

or the continuity of space and deliberately aim for meaninglessness and absurdity. This rejection of recognisable symbolism proves impossible, however, as the iconic scene – slicing through the eye – demonstrates. It gathers symbolic interpretation very easily: in its bisection of the rational Cartesian eye, a position that declares 'I see therefore I am' – the scene signifies a break with the Western notion of the subject 'I' and the world and others as object, and heralds the disorder that follows unconscious thought (Hammond 2000: 26). What is referred to as the 'Surrealist cut' attempts to interrupt reason and narrative (Hammond 2000: 19). And absurdity prevents our attempt to interpret and to find resolved meaning. Much photography that is labelled 'Surreal' translates the fragmented nature of dreams and the Surrealist cut in a literal physical way that superimposes seemingly unrelated objects or cuts up elements of objects in montage, for example in the works of Maurice Tabard.

Besides the obvious reference to a cinematic reality, Wall's *A Ventriloquist at a Birthday Party 1947* (1990), as with much of his work, demonstrates many of these features that confuse reality, fiction and the dream (Figure 15). In many respects a description of this photograph echoes the Surrealist concerns described above, but, rather than 'cutting' or rearranging elements, it uses realism to construct a psychical fiction. The scene contains a lot of ideas, each element contributing to the construction of an allegory that tells stories and provokes numerous associations. Wall's typical focus of gesture here contrasts the hands of the ventriloquist with the hands of the dummy – the real and the fictional. Many of the details deliberately refer to the specifics of literature (Houdon's *Head of Voltaire*, 1778) or history (the 'Eisenhower' jacket of the allied forces adorned with medals). There are also many hidden incongruities; the leg of the dummy (fantasy) is confused with the leg of the ventriloquist (reality). The continuity of time is denied; the clock faces display different times. Appearances are contradictory; the faces of the children are so transfixed that they appear wooden and the balloons appear solid. The space and the source of light are difficult to rationalise and provoke questions. Everything is in focus, presenting an experience of reality that is not one of visual perception. Wall's photographs pictorially manifest an abundance of simultaneous associations. The plethora of detail exceeds the effect of the real, showing itself not to be real: the echoing patterns in the crochet, the window, the light and the numerous small 'still lifes' (Joyce and Orton 2003: 11). Like Calle, Wall utilises photography's capacity to amplify the smallest incident to carry meaning, so that expressions and gestures initiate a series of psychological dramas. John Roberts describes Wall's use of gesture as presenting moments in which people appear to be undergoing 'an experience which places their daily lives in question':

> An example is *Milk* (1984), in which a man crouching next to a wall has just squeezed a carton of milk. The milk spurts out in a violent arc. We do not need to know what caused his compulsive behaviour, only that it represents an externalisation of repressed anger. (Roberts 1998: 188)

And Wall exploits the potential found in the unspoken psychology of small scenes. The fabrication in apparently simple scenes such as *A Woman and Her Doctor* (1980–81) displays a complexity of unexplained gestures that provoke us to speculate:

Why does the doctor look so concerned when the woman is so unconcerned, confident and unengaged? What is he saying to her that she responds in such an amused and entertained way, and yet seemingly with indifference? Is it significant that he is a man and she is a woman? She appears to enjoy being looked at, sustaining his interest. And then the puzzle forces me to look at the detail – they appear to be sitting in a display showroom: the elaborate blue glasses, the cigarette and the very stripy sofa. And what of the foreground figure, at first not noticeable, who looks at them both? Once noticed, this figure assumes my place as the viewer, and appears to be critical to the scene before me and to the interaction that is so perplexing.

Whilst Derrida doesn't talk in psychoanalytic terms about consciousness, he does talk about how our thoughts are represented – as they emerge haphazardly. *A Woman and Her Doctor* articulates what Derrida refers to as the 'intrinsic multiplicity of thought' – within the photograph and in the thinking it provokes. Derrida's consideration of the way we think explains it as messy and self-divided. He critiques the traditional phenomenology of Edmund Husserl, which refers to thought as if it is continuous, perhaps not logical, but understandable and clear. In this view an interior monologue presents an unmediated self-presence that assumes we understand what we are saying even before we say it – as if we had one thought at a time, whereas Derrida insists that consciousness is not self-contained, and the ideal of consistent self-presence is not possible (Derrida 1978: 154–60). Just as perception requires memory and anticipation to make sense of anything, so consciousness requires representation and discourse with other people to recognise itself. He demonstrates (2001) that we cannot entirely control what we think, or what we say, or how we say it. Thought is as multi-faceted as it is simultaneous and disrupted. His description of thinking when responding to others articulates a multi-subjectivity and a process of *invention* that is continuous and inter-reactive. The mesh of uncontrolled, unpredictable factors nascent in thought suggests it is not so very different from fiction.

Psychical fiction: boundaries of convention

Kristeva's writings provide a link between Surrealist aspiration, unconscious desire and the creative process – particularly the aspects that are inexpressible. In her examination of literature [*Desire in Language*, 1979], she makes the connection between psychological motivations, our desire for purposeful stories and the contradictory elements that introduce something we cannot entirely understand. She establishes that the disturbance of conventional order, in any artistic form, surfaces 'as poetry'. And poetry doesn't signify in a clearly defining way. What is challenging, nonsensical or unspeakable in artistic practice is the inevitable consequence of psychology.

Her assertion of what she calls the *semiotic* functions in language and practice as a motivating force keeps total understanding always beyond our reach, and meaning thereby alive and challenging. (Kristeva 1996: 133). The *semiotic* force approaches the 'boundary of what is assimilable, thinkable, abject' (Kristeva 2000: 552). The *abject* originates in those aspects of the psyche that are repressed, either personally or socially or both, and which hold the secret of what will be meaningful or repellent for each of us. In 'Powers of Horror' [1980] she explores the region of the *abject* and describes its manifestation in a material instance of repulsion:

> When the eyes see or the lips touch that skin on the surface of the milk – harmless, thin as a sheet of cigarette paper, pitiful as a nail paring – I experience a gagging sensation and, still farther down, spasms in the stomach, the belly; and all the organs shrivel up the body, provoke tears and bile, increase heartbeat, cause forehead and hands to perspire. Along with sight-clouding dizziness, nausea makes me balk at that milk cream, separates me from the mother and father who proffer it. 'I' want none of that element, sign of their desire; 'I' do not want to listen, 'I' do not assimilate it, 'I' expel it . . . that trifle turns me inside out, guts sprawling; it is thus that *they* see that 'I' am in the process of becoming an other . . . I give birth to myself amid the violence of sobs, of vomit. (Kristeva 2000: 543)

The description above graphically demonstrates the drive that is cognitively repressed, but is bodily irrepressible, as it surfaces involuntarily in encountering material substances. Such experiences are what establish and define us as individuals:

As an individual, distinctly separate from other people, confronting the abject places me at the limits of my identity, where I can either assert myself or become overwhelmed. The contradiction of, on the one hand, being attracted to something, and, on the other, being repelled, touches the origins of my desire and approaches a realisation of the loss of all that has formed me.

Kristeva's discussion of the *abject* in relation to artistic processes developed alongside those practices (many recognised as feminist) that have upturned established norms (Kristeva 2000: 551). As a generic metaphor for not respecting borders, positions or rules, the *abject* works to reference what lies at the edge of what is conventionally acceptable, and acknowledges the shifting relationships between 'pure and impure, prohibition and sin, morality and immorality' (Kristeva 2000: 552). Kristeva's use of the term *abject* inherits Mary Douglas's (1970) notion of 'dirt', which defines the boundaries of acceptable behaviour in any society. The *abject* threatens identity, and the established order of social and aesthetic limits. Social limits determine cultural hierarchies – who and what is acceptable and who and what is sublimated or excluded – usually women or what is deemed foreign and 'other'. In terms of looking at art, we may find ourselves in this same place, confronted by provocative works that articulate the unspeakable or turn our stomachs (e.g. Paul McCarthy's *Hot Dog*, 1974); the abject becomes a regular feature of body art in the 1990s. We can similarly cite the breaking of a number of taboos in examples of photographic practice: instances of indignity and exposure (Mikhailov's *Case History*) or of the sexual act (Robert Mapplethorpe, *X Portfolio*, 1978) or of death and sanctity (Andres Serrano's *The Morgue* series, 1992). Cindy Sherman's work of the late 1980s explores difficult psychological realms, particularly with regard to our relationship to aspects of femininity. Using herself as a means of fictional construction and the body as the focus to encompass fear and desire, her work has visually demonstrated the *abject* territory of the horrific, grotesque and unspeakable (*Untitled #177* and *Untitled #175*, 1987). What have become known as the *Sex Pictures* are confrontational and controversial, utilising a number of taboos such as bodily fluids (saliva, excreta, vomit), sex, menstruation, mutilation, sexual mutation. They confront the parts of us we eject and would rather forget; they render the feminine formless or reduce the body to a hybrid form that is 'inhuman', neither male nor female (*Untitled # 263*, 1992). They are horrific, ridiculous and compulsive.

In Kristeva's considerations of visual practice, her attention to the psychological forces that motivate creative processes confirms the derivation of meaning in what is repressed or absent. As one of the fundamental mechanisms of psychic functioning, the notion of 'rejection' is the negative force that 'reinvents' practice because it perversely reveals, and simultaneously pushes, the limits of aesthetic convention (Kristeva 1984: 147–60). The concepts of the abject and 'rejection', deriving from Freud's discussion of the bodily ego and repression (e.g. 'Repression' [1915], in Freud 1991), establish an outside that is never completely separate from, but which disturbs, the unity of the subject. Within the artistic process, rejection provokes reaction and renewal, as opposed to the repetition of established norms, and is the basis of a 'metonymic desire' that generates and responds to new associations and possibilities for meaning (Kristeva 1984: 178). Artistic practice is a representational form that enables us to confront what is uncomfortable – the 'incompatibilities, rejections and abjections' (Kristeva 2000: 555). Once the abject is visualised, the horror is contained, thereby controllable and something we can face. Images and stories provide an outlet for a process that makes the subject whole again:

> In horror stories or in fairy stories, the fascination with the morbid is also, at least for me, a way to prepare for the unthinkable . . . That's why it's very important for me to show the artificiality of it all, because the real horrors of the world are unmatchable, and they're too profound. It's much easier to absorb – to be entertained by it, but also to let it affect you psychologically – if it's done in a fake, humorous, artificial way. (Sherman quoted in Cruz, Smith and Jones 1997: 8)

The process of a developing aesthetic assimilates material that was once challenging and makes it common currency. In the photographic context, successive disturbance of the normative rules of aesthetics can be seen in the disregard for objective vision (Surrealism), for craft or skill (Ruscha, *Twentysix Gasoline Stations*, 1963), or the use of content that sits on the edge of taste (Serrano's *Morgue* series). However, eventually what was once unacceptable is made safe by, for example, beautifying and sanitising what is repellent or offensive – as with Serrano's baroque use of sensation and sensuous colour. Kristeva, with her background of psychoanalysis, accepts the base and uncomfortable aspects of being human as inescapable and as a positive force that emerges in creative practice. In *Powers of Horror*, she aligns the perverse and *abject* with the 'artistic', because 'art' does not accept prohibitions and makes use of them.

Psychical fiction: absence and loss

Instead of lamenting what is lost, absent or trauma, as Freud and Lacan's theories tend to indicate, Kristeva's conception of a subject constantly in process affirms what is superficially negative, as useful and essential to the creative process. What drives us fundamentally is the motivation to retrieve what we have lost, hence the recurrence and importance of *absence* throughout the process of meaning. Calle's *Exquisite Pain* navigates just *one* passage through her subjective process to reconcile the loss of her lover; there will be many others that she could similarly follow. Her narration of loss depends on the psychological inferences, prompted by objects and details, which may resonate with each of us differently. In psychoanalytic terms, every object of desire is a substitution for the 'real'. In the context of psychoanalysis, the 'real' refers to the chaotic and material world before the acquisition of language, which therefore cannot be represented easily – only the desire for it in its absence.[3] Kristeva emphasises that it is the *processes* of production that satisfy this desire for the 'real'. Desire for what is lost or unattainable perpetuates a fundamental condition of lack. Desire is the contradictory base from which signification begins and keeps us interested. Desire seeps through photographs, by way of associations beside the visible referent or what is absent, and is resolved in representation and fiction as a substitute for that desire (fetish). The idea of the fetishistic object derives from this place of loss, which the photograph can amplify so well, particularly in photographs of people whom we know or have known. Barthes's description of his mother in the Winter Garden is an excellent example:

> I studied the little girl and at last rediscovered my mother. The distinctiveness of her face, the naïve attitude of her hands, the place she had docilely taken without either showing or hiding herself, and finally her expression . . . I could not express [my mother's being and my grief at her death] except by an infinite series of adjectives, which I omit, convinced however that this photograph collected all the possible predicates from which my mother was constituted. (Barthes 1993: 67–71)

Learning that we are similar but separate from others, we are left with the desire to strive for what we hold in common with them; we are motivated to find culturally significant meanings. From a different perspective, Derrida's description of the self-division in thought and interaction with others can be seen as a condition in which we seek both to escape and reconcile in some way – specifically here in forms of pictorial resolution, such as Calle's use of objects as fetish for her pain – the red telephone that coalesces Calle's desire for the lover she has lost.

This chapter has addressed a number of contradictions: that the desire for semblance of real events can be satisfied by fiction; that the desire for narrative is animated by the desire to disrupt it; that the construction of meaning emerges from material presence and conceptual absence; that whilst the photograph cannot escape resemblance, its resemblance to the actual world can construct a world of fiction. The psychological contradiction, of seeking fulfilment in the source of lack, indicates a parallel in representation, where meaning evoked by detail, which speaks to the individual, can be meaningless to others and meaning that is made accessible to all can soon become clichéd and seem empty. Kristeva's thesis explains the contradictory compulsion to cling to stability on the one hand, and to confront and challenge what is familiar on the other. Primal psychical functions explain, from another perspective, the dynamics of meaning (such as *parergon* and *punctum*) that mobilise what is static, move between the intrinsic and extrinsic, the abstract and the material, and determine what is 'poetic' in a photograph. They explain the basis of conceptual transference from one domain to another in metaphor, and the substitution of one thing for another in metonym. Photographers, in consequence, work with the contradiction that photographs satisfy a desire for representation that cannot be satisfied via resemblance alone, and may only be satisfied in unexpected ways. Wall's work has confronted our contradictory desires for explanation, for sensuous pleasure and for the elusive, but meaningful, meaning. For example, *Insomnia* (1994) or *A Woman and Her Doctor* (1980) present us with situations for which we have no explanation and about which we can only conjecture and invent. Contemplating these photographs inevitably prompts psychoanalytical reasoning. Calle on the other hand approaches desire in a methodical fashion – chasing the same thing – the psychological aspects that we don't understand, but desire, and of which we are afraid.

In Chapter Three ('Dialogical Realism'), I argued that the processes of interactive encounter and thought were not so very different from the construction of fiction. Chapter Four ('Poetic Realism') established the tension between absence and presence, and between the actual world and invention. It introduced the possibility that realism need not be constrained by verifiable 'truth' and can be descriptive in different ways. This chapter confirms the photographic break with evidential truth. 'Fictional Realism' aligns photographs with dreams, rather than a form of reality defined by facts, so that they need have no logical consequence or resolved meaning. Rather than truth, photography assumes a fictional functioning and an embodiment of desire in the ready presentation of artifice and fantasy, which need not be narrative. The 'poetic reality' of metonymy and of dreams makes 'sense' of absurdity. Once photography is recognised as being more than a literal translation of its subject-matter, it moves in the direction of fiction: Calle's fiction operates like a dream, a poem or an ideality; Wall's fictional pictorialism takes the visual/verbal dialectic a step further and dispenses with the need for resemblance altogether.

Suggested further reading

Andrew, D. (1984) *Concepts in Film Theory*, Oxford University Press, Oxford

Derrida, J. (1987) 'Parergon', in *The Truth in Painting* [1978], trans. G. Bennington and I. McLeod, University of Chicago Press, Chicago 37–82

Hughes, A. and A. Noble (2003) *Phototextualities: Intersections of Photography and Narrative*, University of New Mexico Press, Albuquerque

Krauss, R. (1985) *L'Amour Fou: Photography and Surrealism*, Abbeyville Press, New York; London / The Corcoran Gallery of Art, Washington, DC

Newman, M. (ed.) (2007) *Jeff Wall: Works and Collected Writings*, Ediciones Poligrafa, Barcelona

Roberts, J. (1998) *The Art of Interruption: Realism, Photography and the Everyday*, Manchester University Press, Manchester; New York

Walker, I. (2002) *City Gorged with Dreams: Surrealism and Documentary Photography in Interwar Paris*, Manchester University Press, Manchester

Notes

1 Translation from the French: '38 days ago, the man I love left me. We were supposed to be landing together in New Delhi on 24 January 1985. He was coming to Paris, me from Tokyo. I had been gone three months, and the thought of this day was the only thing that kept me going. Except that he wasn't at the airport. Instead of our reunion there was a message telling me he'd been hospitalized after an accident. At two in the morning, sick with worry, as a last resort, I dialled his number. To my surprise, he picked up the phone. He had indeed been in hospital: for an infected finger. That's how I found out that he'd met another woman and was leaving me. All this in only three minutes. I hung up. An infection of the finger. Caused by a splinter. That would be me. An infected finger ... incredible. Also called a felon. Funny. But I wasn't amused, not yet. Heartbroken, stunned, I spent the rest of the night in that room 261 of the Imperial Hotel with my eyes on the red telephone. // I spent a whole summer sitting on a chair, at home in Paris. In 1972. Suffering with no apparent cause. Three months in that chair, doing nothing. Stiff, still, eyes open, hands on knees – I stayed in that position for ten hours a day. I have no recollection of the nights. The only visit I remember is the light that came into the room – a dilapidated room, about forty square metres – at around twelve-thirty pm and left at about seven pm. The phone had been cut off. There was no music. The chair was uncomfortable. Why that chair? Because it forced me to keep a certain posture. On a bed, I would have died.'

2 See *Un chien andalou* on YouTube at www.youtube.com/watch?v=Us3DCb__OHk&feature=related, accessed 8 September 2010, and examples of surrealist film at UbuWeb: Film & Video (http://ubu.com/film).

3 In psychoanalytic terms, the 'real' is distinct from more general notions of reality and derives from Lacan's triad of psychic realms (real, imaginary and symbolic) that distinguish it from language and culture (the 'symbolic'). When we are small we are connected to the real materiality of things – skin, milk, smell. When we acquire language we become increasingly separated from the real. Language structures our world and thereafter the materiality and chaotic unstructured drives of the real disrupt order. The 'real' is therefore sometimes described as being pre-symbolic and, because it is drive-based and not motivated by language, it is not accessed by signification. The real refers back to those basic processes associated with the abject and violence. Lacan uses the 'symbolic' as a broad term relating to the order of language, signification and image – the domain of order, logic and rules. In Kristeva's discussion of

poetic language, her use of the term symbolic is more specific and related to syntax and structure in creative production. In the context of semiology, specifically Peirces's, 'symbolic' signs have conventional or culturally defined meaning. The term 'imaginary' – as distinct from imagination – is characterised by what Lacan describes as the mirror stage when a child first recognises herself as separate from other people and objects. It is the part of the psyche that establishes a sense of identity (ego) and initiates the interrelation between subject and the world. The imaginary continues to be present in how we conceive ourselves, and is represented in the processes of creative production in dreams, poetry and art.

6

Phenomenal realism

This chapter explores photographic representation with regard to the way we experience the world, from the contrasting perspectives of phenomenology and postmodernism. I use the term 'phenomenal' to distinguish it from 'phenomenology', which is consistently critiqued by post-structural theories. The term also acknowledges Plato's distinction between conceptions of the ideal and the phenomenal world of appearances (Plato 2003: 340), and Maurice Merleau-Ponty's discussion of what he calls the 'phenomenal field' (1962 [1960]). This chapter considers, first, the impact of a postmodern apprehension of the world; second, a rethinking of vision and the notion of embodiment; third, a discussion of photographies that reconfigure the relationship of the subject-viewer to the image. The photographs discussed disturb our dependence on vision in different ways.

Postmodern vision

Bazin's statement [1958] that the aesthetic potential of photography resides in 'its power to lay bare the realities' expresses what is generally recognised as being the photograph's defining characteristic (Bazin 1980: 242). Chapter One related the cycle of realism in which the photograph, because it references things in the world, initiates a series of assumptions – evidence, authenticity, transparency – reinforcing our conception of both the photograph and reality. Benjamin's observation (1980 [1931]) that photographs remove objects from their context and distort any possibility of authentic reality anticipates Baudrillard's discussion (1983) concerning the distinction between reality and representation. Extending the longstanding discussion concerning the distinction between the original and its appearance in imitations (initiated by Plato), Baudrillard, as a central figure of postmodernism, adds the condition of simulation to the already supposed 'norms' of reality. What is conceived as reality has been transformed by the impact of photographic reproduction that provides the means for endless series, copy and fabrication (simulacrum), and for a pseudo-realism that presents illusory appearance (Bazin 1980: 240). As a consequence of the photograph, we can no longer distinguish between real and imaginary, original and copy, surface and depth. Baudrillard doubts if photographs ever capture any reality at all and suggests further that reality is constructed by the image in a 'panic stricken production of the real' (Baudrillard 1983: 13). What he terms 'hyper-reality' repositions photographs as untruthful documents rather than reflections of reality. The order of 'hyperreality' complicates any representation that might assume there is a simple connection between appearance and reality; there is no adequate analytical system of representation that can refer to the real world as if it were direct or unproblematic. This deferral of direct access to the world is coloured by a concern for the loss of a moral and spiritual perspective, which affects us in a fundamental way. Baudrillard's account presents a reality that is both seductive and repellent.

I am faced with an array of images of different locations and from different perspectives. Some seem to be taken as if underwater; strange landscapes with crabs, trees and monsters. And then I see that this is not a real landscape at all but a fabricated land with model palm trees and a group of primitive homo erectus gathering around water. And then I am confronted with reality – the interior of a dark and dingy nightclub with four naked people – three men, one with his trousers round his ankles, and one woman, performing an absurd and lewd fantasy – or is it fantasy? Two men watch slumped in chairs. This is followed by references to capitalism and poverty, scenes of protest in dilapidated cities, interspersed with neon signs proclaiming products; the interior of a room with cheap television, china figurine, drooping plastic sunflower on patterned linoleum; a framed picture of young smiling girl – perhaps a bridesmaid – in frothy celebratory dress; an elegant girl lying face down on a settee in a shiny office; pompous looking men in uniform smoking cigars; street scenes; a tangle of street paraphernalia, telephones, corridors; red Cadillac and incongruous yellow mattress, surburban garages and a gigantic beefburger; girls and men in sweaty red interiors; men behind desks in hotel lobbies; groups of smiling people in plazas with very white teeth – correction – photographs of people in plazas; a woman cleaning the street; a woman praying; Kate Moss. And only occasionally people talking with each other, closely. Reflections, photographs and photographs of photographs – my experience is confronted by reality and reproduction and fabrication in equal measure. I cannot distinguish between harsh reality and banal fantasy – between sad ordinariness and extraordinary contrast, between crazy frivolousness and political manoeuvring, between beauty product and weapons of destruction. (Response to Nick Waplington's series through cities in South America – *The Indecisive Memento* (1998)[1]

A postmodern vision, suggested by *The Indecisive Memento*, projects a dislocated sense of reality that hides what is meaningful. Baudrillard identifies a series of conditions that remove us from an original interaction with the world. His 'successive phases of the image' describe an increasing separation from reality through history: the first is the transparent reflection of a basic reality determined by rational thought; the second is characterised by the belief that the real is masked by appearance, which perverts that basic reality; the third describes the image as a substitution for reality and thereby masking the *absence* of basic reality; the fourth is described as 'bearing no relation to any reality at all', as an 'ecstasy of communication', which is recognisable as cyberspace and the virtual (Baudrillard 1983: 11). Our understanding of a world mediated by imagery results in an acceptance of inauthenticity and copy so that photographic practice can only create a cycle of *un*-realism (Baudrillard 1999a). Baudrillard's description of photographs as *irreal* (empty, an absence) describes a condition that embodies many of the processes in which photographic practice participates. *The Indecisive Memento* is typical in displaying a self-conscious aesthetic that presents a mask of appearance: images without aspiration to revealing truth, and knowingly without definitive 'moment'. Carlo McCormick describes Waplington's project as 'both off-hand and intentional', a journey into 'the absurdist spectacle of cultural frisson' and 'a world where visual language has become the dominant tongue of all nations' (Waplington 1998). Echoing Baudrillard's discussion of the integration of the simulacrum within perception, Waplington's use of knowing reference demonstrates the dispersal of what we understand as reality and our immersion in a landscape of signs.

Appearance and reality

Masking the absence of reality and being self-consciously fabricated, the photograph can create an implosion of meaning that can be described as self-referential or repetitive. Controversially, Baudrillard sees banality as the inevitable consequence of our expectation of true representation (Baudrillard 1999b: 140). Appearance – and an acceptance of its deception – is what we are left with. As with *The Indecisive Memento*, Beat Streuli's *City* (1999) is characteristic of projects that attempt to present appearance only (Figure 16). This series focuses on people in crowded city streets, which we can encounter every day in every city. It follows the tradition of letting the photograph reveal what we have not noticed, but, like many of his contemporaries, he avoids control by using the preset determination of the long-distance lens and presents a highly edited selection from an indiscriminate number of uncomposed pictures. Its apparent superficiality and lack of concern for the image has provoked discussion as to whether this kind of arbitrary photographic process is sufficiently substantial (von Amelunxen 1995: 55–8). Streuli does not engage with any moral concern and is careful to remove any trace of commentary. His avoidance of interpretative translation aims for a '*feeling* of reality' and acknowledges – implicitly – the impossible project of depicting reality, whilst recognising our desire to be given an illusion of it (Streuli 2000). Series like *City* are indicative of another theme in late twentieth-century photography when they present, in their ordinariness, a state of indifference. A series of appearances picture empty experience and the opaque, dreamlike world in which individual psychology is hidden and no one has an identity. It is as if Streuli had been set the task to produce photographs, stripped of meaning, of all conceptualisation, all differentiation:

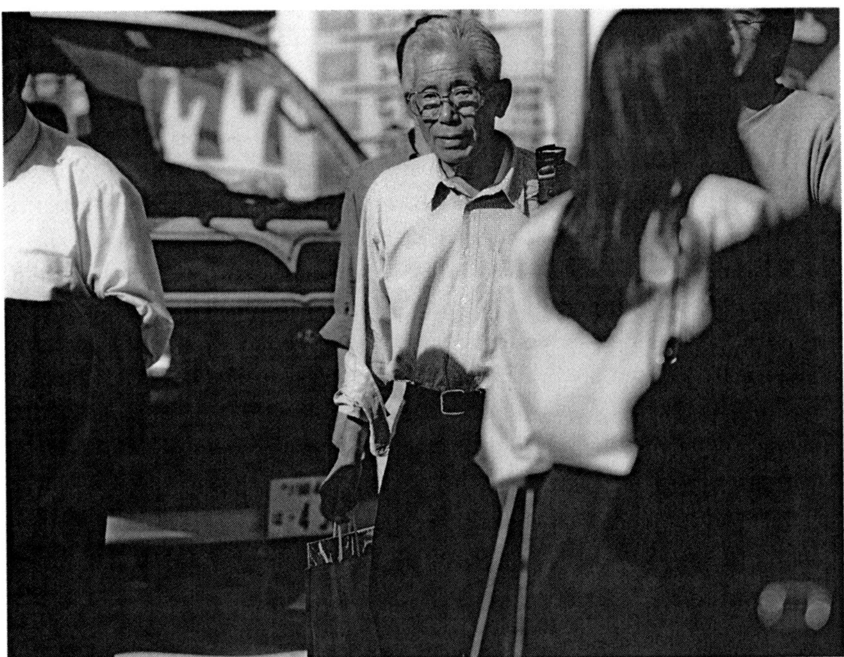

Figure 16 Beat Streuli, *Tokyo 98 II*, 1998.

These photographs present 'others' in a succession of glimpses: people are reduced to visually stunning objects; they compel me to look. They exist for me only to the degree that they appear; they leave me with no experience beyond marvelling at this other world, which happens to be identical to my own. They present my own experience of the street and of my relation to the world and its appearance. They remain distant and removed from me. It is difficult to penetrate their opacity, but despite the lack of emotional contact, they engage my intellect in a play of projection; I am fascinated, but indifferent.

A dislocated 'postmodern' consciousness reduces the dualism of appearance and reality to infinite series that acknowledge a *process* where all one can find is endlessly different and apparently superficial manifestations. However, as Derrida demonstrates, the 'metaphotographic event' is impossible to avoid; metaphor and metonym are held in each of these ordinary event*less* moments (Derrida 1989: 73). Whilst imagery can be bland copy, we compulsively project the meaning of existence onto the most banal of pictures. For example, discussing Streuli's *Oxford Street* (1997), Danto (1998/99: 127) sees the 'modality of being human in the world's cities'. The ordinary street becomes *extra*-ordinary.

Echoing Jeff Wall's disregard for the referent, Baudrillard (1983 [1981]) critiques our acceptance of simulated representation that requires us to move effortlessly between reality and simulacra in 'a kind of frictionless space from the perceptual to the conceptual' (Gane 1991: 3). By playing with this shifting between reality and signs of reality, as if they were logically related to one another, photographs are able to undermine the certainty of visual perception. In the pursuit of 'good' photography, we are used to looking for a hidden reality behind appearance. But because photography has been released from an expectation of authentic representation, it has developed through the play of fictional construction. Fictional photographs such as Wall or Savadov's can be intentionally at odds with their literal appearance and can deliberately not mean what they say, and may be ironic or critical. Both metaphor and irony emerge from an opposition to the literal, and it is the relationship between what is presented and what is intended that distinguishes metaphor from irony. Metaphor shows one thing, whilst referring to something else, so that a journey through the cities of South America coalesces the hyperreality of contemporary life (*The Indecisive Memento*). With irony, the relation between what is said and what is intended is one of contradiction; it can critically comment, so that the same journey shows a beautiful and sensuous world, which results from the ruthless procedures of capitalism and our desire for material products. As a product of the postmodern condition, Andreas Gursky's 'world' is both metaphoric and ironic.[2] His digital manipulation of images rejects the candid straight photograph and strives for 'a condensation of reality' (Beyst 2007). He contrives a reconstruction from a combination of different photographs and presents us with spectacular panoramas that include the acute clarity of the smallest detail – not possible by direct perception. He relinquishes the single-point perspective that privileges the observing subject as central to experience, and assumes multiple viewpoints that visualise the hyperreal condition. So removed are Gursky's constructions from the real world that they amount to a form of abstract expressionism, which manipulates the signs of reality as if they were painterly elements, without any regard for what is true or real. His exploitation of colour, size, symmetry, pattern and high resolution visually demonstrates Baudrillard's 'ecstasy of communication'. Beyst's desciption of Gursky's confusion of appearance and reality exemplifies the disturbance of appearance, vision and thought, which I discuss in this chapter:

> [Gursky] is unable to see the invisible that goes hidden behind all that visual profusion. The accumulation of details is a substitute for the invisible whole that remains inaccessible to Gursky's camera ... The 'reality' that Gursky wants to show through his 'construction', is not the 'deeper reality' that goes hidden behind the visible appearance, rather a reality that is, if possible, still more superficial than the visible appearance itself: so mercilessly visible that there is no longer anything to see at all. (Beyst 2007)

Rethinking vision: mind and body

Hyperreality emphasises a world dominated by visual appearance. This next section considers a reconfiguration of subjective consciousness from a perspective that upsets the privileging of vision over other senses. The correlation of experience with sight is habitual: Sartre's existential approach and Barthes's amplification of being photographed in *Camera Lucida* each describe subjectivity defined by looking and being looked at (Barthes 1993b: 10–15). Barthes describes how we might split ourselves when being photographed and present a mask to the world. Lacan uses the metaphor of looking into a mirror for the moment that defines individual subjectivity. And, since photography, our sense of identity is modified by seeing our bodily appearance in photographs so that, in a sense, experience of ourselves is reduced by vision to a kind of passive observation. Philosophical assumptions that frame our understanding of experience have tended to reduce the world to a spectacle observed by a disembodied mind, which reconstitutes perception into a function of rational thought and judgement (Jay 1994: 308). Traditionally the mind has taken precedence, bypassing biological functions, and the body has been sidelined. Maurice Merleau-Ponty's discussion of the 'phenomenal field' [1960], which incorporates perception, psychology and philosophy, has been a major influence on changing attitudes to subjective consciousness, particularly for feminist theories developing later in the twentieth century.[3] The 'phenomenal field' is not confined to vision only or to the inner world of introspection (Merleau-Ponty 1962: 54–7). His critique of the Cartesian view of perception, which looks on the world from the outside and is defined by vision, seeks an alternative to the dualism of the thinking subject and the body-as-object. He refers to a sensory state, which is prior to the differentiation of the senses that prioritises vision (Merleau-Ponty 1964: 197). He conceives perception as a unity of bodily being and subjectivity, not as a meeting of opposites, but as a single reality – both material and spiritual – and incorporating rational intellect and artistic imagination (Merleau-Ponty 1968: 39). Since the time of his writing, the more contemporary term 'embodiment' describes a subjectivity in which our psychology arises from both brain and bodily experience. The conception of 'perception' has been adjusted as a function of us 'being-in-the-world' – an inter-subjectivity that is not distanced and separate, and is visual *and* emotional (Jay 1994: 311). What is seen is not restricted to only what is intelligible in terms of known facts, but is more qualitative – more sensed – by the body.

The body has been seen traditionally to represent the abject and chaotic dimensions of humanity (often associated with the feminine) and as something other than our true self, which resides in our mind. When the question of representation incorporates psychoanalytic and feminist revisions, the notion of subjectivity shifts from looking (from a distance) to include embodiment. Kristeva insists that the subject is determined by repressed bodily experiences and therefore grounded in material reality. Her attitude, exemplified in her description of the *abject*, offers a contrast to attitudes characterised by the Cartesian 'I' or Sartre's self-absorbed individual (Kristeva 1996: 132–3). Kristeva's *Powers of Horror* (2000 [1980]) provoked a response in feminist theory and practice that acknowledges the significance of corporeality. And Kristeva's concern with a changing subjectivity *and* the constitution of meaning [1974] argues that theoretical processes cannot, *should not*, be disentangled from our bodies and desires, because they are inseparable (Kristeva 1984: 30).

Mary Kelly's *Post-Partum Document* (1973–79)[4] illustrates a radical departure in representation that is demonstrative of this development of ideas, because it graphically visualises the corporeal, unregulated aspects of ourselves, alongside the intellectual. *Post-Partum Document* presents an analysis of the mother and child relationship from two traditionally separate perspectives: a theoretical perspective and the subjective experience of motherhood. It consists of 135 small units – a mixture of the visual, the sensual and the cognitive – that range from her son's soiled nappies to reflective written commentary. The manner of documentation therefore refuses the usual separation of the sensuous appeal of visual imagery from theoretical discourse. Its structure echoes Kristeva's *Stabat Mater* (1987 [1977]), which presents similarly contrasting perspectives of maternity in parallel. *Post-Partum Document* juxtaposes the voice of female subjectivity against the density of theoretical discourse, by presenting her son's first drawn marks alongside her written text. Specifically, it discusses the psychoanalytic perspective with regard to maternal fetishism. More generally, it addresses the debate that concerns the contribution of nurture (represented by her son's acquisition of language) and nature (represented by the everyday realities of childhood, such as soiled nappies) to the constitution of subjectivity. A number of arguments are contained in this visual presentation: gender does not emerge from biology but from institutional discourse – medicine, psychoanalysis, history; the feminine, traditionally and metaphorically aligned with the un-nameable and the other, is promoted and openly displayed; bodily reality forces another dimension to theory, which has been habitually separated from the emotional and corporeal. *Post-Partum Document* subverts the dualism of mind and body by presenting text (representing intellectual ideas) alongside corporeal realities (represented by soiled nappies) alongside emotional response (represented by accounts of loss and memory).

Art and embodiment

The separation of mind from body that has dominated modern thought has perpetuated the primacy of vision in discussions of art and aesthetics. In consequence, our thinking about art and its materials (including the photographic) develops further divisions: between vision and feeling, between matter and form, between art and language. Philosophical conceptions regarding the relationship between mind, body, vision and language influence the many definitions of art, for example:

Art defines meaning as something originating in the artist's mind; or distinguishes between non-art and art by determining what is available to the intellect rather than the senses; or language communicates cognitive meaning whereas art communicates emotive meaning; or art is a material embodiment of an inner emotional state.

Susanne Langer's writing provides an example of a traditional view that makes a clear distinction between *discursive* and *non-discursive* or *presentational* symbols (Langer 1953: 162), where the *discursive* is aligned with communication and the arbitrary use of signs to denote meaning by association, as described by Saussure. Conversely, *non-discursive* symbols do not mirror an external world or condition; they mirror the artist's inner conditions or feelings. *Non-discursive* symbols articulate knowledge that is not readily communicated using language (Langer 1953: 240–1). In this way of thinking, an artwork represents feelings, as with Stieglitz's *Equivalent*, which attempts to resemble an internal world, rather than an external one that is visually perceived. The theory falls short when considering art that includes more conception than feeling, or which is complicated by the inclusion of readymade objects from the real world, or processes, actions and events. It accounts for the emotive meaning of paintings, photographs or sculptural objects, but does not take into account more ideological meaning. It cannot therefore encompass a substantial amount of practice since the 1960s. The divide between the *discursive* and *non-discursive* assumes that art and language serve different functions and are not comparable: artistic meaning, which is 'beyond the sayable', cannot be captured in language. Art continues where language finishes; it is a symbolic activity, which conforms to certain codes of its own: for example, the gestural painted mark or the photographic 'decisive moment'. This attitude, which confirms Foucault's analysis that resemblance in visual representation has been historically separated from what we understand as discourse, continues to influence our response to photographs.

Greenberg's statement from 1960 that 'visual art should confine itself exclusively to what is given in visual experience' typifies a modernism that gives primacy to vision (Greenberg 2005: 774–5). This and the refusal to reference anything outside itself are the defining characteristics of abstract expressionist painting. A self-referential practice is defined by whatever is unique to it as a medium – hence Paul Strand's 'essence of photography' being a photographic objectivity (Strand 1980 [1917]). A rethinking of vision and the notion of embodiment introduce different ways of understanding and alternative forms of art practice from the focus on the visual. Much art of the 1960s and 1970s attempted to radically change attitudes to the art object. Minimalism pushed the boundaries with regard to illusion and perception of the object, and Conceptualism with regard to ridding art of the material object altogether.[5] Modernism attempted to transcend the object, and Minimalism, influenced by Merleau-Ponty's *Phenomenology of Perception* (1962 [1960]), attempted to engage the body in response. Artists like Robert Morris rethought the viewer's response in trying to achieve a whole presence (gestalt), rather than a projection of an idealist conception. Practice has continued this adjustment in attempting to change the viewer's engagement with work by intervention or by provoking interaction. Feminist art practices in particular, such as those of Mary Kelly or Cindy Sherman, have disrupted the primacy of language in constituting meaning by confronting the irreducibility of the body and de-mystifying its power by including representations of *abject* processes. The notion of embodiment disturbs the primacy of vision as the norm and leads to forms of representation which create a more *haptic* experience that can be as much auditory and tactile as visual. What is termed *haptic* perception responds to the particularity of the material and sensation, and incorporates the visual, the bodily and the experiential. And whilst it seems doubtful that photography, which amplifies vision, can contribute to a demonstration of embodiment, it does contribute to the continuing breakdown of *discursive/non-discursive* dualism by demonstrating, implicitly, changing attitudes to subjectivity and perception.

Rethinking vision: body and identity

Feminist theories have asserted a subject-in-process that is psychical, corporeal and cultural, and introduced a more subtle emphasis to our thinking about the construction of identity and the nature of our relationship with others. Subsequently, discussion of the individual acknowledges a mesh of sociological, political and psychological influences. In photography, the address to corporeality can be seen in two respects – confrontation with the body as signalling identity, and with regard to the subject-in-process in attitudes to photographing others. Photographs depicting the appearance of physical bodies do not subvert mind/body dualism as such, but they are indicative of a changing emphasis. Those that focus on intimate fragments of the body, as with Hannah Villiger's compositions (e.g. *Block XXIV*, 1990) or display *abject* content (Sherman's horror pictures), can provoke a visceral rather than mindful response. A very different and profound adjustment to how bodily subjectivity might be represented is evident in the dialogical series by Jo Spence (*Putting Myself in the Picture*, 1986). Spence's naked self-portraits, following breast cancer surgery, challenge assumptions that align visual appearance with subjectivity, and confront the possibility that the structuring of the psyche is constrained by corporeality. Spence's work, like Sherman's, presents uncomfortable topics such as menstruation (*Libido Rising*, 1989, with Rosy Martin) and disease (*The Picture of Health*, 1982–86, and *Narratives of Disease*, 1991, with Tim Sheard). Borrowing methods from psychotherapy during the 1980s, Spence and Martin developed the process of 'phototherapy', which used the technique of restaging family scenes from different points of view – as child, as parent, as authority figure, as 'inner child'. The practice visualises in photographs a series of perspectives from which to observe how, as 'subjects in process', we inhabit contradictory positions with different people, within different discourses and at different times. In photographing others, it is the manner of engagement that is most significant; we have seen how the participation of the photographer can demonstrate a different relationship with the photographic-subject – as with many of Goldin's series, which represent her experience in the guise of her friends. Antoine D'Agata displays a more physical participation in which he and the photographic-subject often appear inseparable (e.g. *Insomnia* series 1998–2003). Frequently concerned with sexual encounter, the photographs attempt the representation of experience and the incorporation of feeling, over visual appearance. Magnum Photos describes his work as telling us how he is part of this world:

> We find ourselves swept up in the chaos and turmoil of his nights: sordid and artificial purgatory, slices of wounded and famished flesh, desperate promiscuity on vacant evenings, and constellations of depraved and violated private lives. This is crudeness of the state of being seized photographically.[6]

Bodies present the appearance of identity; the body is marked by its response to experience and to others' behaviour – it is a constant process of re-*action*. Bodies are representations of cultural *habitus*, the process of becoming subject, of establishing an identity; identity is not stable and is performed according to habit, so that body image is a combination of cultural and individual construction. On a simple level, Lorna Simpson's photographs (e.g. *ID*, 1990), in recognising cultural embodiment, question codes of representation and how we define identity. *ID*, by playing with the shorthand 'ID', points to the confusion of identification by means of classification, with alternative evidence of individual identity. Simpson avoids the usual things that communicate identity, that define by stereotype, and which characterise traditional strategies of the portrait, as seen in the works of Karsh. Rather than aiming for an essential subjectivity, Simpson focuses on the particularities of bodily gesture or clothing that point to the minute differences between us. Her reference to bodies, specifically black bodies, focuses on hair and skin – those aspects of the body that grow continuously and shed themselves irrespective of cutting, removing or grooming. Thus, in its use of material and corporeal signs, the work addresses control and uncontrol, resistance and perpetuation, living matter and dead matter. Many of Simpson's works challenge our tendency to generalise, by presenting a visual catalogue of identifiable features as signs for culture and history – such as hair – that may indicate a particular racial 'type' or a point in history, but which in themselves will never sufficiently describe an individual subjectivity. Works such as *Bio* (1992) refer to the many aspects that constitute subjectivity – biography, biology and biopsy – *Twenty Questions* (1986) presents alternative interpretations – 'pretty as a picture' or 'black as coal' – and *Stereostyles* (1988) offers an array of clichéd descriptors – 'country fresh' or 'smooth and silky' – that are familiar from shampoo adverts.[7] The photographs present the argument that whilst we can be easily persuaded by visual appearance as this or that or verbal descriptions such as 'pretty as a picture', the individual is none of those things. Simpson inserts an additional tension in her attempt to address stereotype that is not dominated by race – that insists once we see a black face, we cannot see 'everyone' or women in general – and to talk of universal issues rather than those defined by racial stereotype.

Peripheral vision

Practice has changed the viewer's expectations of the relationship to vision, not only by inserting consideration of the body, but in terms of the division between vision and conception. In different ways, works by Waplington, Streuli and D'Agata shift the viewer's perspective so that it is frustrated or dispersed. The displacement

Figure 17 Uta Barth, *Field # 14*, 1996.

of vision is also evident in uses of photography that appear to deny photographic focus (Figure 17). This section discusses the consequences for our relationship to photographs in which the content is presented as tangential. Practices that resist representation of graspable or even visible things do not mirror tangible external conditions and disturb our fundamental desire for visual resemblance and transparent meaning. For example, Uta Barth's subject-matter is visual perception itself rather than objects or people (*Field #21*, 1997, Figure 18):

What am I looking at here? It is blurry, but not in the sense of a painterly rendition of an object or place. It is rather a photograph of the state of 'blurriness'. It presents me with something I cannot see clearly, and I must use memory, knowledge and imagination to puzzle it out; it presents the experience of vision itself. In what looks like a street scene – I see two buildings separated by a square void of space – I detect a dark lozenge shape that may or may not be a figure. If it is a figure, it hovers in a horizontal plane of hazy light. The dark vertical light to the right divides the picture and may point downward to another figure. Because it is blurry, the photograph invites me to engage with the act of looking.

This photograph relies on our inability to recognise what we are looking at, whereas in another series *Nowhere near* (1999) we can see what is there. Here Barth removes obvious subject-matter and focuses our attention on what we normally

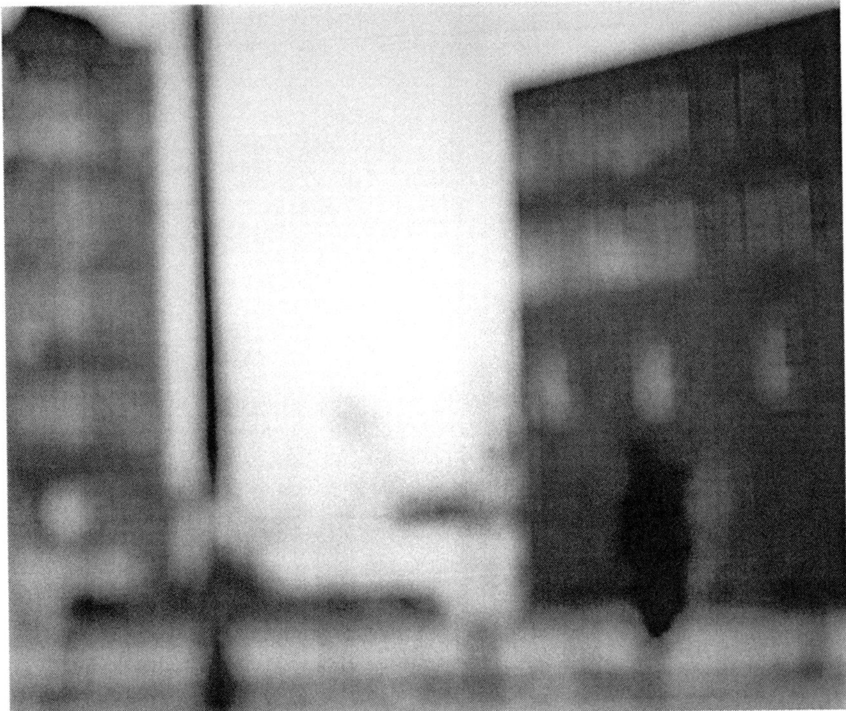

Figure 18 Uta Barth, *Field # 21* 1997.

ignore in the process of filtering what is important – such as the outer reaches of trees, telegraph wires against grey and dull skies, the peripheral play of light or shadow on walls and sofas. Images are presented in groupings of twos, threes and fours, each element describing a different perspective or moment within a sequence: zooming in or out; in focus or out of focus; moving to the left or right of a previous frame. Barth's work displays an interest in phenomenology and the experience of durational time (Tumlir 2004). It addresses our relationship to perception – and the degree to which we conceive ourselves either as an object in the world, like all others, or as a thinking subject who looks upon that world from a distance. It plays with the 'phenomenal field' at the intersection between vision, thought and imagination. In this way, by depicting a series of moments abstracted from the duration of looking, Barth makes a literal attempt to picture consciousness.[8]

Jean Luc Mylayne's photographs address consciousness in a more oblique and figurative way, because their ambivalent subject-matter forces the focus upon *us* – in the process of looking at them (Figure 19). Works by Mylayne disturb realistic representation on several counts: confusing how the viewer can relate to the work; invoking doubt rather than comfortably confirming what is familiar; confusing the distinction between object-being-in-the-world and subject-looking-at-the-world. Mylayne's photographs present us with a paradox; whilst birds are the conceptual focus of his photographs they are frequently *not* focused in the literal sense of presenting a central presence. More often they are out of focus, hidden or obscured and featured as a tiny addition within the whole frame. As subject-matter, the topic of 'birds' is sidestepped. Mylayne tracks birds, isolates one among many and photographs it as the central 'player', not with the ornithological purpose of selecting a prime specimen and characterising the essential features in a clear, close-up view, but in a way that directs attention ultimately to the manner of representation (Mylayne 2007). These are encounters with *individual* birds, rather than with a species, and more concerned with articulating their location in relation to us, to our experience of the world, than depicting its visual appearance. These photographs are not wholly comprehensible as pictures-of-birds and appear to present something other than literal things (birds). It is the metaphoric visual operation of *focus* and the implications provoked by the birds as tangential additions to the photograph that is of particular interest here.

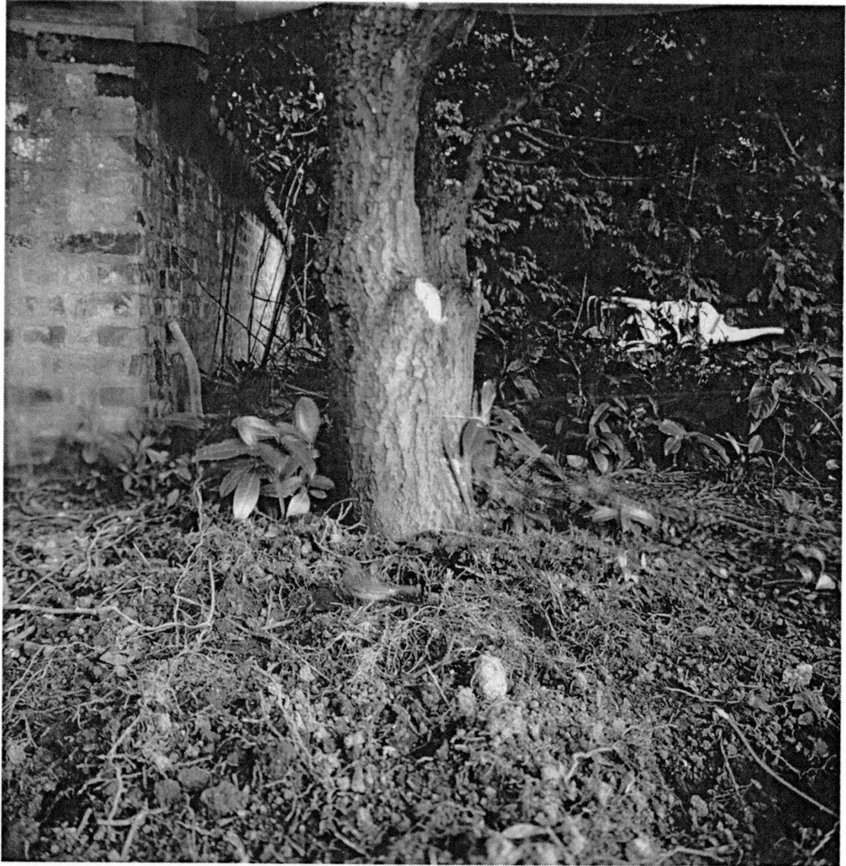

Figure 19 Jean-Luc Mylayne, *No. 131 Décembre 2000 Janvier 2001*.

Mylayne's work provokes lengthy attempts to articulate what is extremely elusive. Either the mechanical process is described, or our existential condition in relation to them. Both testify to the fact that the effect of the scene is difficult to describe in words. Lynn Cooke suggests that the barely visible birds exist in a liminal zone, 'barely conscious, barely known' (Cooke 1997: 104). Anne Bertrand questions what the 'real subject' is and suggests that the birds become agents for 'our possible point of perception of the universe' when we 'forget ourselves' (Bertrand 2006: 25). Didier Arnaudet responds with a poetic reverie about perception and what the 'eye' gives us in apprehension, using terms such as 'immersive' and 'contemplative', and the imagery of metaphysics in references to 'infinity and finitude, of light and matter'. Arnaudet's descriptions indicate the desire for a dimension of knowledge that cannot be described, nor perhaps understood. He refers to what is ungraspable and the desire for a 'sort of excess that overflows from simple things' (Arnaudet 1997: 122–3). Whether we might imagine ourselves as the bird in question, as Bertrand suggests, or that each image confronts either our immersion in, or our detachment from, the scene, they do demand some sort of engagement with our understanding of vision, representation and knowledge:

Whether it is the bird, or my looking at the bird, they point to my own presence in the attention I give to its momentary appearance and its near absence. The birds, the location of the birds and my response to the birds introduce a confrontation with peripheries and contradictions. They indicate the limits of my vision and consciousness, and they represent the impossibility of my comprehending the complexity of my experience.

With this experience in mind, we can see how the mechanical or formal process, which is typical of many discussions of Mylayne's work (including Mylayne's), operates in the form of generic metaphors (indicated by italics within brackets below) for our experience and its representation, which remind us also of the photograph's ontology:

> [Mylayne] implicates [birds] in an articulation of resistance and abandon, of infinity and finitude, of light and matter [*metaphysics*]. This articulation echoes a balance of opposites [*dualisms*], a new communication between the periphery and the centre [*essence*], a source of sight and sense unfolding in the space of things brought close to us [*aesthetics*] ... [and which] neither invalidates nor exasperates contradiction but rather balances them in bright, calm space. (Arnaudet 1997: 123)

Mylayne describes his use of fifty personally designed lenses, which give him multiple focal point perspectives within a single exposure:

> I start with a standard-focus lens, and then put the other lens over it [*multiplicity of vision*]. These lenses allow me to change the positions of the planes in front of me – the foreground, the middle-ground, and far distance – to have several different focal points on one image [*phenomenological perspective*]. For example sometimes the bird is soft and the landscape is sharp. Or I can do the opposite: the bird is sharp and the landscape, out of focus [*coexistence of opposite conditions*]. The lenses can turn in the camera, so I can be

> in the same place but have different points of view, different points of focus [*subject-object relation*]. You can see that the focus I get from the lens is not the same as reality [*opaque vision*], or the way the eye perceives perspective and distance [*differential positions*]. With these lenses I can reconfigure the landscape to make it look just as it would as if we were to perceive it with our eyes [*phenomenological reversal*]. (Mylayne 2007)

What occurs in these photographs is the amplification of the peripheral and what is nearly out of sight. The bird is the central focal point and, at the same time, sometimes it is the single most incidental thing. Superficially this resembles attitudes, explored by Surrealism, which look elsewhere besides the central figure in forgotten elements, where no one thing is signalled as being more central than any other, and nothing is insignificant. Yet, at the same time, significance is actively avoided. The difference with Mylayne's work is that attention to something fleeting is not *found* to be incidental by chance, but actively *constructs* that fleeting thing as incidental. The birds are not aestheticised into an object of display in the way we have come to expect with photography. The manner of significance is strangely reversed; instead of the insignificant being elevated, the apparently significant focus is visibly reduced.

Representation: difference and doubt

Chapter Five, 'Fictional Realism', introduced Derrida's discussion of *parergon*, which calls into question what is understood as aesthetically important. This chapter pursues photographic reference to what exists on the periphery, but which is also intrinsically important, as is the case with Mylayne's photographs of birds. Derrida challenges the aesthetic expectations we have inherited from Kant's reasoning (1952 [1790]) that persuades us that aesthetic quality derives from the object that pleases, rather than from ourselves as viewers, whose 'disinterested pleasure' is supposed to be objective (Derrida 1987: 45–7). Mylayne's work indicates two points of significance that echo Derrida's discussion: first, it demonstrates an ambivalent focus, which is both central and peripheral; second, it questions where the understanding of quality comes from and shifts position, from its origin in the self-sufficient value of the work, to the attitude of the viewer. Kant's logic suggests that placement must be *either* integral and essential *or* detached and external. Here, in Mylayne's photographs, there is no question of where the *parergon* might be; it is the bird – if we can find it. Rather than being supplementary in terms of a literal, peripheral element, like drape or frame as discussed by Kant (1952 § 14: 68), the birds confuse the logic of supplement because they *are* the figurative focus, if not the literal one. Mylayne's birds present the same questioning as Derrida's, but entirely visually; they are 'neither outside nor inside, accident nor essence' (Derrida 1982: 43). Because we cannot detach the birds from the picture, they function to hold the image together and animate it conceptually, giving each work a purpose without which the work would be meaningless. Their peripheral position assumes centre stage and we, the viewers, are forced to look for that centre, which is visually peripheral:

These photographs compel me to scrutinise their space. I am drawn to the tranquility and contemplative nature of each picture; they are simply beautiful and yet empty. I struggle to find content that makes sense and yet I keep searching for it; I keep questioning. Some remind me of familiar places in my past and some are more exotic and alien to me, and it is this I respond to; the bird is but a diversion and a supplement. What does this obscurity say to me? What is my experience? What is it that resonates? Perhaps any experience that challenges me will be one of perplexity. And perhaps the invocation of perpetual uncertainty and doubt is what satisfies me.

These photographs incorporate a number of contradictions that seem to be in opposition: absence and presence, lack and fullness, centre and periphery. Much of Derrida's writing addresses that which is contradictory or is inconsistent, and is concerned to uncover the paradoxical nature of thinking. 'Right of Inspection' demonstrates that photographs can be read in different directions: there is 'reversibility, irreversibility, diachrony, and simultaneity' so that they can provoke, divert and confuse, as Mylayne's do here (Derrida 1989: 42). Derrida's critique of how we understand thought, language and meaning exposes the fundamental polarities on which that understanding depends (such as mind/body or centre/periphery). He reminds us that the reduction to binary oppositions is but a habitual way of thinking and that we create borders and oppositions in order to dispel uncertainty. Uncertainty is at odds with our desire to make sense of things and to find resolution, and so deviation from certainty requires a fundamental adjustment to how we might understand representation. Derrida uses several metaphors to demonstrate how meaning is not certain but is indeterminate. His exploration of *supplément*, which in French means both substitute and addition, promotes the coexistence of addition and substitution – his use of *pharmakon* (poison and remedy) and *parergon* (outside and inside) work similarly. These paradoxes present what appear to be contradictions – the coexistence of difference, rather than binary opposition. No one meaning is privileged over another, because as soon as one meaning is established it is differentiated from others, which unlocks further possibilities. The many manifestations of difference become as important as certainty and are evident in photographic works that represent identity – such as those by Sharon Lockhart and Lorna Simpson. For example, Simpson's *ID* and *Bio* explore this fact of difference by offering a number of directions simultaneously, so that 'this' or 'that' are not necessarily alternatives but different aspects of the same. And we can see how Mylayne's photographs display the minutiae of difference between one seemingly insignificant bird and another, yet make no attempt to effect close-up or to privilege any different feature as being more significant. The birds – and the intervals in space, time and focus that they inhabit – present the paradox of their conceptual presence and visual absence. They present the coexistence of contrary elements in the same way that 'semantic models' refer to our capacity to conceive them simultaneously. This coexistence deconstructs a logic that insists on 'either/or', and signals the possibility of any number of modes of being and diverse elements that may be simultaneous and incongruous. This approach to understanding representation recognises that apparently incongruent or absurdly associated elements coexist. It shifts the goal for interpretation from finding resolution to a discursive exploration of different possibilities.

Without purpose

A photograph without a clear central subject or universal symbolism invokes doubt; it is one thing (and it is this and this and this) at variance, inconsistent and sometimes seemingly purposeless. I am not suggesting that Mylayne's photographs are deliberately purposeless but that their purpose, being visually displaced, challenges some of the still dominant 'rules' associated with photographic aesthetics and how we determine meaningful photographs. In terms of establishing aesthetic value, assumptions, originating in words such as 'purpose', 'significance' and 'meaning' as essential attributes, assume that a lack of these must therefore be inferior. For example, the expectation that the meaning in photographs is equated with narrative relies on another expectation – that it must be authorial narration that constructs what is meaningful. These expectations result from the persistent distinction between photographs that give us information and those that make authorial comment. An expectation that equates meaningful with purposeful assumes the priority of authorial purpose, which is seen as more desirable than a photograph being merely descriptive and not expressive. And the modernist tradition assumes a very purposeful authorial expression. Otherwise a simple, informative depiction leaves us with nothing, besides being a sign for a certain type of a thing. In this scheme of values, seeming purposelessness is problematic – and here lies the subtle contradiction of the poetry in straight depiction – that a photograph of an object, which may appear merely descriptive, can be purposefully determined by the photographer's aspiration to transcend that object. Thus the clarity of intentional purpose is central to the condition of meaningful quality and at odds with the possibility that quality may arise in an ambivalent, purposeless way. The uncertainty of the location and purpose of Mylayne's birds is significant because their effect, which lies somewhere between description and expression, is one of ambivalence.

How can Mylayne's photographs be resonant when their representation is so ambivalent? Derrida's discussion suggests that artworks which do not aim 'to represent, show [or] signify', but which introduce visual paradoxes, can also be potent (Derrida 1987: 97). In another encounter with Kant, Derrida disturbs the conception of 'beauty' by identifying alternative possibilities for understanding how the meaningful value of an artwork is determined (Derrida 1987: 83–118). 'Beauty' is a problematic term in this context, so where I refer to 'beauty' I have in mind the alternative term 'resonance' that similarly indicates quality, but which is not loaded with connotations allied to pleasure. Derrida's play with words in this essay demonstrates the term *sens* (sense) as particularly ambivalent: his deliberate use of the French word *sans* (without) refers simultaneously to *sens* (intelligence), *sens* (phenomenal), *sens* (reference) and *non-sens[e]*. Derrida examines the inconsistencies in Kant's criteria for beauty and, in particular one of them (Kant's 'third moment'), which describes 'beautiful' as present in work that has finality but is 'without end' – without purpose (Kant 1952: 61–80). Derrida proceeds to argue that, if something can only be beautiful without a purpose, yet appears to strive towards one, it is this *lack* of purpose that is essential to the property of 'beauty'. Thereby 'beauty' (or resonance in this context), which depends on the 'absolute interruption' of purpose, gives an emphasis to *lack* rather than to possession or property. Derrida pursues those spaces (without-concept, without-purpose) that appear to lack something or that lie in-between the more easily definable aspects in pictures. Aesthetic quality may be dependent on what is not described, or what is lacking just as, for example, Waplington's *Indecisive Memento* lacks decisive moment or any self-sufficient image. In Derrida's terms, the logic of intrinsic value requires an absence – *without* is not a lack in a negative sense therefore, because it is a required component of resonance (Derrida 1987: 87). He establishes the significance of absence and lack as being necessary for aesthetic quality.

We arrive again at an apparent contradiction: that 'the essential thing' is edgy, ambivalent, and is on the edge of purpose, as it strains towards it. Derrida's 'logic', of resonance found in lack and purposeless-ness emphasises conditions that disturb the urge to find resolution. Kant's desire for certainty requires either-or definitions, which the photograph does not easily concede. Photographs constitute works 'without end' in three respects: 'without end' (in the sense of purposive intention) is inherent in the accidental property of the photograph that incorporates whatever the camera is indiscriminately 'pointed' towards; 'without end' (in the sense of termination) is found in the photograph's propensity for endless connotation and interpretation; 'without end' (in the sense of lack) resides in the photograph's capacity to reference what is absent. The property of *without* contributes to an aspect of art-photography that misplaces content or significance, and which switches emphasis from what is literally described, to an exploitation of what is not there.

Representational reversal

Modern philosophy has privileged the observing subject as central to experience:

What I think of as my experience is ordered by an interior subjectivity that interprets what is presented to me; naming and positioning things helps me to determine my relationship to those objects. As I am responding to images, I name what I see – this is a bird – here is the bird and here I am – which confirms my existing conception of the world. Photographs are supposed to picture something: I assume that photographs represent the world for me and the history of photography presents a series of realities for me, as I am central to that world. With that as a founding premise, the focus in the photograph will determine my relation to it and photographs that disturb this relationship make it difficult for me to do that.

Derrida is among those thinkers who question processes of thinking that focus on the centred subject – 'I'. As with Mylayne's 'several different focal points' that indicate variable subject positions within and without the photographic frame, Derrida's *perquisition* assumes a similar approach in the reading of photographs as a dialogue between the photograph and the reader; it blurs the distinction between the 'I' and the objects in the image, which are each given a voice. In this process, a photograph supports coexistent subject positions and is active in describing at the same time as being described. The apparent misplacement of 'end' in Mylayne's work, in terms of focus, completion and purpose, highlight two issues: the confrontation of purpose and purposeless-ness, and the phenomenological activity of looking, both of which affect the nature of representation. Mylayne's photographs are indicative of a shift in rational representation because they refuse the expectation of simple cause and effect. The photograph misplaces what is represented (the birds), and does not conform to a system that assumes a clarity of representation. With this misplacement, the lack of focus becomes significant, not only because it provokes a tension, but also because it suggests that the focal point (purpose) is not in the photograph at all but resides in the concentrated effort required by the viewer to find the focus: *The bird assumes a number of roles: the represented object, the purposeful focus for the author and the subject that forces my contemplation. As I am forced to look within the frame, the distinction between the bird (as the object of scrutiny) and I (as the subject) collapses. It is this disintegration that becomes the formal aspect of the image. I become my own subject-matter. I become the object of discussion. These photographs present a paradox because their purpose is reflected back on me.* The misplaced focal point (location) adjusts the norms of representation by forcing the viewer's active involvement. It becomes clear that the 'essential subject' of these photographs is the looking activity by both author and viewer; it is not solely within the work. The location of significance is shifted from the work to the viewer. It may at first appear that this reversed focus on the viewer represents a return to a projection of interiority within the material image, as with Langer's non-discursive symbols and Alfred Stieglitz's *Equivalent*. Stieglitz exemplified the modernist search for endless presence. His claim for photographs, as a direct communicable essence or as 'equivalents of my profound life', equated photographs with feelings and privileged the inner depth of the individual expressed by the photographer, over external appearance. However, Mylayne presents something fundamentally different from this because our immersion in the photographs as viewers does not privilege the photographer's purposeful vision. This is a project that confuses the 'rules' of both 'objective' and 'expressive' representation because it depends on Mylayne's simultaneous subjective obsession and objective stealth and preparation, together with the viewer's interiority.

This chapter has introduced the possibility that photographs can force an interaction between us as viewing subjects and the world of objects. Feminist practices, such as Kelly's, have importantly contributed to the disassembly of the primacy of language in constituting meaning, and confronted the exclusion of corporeality in representation by de-mystifying its power. Photography has provided the ideal means with which to confront difficult subject-matter, and feminist practices have exploited its use in their concern to counter hierarchies and to address the processes and the associated prejudices of subjectivity. In a very different way, the discontinuous space of the photograph, exemplified by Jean-Luc Mylayne's project, illustrates a re-negotiation of our subject position in relation to vision, looking and representation. Baudillard also questions the nature of representation and, more specifically, our relation to the object as a result of it being photographed. He asks: 'can the photograph move beyond representation?' (Baudrillard 2004: 95) He suggests that it is unlikely that any photography can be meaningful in the aftermath of the *irreal*, and yet acknowledges that we keep trying to achieve meaning, despite the convoluted condition we live in and the photograph's facility to nullify horrific content. In taking photographs in the 1980s and 1990s, he attempts to remove himself as subject in order to recover 'anthropological status' or 'purity' for the photograph (2004: 89).[9] This position is reiterated in many other photographic projects that seem intent on presenting banal and 'meaningless' content uninfected by the photographer's expression. But despite photographers' strategies to avoid purpose or to deny an aesthetic, it seems that the photograph returns us to 'the objects' own magic' (Baudrillard 2000), its 'unsiezable enigma' (quoted in Zurbrugg 1997: 28). Whilst Baudrillard resigns himself to meaningless-ness, his comparison of the quality of photographs with, for example, the strange or intimate light of Edward Hopper and Jan Vermeer's paintings betrays a desire for the 'exceptional image' (Baudrillard 1999b: 145). Despite the abundance in this era of photographers' strategies to rid the representational operation of tradition and significance, something remains behind as inexplicable. It is still the elusive quality – Barthes's *punctum* and Baudrillard's *poetic transference* (1999a) – that defies logic, which is simultaneously pursued and obscured, repeatedly, in late twentieth-century practice:

> At best a few images (as a thought, a few ideas) can gesture discreetly to one another across space. That is in itself not a bad achievement. The only true photograph is the one which eliminates all the others. In the best cases, you can, when you have looked long and hard at such a photograph forget that you took it . . . as though you had dreamt taking it, as if it has come from somewhere else. (Baudrillard 1999b: 145)

This book is concerned with the manner in which photographers have played with reality, using photography's 'own logic, within its own processes' (Baudrillard quoted in Gane 1993: 137–8). This photographic logic is seen to be one of paradox and not so much to do with vision as we had thought. Baudrillard's quote above correlates photographs with ideas and thoughts, and suggests that the best photographs, which prove to be most meaningful, are those that occur in the same haphazard and interactive manner as thought itself, as Derrida describes. The photograph *as object* – the frame, the focus and the fragment – assumes a meaning after the act of it being taken, in spite of the world it depicts, and asserts a life of its own. This is not to say that the meaning resides in the photograph as some sort of transcendental truth.

The photograph's meaning requires our interaction with it to put it there – and this is dependent on the culture and context in which it exists. But the object that is photographed continues to 'surprise us' (2004: 90), and functions as an independent intermediary between thinking and the construction of meaning. Photographic space *demands* a relationship with it. This adjustment to the relationship between the photograph and viewer contributes to a post-structural move of digression and deferral that demonstrates how photographs can 'think' (Derrida 1989: 76; Barthes 1993: 38). This adjustment in thinking suggests that if we were able to switch focus from considering photographic representation as solely concerned with the object depicted to consideration of the photograph as a representation of thinking, we could consider the possibility of abandoning the literalness and trickiness of reality and consider alternatives in fiction, doubt and discourse.

Suggested further reading

Baudrillard, J. (1983) *Simulations*, trans. P. Foss, P. Patton and P. Beitchman, Semiotext[e], New York

— (1999b) *Photographies 1985–1998*, ed. P. Weibel, Hatje-Cantz Publishers, Ostfildern

Butler, J. (1997) 'Performative Acts and Gender Constitution: An Essay in Phenomenology and Feminist Theory' [1988] in K. Conboy, N. Medina and S. Stanbury (eds), *Writing on the Body*, Columbia University Press, New York

Grosz, E. (1994) *Volatile Bodies: Toward a Corporeal Feminism*, Indiana University Press, Bloomington; Indianapolis

Jay, M. (1994) *Downcast Eyes: The Denigration of Vision in Twentieth-Century French Thought*, University of California Press, Berkeley; Los Angeles; London

Marks, L. U. (2002) *Touch: Sensuous Theory and Multi-Sensory Media*, University of Minnesota Press, Minneapolis

Merleau-Ponty, M. (1964) 'Eye and Mind' in *The Primacy of Perception, and Other Essays on Phenomenological Psychology, the Philosophy of Art, History and Politics*, Northwestern University Press, Evanston, 162–5

— (1968) 'The Intertwining: The Chiasm' in *The Visible and Invisible* [1964], trans. A. Lingis, Northwestern University Press, Evanston, 133–6

Sobchack, V. (1992) *The Address of the Eye: A Phenomenology of Film Experience*, Princeton University Press, Princeton

Notes

1 http://nickwaplington.co.uk, www.cesta.jp/nwns.htm, accessed 31 August 2012.
2 Search Andreas Gursky 1990s, for example – www.moma.org, www.guggenheim.org.
3 See for example, Grosz 1994: 86–110 or Sobchack 1992, and Olkowski and Weiss 2006.
4 www.marykellyartist.com/post_partum_document.html, accessed 31 August 2012.
5 See Lippard 1973.
6 See Antoine D'Agata's work at www.magnumphotos.com, accessed 8 August 2010.
7 http://lsimpsonstudio.com, accessed 8 August 2010.
8 'Uta Barth: In Between Places', Henry Art Gallery, www.tfaoi.com/aa/2aa/2aa239.htm, accessed 31 August 2012. See also Barth 2000, Higgs 2004.
9 See examples in Scheer 2006 and Coulter 2010.

7

Political realism

This chapter discusses the influence of political theories, specifically feminism and post-colonialism, on the photographic documentation of peoples, places and relationships. It discusses the overarching critique of representation – of identity and its political implications – and focuses initially on projects that assume documentary as a style. It considers the emergence of a concern for the political responsibility of context and social function, along with attitudes to documentation, expression and politics, and introduces the debate regarding authenticity and aesthetics. The photographic works selected serve as markers for aspects of history, identity and difference.

Documentation and responsibility

> For me what was important was to record everything I saw around me and to do this as a methodically as possible. In these circumstance a 'good photograph' is a picture that comes as close as possible to reality. But the camera never manages to record what your eyes see, or what you feel at the moment. The camera always creates a new reality. I have always been concerned with the disjunction between experience and what can be recorded photographically. In the case of Rwanda, the disjunction was enormous and the tragedy unrepresentable. This is why it was so important to speak with people, to record their words, their ideas, their true feelings. I discovered that the truth of the tragedy was in the feelings, the words, and ideas of those people, and not in the pictures. (Jaar, quoted in Levi Strauss 2003: 91)

In doubting the photograph's ability 'to record what your eyes see', Alfredo Jaar's statement introduces the issues that continue to perplex photographic documentation: those of truth, reality and experience. His statement articulates a reversal in attitude with regard to the photograph being relied upon to depict reality. In 1994, Jaar took over three thousand photographs and recorded numerous accounts of witness to the genocide in Rwanda. However, his photographs do not directly depict scenes of violence and destruction. Concerned to do the situation justice and not

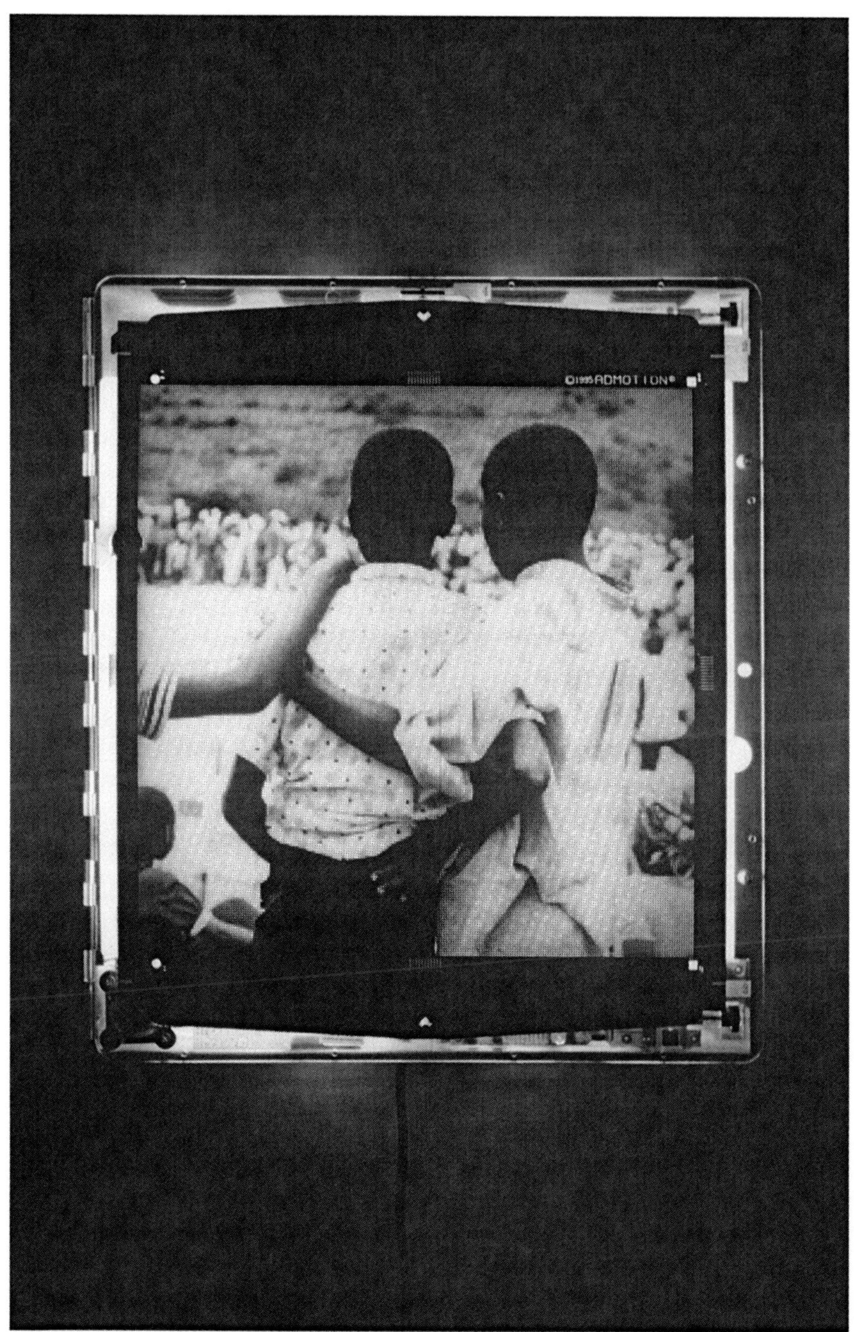

Figure 20 Alfredo Jaar, from *Let There Be Light*, 1996.

merely add to the ubiquitous news imagery that tends to have no impact on us, he did not show these photographs for nearly two years whilst he considered how to present them. And his first display, *Real Pictures* (1995), shows no photographs at all. The installation consists of stacked black boxes in eight piles, each concealing a photograph of one incident; on top of each there is a description of the photograph within. For example:

> This photograph shows Benjamin Musisi, 50, crouched low in the doorway of the church amongst scattered bodies spilling out in the daylight. Four hundred Tutsi men, women and children who had come here seeking refuge, were slaughtered during Sunday mass. Benjamin looks directly into the camera, as if recording what the camera saw. He asked to be photographed amongst the dead. He wanted to prove to his friends in Kampala, Uganda that the atrocities were real and that he had seen the aftermath. (Jaar 1999: 25)

Let There Be Light (1996) is an installation in a darkened space that combines the illuminated names of ten sites of Rwandan massacres (e.g. Kigali, Mibirizi, Butare) together with a looped sequence of four projected images showing two boys, each of whom has his arm around the other. They are standing with their backs to us and are looking at something that we cannot see. There are few clues to what is being witnessed other than, with each image, they draw closer together (Figure 20). As with *Real Pictures*, we are forced to imagine the scene. In 1996, Jaar presented an installation (*The Eyes of Gutete Emerita*) in which an illuminated text relating Gutete Emerita's story is followed by a projected image of her eyes which flashes before us for a momentary one-fifth of a second:

> Gutete Emerita, 30 years old, is standing in front of a church where 400 Tutsi men, women and children were systematically slaughtered by a Hutu death squad ... Killed in front of her eyes were her husband and her two sons ... Somehow Gutete managed to escape with her daughter ... They hid in the swamp for three weeks, coming out only at night for food ... Her eyes look lost and incredulous. Her face is the face of someone who has witnessed an unbelievable tragedy and now wears it. She has returned to this place in the woods because she has nowhere else to go. When she speaks about her lost family, she gestures to corpses on the ground, rotting in the African sun. (Jaar, quoted in Levi Strauss 2003: 96)

It is noticeable that the descriptions are as factual as possible and attempt to supplement the image without imposing obvious interpretation. In another version of *The Eyes of Gutete Emerita*, the viewer is primed with her story before confronting a large light box on which one million slides are heaped. Slide magnifiers are placed along the edge of the table through which Gutete's eyes can be viewed in close-up. *Field, Road, Cloud* (1997) is an installation of what appears to be three simple cibachrome prints of a field, a dirt track and a single cloud in a clear blue sky. The three photographs are each displayed next to a drawing that indicates a location marking a site of genocide. Jaar's Rwanda project identifies a number of significant issues that exemplify changes in attitude to representation and which I discuss below: a suspicion of photographic documentation; the viewer's habitually fleeting reading of photographs; the fabrication of photography; a responsible telling of history; the photographer's indifference and/or subjectivity; the specifics of locality and difference; the possibility of an aesthetic political comment.

Document and representation

Photographic representation is complicated by contrasting attitudes to the inheritance of the photographic document and to what is considered to be truth or realism. Tagg argues that a photograph is not a mysterious phenomenon that satisfies existential desires, but can be explained by the specific context in which it is found. His approach is one of assessing the image not aesthetically, but in terms of its cultural value and what it tells us about the referent and the agency of the photographer. Tagg emphasises the photograph's ideological existence as a material object, as a historically specific social practice and not as something 'outside' reality (Tagg 1988: 188). If we see that a neutral representation is unlikely, then we need to ask how subjectivity is incorporated and to what degree that subjectivity is self-conscious and deliberate. This thinking prompts questions such as: If this is not a transparent picture of the world, what is mediating it? (Tagg 1988: 3–4). In contrast, since photography has been accepted as an art form, an argument persists for a more lyrical response that resists translation. Gerhardt Richter represents the artist's point of view that says pictures do much more than make historical record. In discussing representation, iconographic significance and his use of photography, he speaks of the difference between what the artist experiences, the visual appearance of the referent in the photograph and the intentional meaning provoked by that referent. He states [1986]: 'A picture of a dead dog shows a dead dog. It only becomes difficult when you want to communicate something beyond that, when the content is too complicated to be depicted with a simple portrayal' (quoted in Harrison and Wood 2003: 1148). Similarly, Berger comments on the photograph's ambiguous and sometimes contradictory presentation: the difference between what is realistically depicted and the significance potentially available to us when looking at it. He asserts that no amount of documentary detail will account for what is felt (Berger and Mohr 1995: 87). Representation of the emotional response as well as the visual and factual evidence demands more rhetorical methods – such as Jaar's.

Chapter Five introduced the mechanisms that construct realism, which are determined by the sociological dimension of our assumptions and ideals. Documentations, whether filmed or photographed, insert authorial perspectives so that there are only degrees of objectivity, which are dependent on different levels of ideology and subjectivity. John Grierson, a major influence on social commentary film, identifies that filming 'actuality' does not constitute 'truth', and that a filmmaker can only present a creative treatment of 'actuality' that makes a 'statement *about* reality' (Nelmes 1999: 213). He points out that there must always be some intervention. John

Corner identifies three degrees of motivation that drive the construction of social documentary: the description of social conditions indicating the impact of something on human lives, where criticism remains oblique; more overt social criticism where the intention is to make the audience conscious of injustice; and social protest that expresses anger and intends to induce outrage (Jerslev 2002: 146–8). But it can be difficult to distinguish realistic aspects from those of protest or imaginative fiction. Robert J. Flaherty's film *Nanook of the North* (Canada, 1922) demonstrates how easy it is for a film or a photograph to deceive, when what is presented-as-reality appears to be unmediated. In fact, Flaherty changed reality by restaging past practices and ignoring the political dimensions informing the situation. His underlying intention was to recall a former, more primitive way of life, which would appear to the Western world as pure and noble, and confirm an existing mythology. In so doing, his nostalgic authorship effectively removes the realities of life from its context (Nelmes 1999: 217–19). Barthes critiques *The Family of Man* exhibition (1955) for similar reasons. His essay [1957] discusses the myth of community that functions in images that stress the differences in human appearance, behaviour and culture whilst pointing to a unity of essential existence (Barthes 1993a:100). We cannot rely on photographs to tell the truth because subjectivity and ideology are always present in any communication and so truth is complex. Photographs will implicitly display the photographer's motives. Berger distinguishes three uses of photography – scientific, political and communication – and thereby three kinds of truth: there is no *one* truth. And because the three functions are generally mixed up, the notion of truth is oversimplified and reduced to what is evident in one moment (Berger and Mohr 1995: 100). Different kinds of content require a different order of truth and, if no distinction is made between communication and politics, no distinction is made between different kinds of truth – photographs can tell lies (Berger and Mohr 1995: 97).

In addition, the debate concerning ethical uses of photography is longstanding. Sontag observes that photographs very easily beautify, however awful the content, and the ease with which photography creates stereotypes has consequences for their effectiveness for political ends (1979: 102). Barthes states [1979] that images which intend to convey horror often fail to do so. Because we look at them from the safe distance of our freedom they have no history or meaning for us, or because the photographer adds to the facts by pointing out contrast and parallels we cannot *invent* our own response because the photographer has already translated them for us (Barthes 1997: 71–2). Beautiful images might invite admiration but may compromise their status as documents; they can dilute images of horror or create the illusion of consensus, lulling us into a state of acceptance. They may therefore be less effective as a political call to action. Sontag cites photographs by Sebastião Salgado (e.g. *Mali*, 1985) as being typically problematic because they are seductively beautiful but ultimately idealistic and indifferent to the context of the subjects portrayed (Sontag 2003: 68). Such photographs threaten the boundary between aesthetics and politics leaving some to conclude that they should remain separate and that documentary photographs should be political and not confused by aesthetics. Victor Burgin comments [1976] that, if the photograph creates myths and clichés by facilitating acceptance of what appears 'natural', a task for socialist art practice is to deconstruct these codes by exposing the devices through which they are constructed (Burgin 2005: 940).

Democratic documentation

Allan Sekula's use of the term 'communication' is different from that of Berger or Richter. Sekula is both a theorist and a practitioner whose post-structural attitudes are implicit in his use of photography and his writings, which aim to clarify his overarching endeavour to promote a democratic photography. As with Tagg, he is wholly suspicious of photography that claims a documentary truth. Rather than a photograph being thought of as natural, it is culturally determined so that, in reading a photograph, it is important to question its rhetorical function and look for its agency and the investment that lies behind it. Sekula points out the disparity in a reading of photographs as evidence that assumes it can divorce the inherent translation of the facts from the agenda that drives interpretation. His early essay 'Dismantling Modernism, Reinventing Documentary' [1976/78] discusses the complexity of the photographic document and, more specifically, the division between photography-as-document and photography-as-expression. He starts his essay: 'Suppose we regard art as a mode of communication, as a discourse anchored in concrete social relations, rather than as mystified, vaporous and ahistorical realm of purely affective expression and experience' (Sekula 1999: 118). This statement challenges what he calls the 'cult of the self-sufficient visual image', which expects an 'unqualified objectivity' (Strand 1980 [1917]) or photographs that symbolise ideology and 'that transcend the perceptual'. His argument with the 'self-sufficient image' is that it represents the photographic preoccupation with the possibility of a 'complete' image or, by implication, with its promotion of the author as artist/genius (Sekula 2003a: 246). His is a socialist premise that advocates something other than the elitism of the privileged author and something other than the modernist inward-looking critique of the kind that Greenberg advocates.

Photography has claimed its status as art by aspiring to a depth of meaning exemplified in work such as Evans's 'lyrical documentary style' [1964], which articulates a documentary form touched with expression (the artist's mark) and suggests that photography can be both factual and expressive (1994a). However, Sekula argues that once documentary becomes art then its referential function is swallowed up by its expressive form and it too becomes subject to mannerism and style (Sekula 1999: 123). Rather than being desirable, this can be seen to undermine the photograph's political potential. Sekula's position is one that questions the modernist view typified by Stieglitz's 'expressive realism', which promoted shapes and tones as describing emotion. Sekula argues that the translation of people and places into shapes, as metaphors for the artist's feelings, abstracts people and places from their context, and that this translation functions as a form of fetish – of the imagination. He identifies two opposing features in art-photography, characterised in the works of Lewis Hine and Alfred Stieglitz, whose apparently similar photographs represent two radically different contexts. Hine's work (*Immigrants Going Down the Gangplank, New York*, 1905) was originally published in a journal devoted to social welfare, and Stieglitz's work (*The Steerage*, 1907) in an avant-garde art journal. One is concerned with discourse and communication (documentary) and the other is mysterious and to do with expression (art) or, as Sekula suggests, with fetish. Hine's is a realism concerned with reportage; the other is a 'pure symbolist autobiography' in which 'the photograph is believed to encode the totality of an experience, to stand as a phenomenological equivalent of Stieglitz-being-in-that-place' (Sekula 1982: 100). Hine's work is positioned as an example of photographic document that avoids this pitfall because the subjects are not objectified as a formal idea and they provide photographic witness, to some degree, of fact. Photographs move between a realist truth and a symbolic (inner) truth and between the photograph's capacity for both metonymic and metaphoric signification. Sekula suggests that Diane Arbus's portraits encompass both these views. On the one hand they are seen as transparent, metonymic vehicles for the psychological truth of her subjects, and on the other as a metaphoric projection of her tragic vision confirmed by her suicide (Sekula 1984: 58).[1] These capacities coexist and, despite the contradiction, enhance each other. Whilst documentary is aligned with objectivity, and expression with subjectivity, both amount to mythic truth positions. Concerned less with objectivity than with political manoeuvring, Sekula sees the art-photograph as a form of ideality that reduces the potential of its original reference and political condition, which, in his terms, is the more fundamental reality. What Sekula despises is removal of the specificity of the photographic-subject, which transforms meaning into generality and myth and substitutes 'mystic trivia' or 'abstract fetish' for authorial feelings. Concerned to escape the ego of authorship, the cult of the transcendent image and the 'expressionist liberalism of the find-a-bum school of concerned photography', he is severe in his advocation of document at the expense of expression (1999: 126). In the face of these considerations, Jaar's problem with *how* to present the Rwandan photographs is understandable.

Following Sekula's premise much of the photography that assumes a documentary style is influenced by this polarised view, but can be deceptive – Martin Parr's work, for example, has the look of documentary but it is very much entrenched in the art market economy.[2] If art is supposed to be authentic, there is a fundamental conflict because aesthetics is seen to distort authenticity. In this way of thinking it is questionable whether politics can have a place in art, or art in politics. Sekula's argument suggests that it is not possible for a photograph to be both political and aesthetic, in the sense of being visually and conceptually compelling. To remain compelling there must be tension and some room for contemplative resonance. Alfredo Jaar presents an alternative to Sekula's extreme view because not only does he aim to be democratic but his work is undeniably 'aesthetic'. It incorporates document, expression and metaphor in representations of specific contexts, individuality and locality. Jaar uses structural devices that present events obliquely, projecting a sideways look at reality in what is absent or not said. Rather than relying on definitive descriptions, the function of image is shifted from indexical record to one of *integrational* effect as he focuses on details that rely on associations and imagination to build a reality. He uses the photograph to allude, slowly building a different realism in our response to a single, and sometimes peripheral, element. In its extreme form, the effect of absence refers to what is unspeakable horror. Jaar makes a number of versions of the Rwanda project, which gives him the freedom to emphasise different aspects of the situation. He deliberately restricts the information given to us, forcing us to ask questions: What are they looking at? Why are they standing close together? What is happening? Why is it happening? As meta-fictions, he includes reminders of the photograph's distance from reality by including reference to their manufacture, acknowledging photography as a form of performance and fiction. He demonstrates the closeness of fact to fiction, and of memory to evidence, in documenting events, people and places. The function of subjectivity in Jaar's work is to describe subjective experience rather than documentary fact. His version of photographic document is implicitly conceptual and inherits, for example, the awareness of the ironies and contradictions present in any reality. Jaar's anxiety to respect the individuals concerned and to achieve a significance that does justice to the situation demands methods that force a response. His procedures are wholly fabricated and deliberately designed to make us react, rather than just to look and accept. He does not document a statistical history referring to anonymous thousands, which becomes, in abstract terms, 'the tragedy-of-black-Africa'. Instead, he shifts emphasis from the abstract and universal to the particular, by focusing on one tragedy, one local history, at a time. Jaar's rhetorical approach forces us to interact with the specific incident of a political reality and its effect on individuals. He interrupts our perception and response, in a way that moves merely looking to a reading of duration.

The politics of representation

History is constructed by its representations – written descriptions and photographic documentation – and is defined by the perspective from which we look at it. Photographs demonstrate implicit histories, relationships and the values embedded in our view of the world. They display unspoken attitudes and agency in the way something is documented, in recording physical appearance. Claude-Joseph Désiré Charnay's photograph *Women of Madagascar* (1863) pigeonholes all Madagascan women as having a common and shared identity defined by costume, with no individual status, personality or name.[3] It clearly displays a paternalistic imperialism and the divide between Western and other cultures. Global economic change and post-colonial debate have forced a reappraisal of attitudes with regard to peoples and cultures, and assumptions concerning representation and subjectivity have since been re-adjusted. Following Foucault, we are aware of the implicit presence of power defined by systems of classification. Following post-colonial theories, we are aware of the ubiquity of cultural generalisations and the subsequent abuse of power. We now ask questions such as: What is implicit in this image? What histories have influenced what it shows us? Art practice can ask the same questions by reflecting an awareness of subjectivity and identity. Photographs can display interpretations of history and political response to situations, sometimes overtly and sometimes allegorically or obliquely. For example, accounts of war, such as Robert Polidori's *Samir Geagea Headquarters #1, Rue de Damas, Beirut, Lebanon* (1994), or Simon Norfolk's of Afghanistan (2001), are touched with the knowing irony of photographic beauty presented in the aftermath of violence.[4] Attitudinal changes are not necessarily evident in content that is *about* subjectivity or *about* politics or *about* the history of a culture, but are implicitly present in the photographer's methods of engagement with culture, history and politics. Photography has the potential to interact with history and ideology in a completely different way from verbal debate. History is constructed – even invented – and art practice can disturb the processes and views of history or demonstrate subtle displacements.

Many photography projects that adopt the appearance of documentary incorporate an awareness of the conditions of power in the careful avoidance of directorial authoring, or in an assertion of difference over general statement, or in the adoption of elaborate strategies that declare cultural awareness. For example, Fazal Sheikh, rather than presenting photographs of anonymous individuals to represent a people or a situation, pointedly names his photographic-subjects and their circumstance (*A Sense of Common Ground*, 1996). Susan Meiselas's web project *Kurdistan: In the Shadow of History* (1997) builds 'a collective memory and cultural exchange with a people who have no national archive' and invites the Kurdish community to contribute their individual stories by submitting their own photographic documents.[5] Sharon Lockhart's *Apeú-Salvador: Families* (1999) attempts to create a democratic document that does not objectify or categorise people in the same way that Charnay's photographs clearly do. *Apeú-Salvador* is typical of a concern to use photography as a social practice and to expose the myth that documentary accesses photographic truth. She deliberately selects a range of methods and contexts in order to engender a participative commentary with the people, and to present different aspects of their lives. In making portraits of the families and individuals she is careful to make a negotiated documentation. The families select their location, pose and, using a Polaroid camera, review the results before repositioning themselves as they choose. The resulting images are somewhere between portrait and self-portrait so that the photographic process is reciprocal. She includes a more obviously symbolic ('aesthetic') series of photographs of *Apeú-Salvador: Maria da Conceicão Pereira de Souza with the Fruits of the Island*. She uses snapshots that the families have taken themselves and re-photographs them. Echoing Sekula's concerns, Lockhart produces an extended, horizontal document, describing the different dimensions of cultural identity, which is not dependent on the success of any one individual photograph and not interested in the individual style or expression of the photographer.

The politics of representation: difference

In simple terms, 'post-colonialism' refers to the consideration of countries following colonialism. But it has come to represent a political position in response and resistance to colonialism. Theorists such as Frantz Fanon (*Black Skin, White Masks*, 1991 [1952]) and Edward Said (*Orientalism*, 1995 [1978]) have forced recognition of the implicit powerbase of Westernism and its imposition of culture, politics and society, which is visibly evident, for example, in colonial architecture. Said explains the term 'oriental' as a Western construction that encapsulates a mythology of 'otherness' that is distinctly different and exotic. The term post-colonialism is contested and its association with postmodernism is seen as problematic because it suggests a resignation, a completion – of position and of argument. Gayatri Chakravorty Spivak prefers the term 'post-coloniality', which implies an ongoing process (Boyce Davies 1994: 91–2). As with Spivak, Homi K. Bhabha represents a position that resists the fixed chronology of one state following another suggested by the prefix 'post'. As a cultural theorist, Bhabha is concerned with colonial, post-colonial, modern and postmodern debates. Writing in 1994, he discusses the shifting position of the 'realm of beyond', by which he does not mean a mysterious transcendence but a concern with disorientation and change. He characterises the prevalent themes leading up to the turn of the century as 'difference and identity, past and present, inside and outside, inclusion and exclusion' (1994: 1). And, writing from the perspective of cultural difference and direction, his concern is that of a way forward in the face of the past histories of colonialism and subjugation. Like Kristeva, his focus is on processes of identity rather than fixed narratives of the past. But rather than individual subjectivity he emphasises the articulation of cultural differences and 'the idea of society itself'. Theorists such as Fanon established the importance of reasserting the histories pertinent to any subordinated peoples, who have incorporated the culture of their colonisers and thereby confused and even lost their own. As a result of a history that nurtured inferiority, the desire for a cultural presence in a post-colonial society can be a negating activity. Bhabha's is a positive interpretation of post-colonial awareness. He points out the dangers in mythologizing and fixing a past history rather than promoting the process of a living culture that continues to change and evolve. He uses the metaphors 'between' and 'borderline' to provide focus for representing cultural and racial difference, incorporating both antagonism and negotiation. He asks 'How are subjects formed "in-between" elements of difference (usually described in terms of race/class/gender etc.)? How do strategies of representation or empowerment come to be formulated?' In common with many of the theories already outlined, Bhabha's emphasis repositions assumptions of received tradition or the idea of originary identity and challenges 'normative expectations of development and progress' (Bhabha 1994: 1–2). Interestingly he uses Sekula's *Fish Story* as an example of the metaphor 'borderline', which narrates an instance of critical displacement, evident this time in the more specific borderline of 'harbour', between land and sea (Bhabha 1994: 8).

The cultural theorist Stuart Hall emphasises cultural identity as being a process of 'becoming' and as something that must be considered through different and specific subjectivities (Hall 2001: 104). Like Bhabha, he sees this as an evolution, belonging to the future as much as the past. He refers to 'black' as not indicating any particular racial group but a politically and historically contested idea, which continues to evolve. Race, he says, is a discursive form that constructs and justifies divisions; it is 'more like a language than it is like the way we are biologically constructed'. Skin is a signifier, not of a fixed inner nature, but of 'a sea of relational differences' (Hall 1997a). Hall and Sealy's collation of works by black photographers in *Different* (2001) provides a useful overview of the disruption of processes of identification demonstrated in photographic projects at the end of the twentieth century. The book is concerned to consider this notion of becoming as being fluid rather than fixed. It focuses on imagery that subverts the traditions of portraiture and documentary, indicating a loss of confidence in documentary being able to describe the process of identity. Rotimi Fani-Kayode expresses this very clearly:

> My identity has been constructed from my own sense of otherness, whether cultural, racial or sexual. The three aspects are not separate within me. Photography is the tool by which I feel most confident in expressing myself. It is photography therefore – Black, African, homosexual photography – which I must use not just as an instrument, but as a weapon if I am to resist attacks on my integrity and indeed, my existence on my own terms. (Fani-Kayode 1988: 42) [6]

Hall and Sealy state that the photograph, as a symbolic space, always entails 'a politics of truth' and a 'politics of desire', which put identity into question (Hall 2001: 36–8). The body, which represents a person, will always re-present identity and subjectivity and thereby always address aspects of race, gender and sexual difference. Hall's lecture 'Representation and the Media' (1997b) very clearly explains representation as either presenting again (repeating or copying) something that was already there, or standing for something else. Most often this substitution is ideological, so that, for example, the black male body assumes a mythic and stereotypical status. Further to this, Hall refers to the equation of 'black' with 'abject' or 'other' and discusses black photographers who actively reverse existing Western hierarchies such as whiteness and heterosexuality. This can be effected by simply replacing one privileged norm with an opposite position – for example, Fani-Kayode's *Every Moment Counts* (1989) shows a black Christ-like figure. Works by Fani-Kayode force a re-adjustment of our acceptances of normative dualisms: black/white, feminine/masculine, erotic/spiritual. As we have seen, Lorna Simpson raises questions about

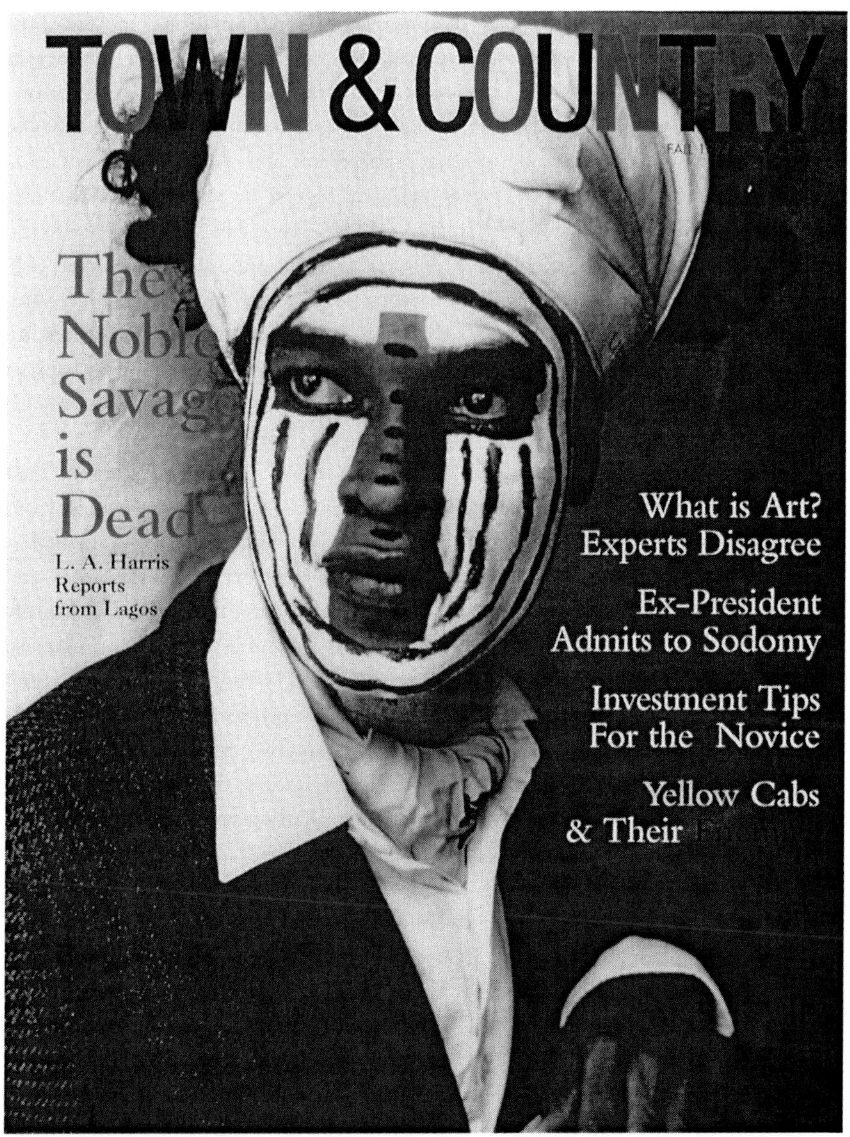

Figure 21 Iké Udé, 'Town and Country', *Cover Girl* series, 1994.

how 'identity' is assumed on the basis of appearance. Iké Udé critiques media representation by producing a series of fake magazine covers on which he appears in different guises (*Cover Girl*, 1994).[7] He pokes fun at conventions in a series of contradictory statements: 'Town and Country' announces a feature entitled 'The Noble Savage is Dead' next to which he wears a tailored suit and cravat whilst his face is painted in Igbo Uli tribal stripes (Figure 21). 'Real Men Wear Make-up' also features him wearing a suit but this time with lipstick and false eyelashes. But, contrary to the attempts of much post-structural commentary to avoid oppositional reversal, Udé advocates a reversal of the classic dichotomous positions of appearance and reality or artifice and naturalism. He suggests that what is more natural now is artificiality and performance, and that 'being natural is tantamount to advocating going back to the wilderness'. He takes an acceptance of fiction and falsity to its extreme conclusion – that mimicry and fake are routes to truth (Hall 2001: 48–9).

Destiny Deacon's reference to 'blak' is confrontational and more irreverent than Hall's measured critique, but makes the same points. Deacon is descended from the KuKu and Erub/Mer peoples of Australia, and her whole practice is steeped in the implications of representation and colonial history. It presents an extreme and uncanny contrast of photographic process and political intention whereby absurdly constructed tableaux represent the realities of injustice and prejudice. *My Boomerang Did Come Back* (2003) presents a blurred image of a hand holding a boomerang – both of which are smeared with blood (Figure 22). *My Boomerang Did Come Back* recalls Charlie Drake's absurd chart song 'My Boomerang Won't Come Back' of 1961, which ignores any regard for Aboriginal culture or experience. At the time of its release, indigenous Australians could not vote in the Australian elections: 'what Drake had failed to mention in the context of dispossession, massacres and introduced disease was that it was scarcely surprising that Mack's boomerang wouldn't come back' (Broker 2003: 19). Motivated by feminism and political activism, Deacon's satirical use of photography not only recalls its use in history to represent people as objects of curiosity (*Women of Madagascar*, 1863) but also harnesses the metonymic power of objects described here in Chapter Four ('Poetic Realism'). Deacon demonstrates photography as an effective tool for satire and critique. Described as wielding her camera to argue (McFarlane 2004) and cutting through 'the absurdities of racism' (Broker 2003: 16), the images are noisy, rebellious and defiant and full of humour whilst being implicitly critical of Australia's social history. Her humour is laden with irony that subverts assumptions about race, difference and subsequent post-colonial critique. She describes, for example, 'an ongoing series where I take pictures of men and white men as well – I'm not prejudiced'.[8] Deacon's use of photography is deliberately and technically careless, paying little heed to the conventions of 'good' photographic composition. She avoids sophisticated digital applications, simply scanning Polaroid photographs into the computer. Her use of objects is described as 'fighting reification' because they are actively 'performative' (Langford 2005: 105). Using an assortment of cheap but potent souvenir objects – Union Jacks, sceptres and golli-

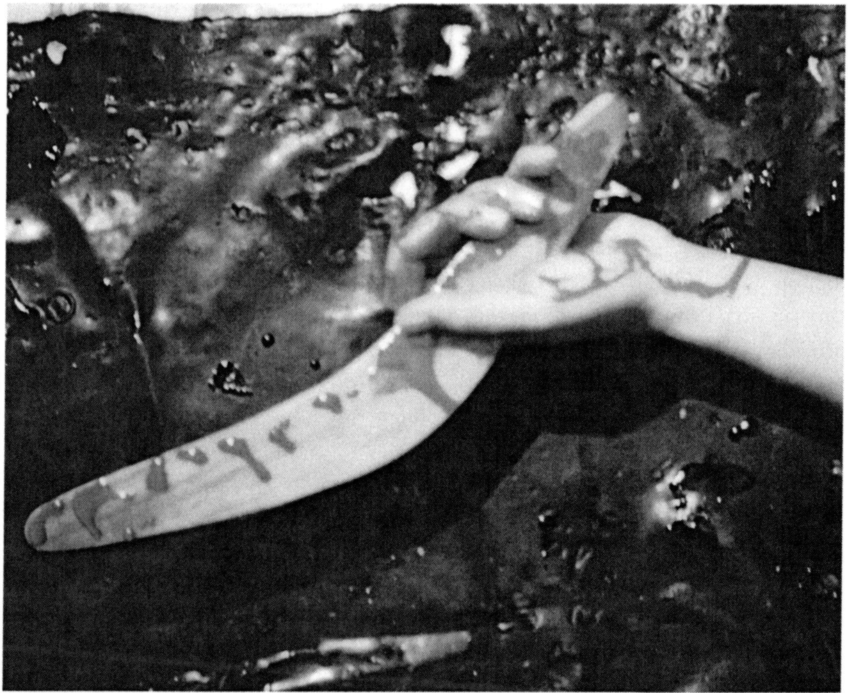

Figure 22 Destiny Deacon, *My Boomerang Did Come Back*, 2003.

wogs – the objects recreate the racial and sexual politics of everyday life, including imagined scenarios from her mother's life growing up in Queensland (*Postcards from Mummy*, 1994). Casting 'blak' dolls as her principle 'actors', she is able to manipulate them physically in extreme ways, which suggest emotional and violent abuse: stuffed into crates, enacting kitchen scenes with broken crockery, dressed up and carrying handbags in elaborate kitsch set-ups, headless and placed in a scooped-out melon (*Melancholy*, 2000) and laid out in paper cake cases in various states of undress (*Adoption*, 1993/2000). Her work provides a running commentary of a post-colonial society that is simultaneously disturbing and humorous.

Politics of representation: privileged or reciprocal gaze

Charnay's image *Women of Madagascar* also positions 'women' as being the same wherever they are. Laura Mulvey's essay 'Visual Pleasure and Narrative Cinema' [1975] is indicative of feminist theory that questioned the attitudes implicit in visual culture. Drawing upon ideas from psychoanalysis, Mulvey introduced a discourse that considered the activity of looking, the passivity in being looked at and the consequent processes of desire, display and the mask of presentation, so obviously evident in the spectacle of film. Her essay describes a patriarchal world that identifies the male as active, whilst the female passively displays herself in a manner styled for erotic impact:

> Woman ... stands in patriarchal culture as a signifier for the male other, bound by a symbolic order in which a man can live out his fantasies and obsessions through linguistic command by imposing them on the silent image of woman still tied to her place as bearer, not maker, of meaning. (Mulvey 1989: 15)

The above quote concentrates a number of central points for reconsideration of the representation of women: the hierarchy of male/female dualism; the primacy of language in constituting meaning; the significance of the image – literally in terms of providing a resource for male fantasy and metaphorically in terms of the expectation of women as passive participants in the constitution of meaningful life. Awareness of Mulvey's analysis can be seen visually demonstrated in a number of photographic translations. Cindy Sherman's work presents an extended study of looking and being looked at. The earlier *Untitled Film Stills* (1977–80), using the conventions and stereotypes of filmic construction, display Mulvey's 'to-be-looked-at-ness' and the phenomenological subject we are familiar with – of being looked at as-picture and as if captured by the gaze (Mulvey 1989: 25). Jeff Wall's *Picture for Women* (1979) simultaneously articulates and challenges the gaze, as described by Mulvey, by visually confusing who is looking at whom. Barbara Kruger's work builds a political critique of representation: *Your Gaze Hits the Side of My Face* (1981–83) refers, as if directly, to Mulvey's discussion of the mediation of self and language by injunctions that emerge in social structures. It makes implicit and explicit reference to woman's vulnerability in the face of the photograph, the film and the gaze. Echoing Barthes's exposure (1993a [1957]) of what is seen as natural or 'what-goes-without-saying', Kruger's work explores the consequences of nature being subsumed by culture, and thereby understood as natural. She presents confrontational photographic statements, in combination with text, that expose cultural stereotypes and behaviour. These image-statements, cropped and manipulated for rhetorical effect, protest about the representation of norms, relationships and oppression. Each incorporates a declaration that questions high art, mass culture, sexual politics or cultural power. Kruger's use of personal pronouns (Your, My, I, You, We) personalise the exchange between spectator and image and address us as individual 'subjects'. *We Won't Play Nature to Your Culture* (1983) comments on representation in the male–female relationships of patriarchal politics. It declares that 'We' – translating as the viewer, any individual or all women – will not become what 'You' – a particular individual or all men – have constructed as an idea of 'Me', the ideal woman. Like Mary Kelly, she uses the contrast of personal reality with political argument: the subjective pain of specific relationships together with a more distanced political anger.[9]

Discussion of the gaze has been extensive, particularly in the context of the cinema (Sobchack 1992; Silverman 1996). In 1981, Mulvey revisited her original analysis of male/female opposition and considered the 'female spectator', reminding us that the activity/passivity function is metaphoric and continually shifts position. The conventional oppositional stance has been challenged, and reconfigured in the contexts of racial difference and sexual orientation. The gaze can be adopted by both male and female and is not confined to heterosexual subjects. Robert Mapplethorpe's *X Portfolio* (1978) is an effective visual critique in its confrontation of normative dualism and desire. Late twentieth-century uses of photography have subverted the 'gaze' in various ways: Sherman's *Untitled #175* (1987) refers to the gaze indirectly, reflected in a spectacle frame lying in vomit, and the objectifying gaze is deliberately averted by denying any direct contact, as in Yokomizo's *Strangers* (1998–2000). Wall's *The Mimic* (1982) subtly colludes with the viewer in its critique of the prejudicial gaze; it exploits the casual survey of photographs in its use of a barely perceptible, but hugely significant, gesture that refers to racial attitudes.

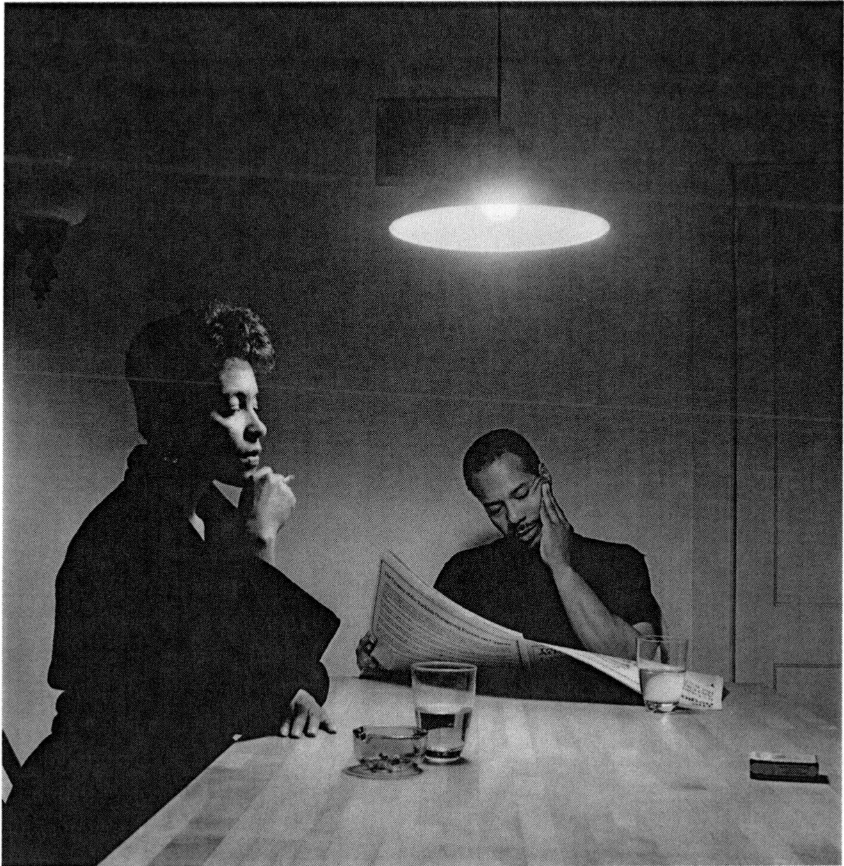

Figure 23.1 Carrie Mae Weems, *Untitled (Man Reading Newspaper)*, from *Kitchen Table* series, 1990.

> A woman didn't know how to construct an image of herself. The image-making was starting to follow the theory of Laura Mulvey, etc. rather than the other way around! There was a fear on the part of visual artists to take control of our bodies, our sexuality. I was trying to respond to a number of issues: woman's subjectivity, woman's capacity to revel in her body, and woman's construction of herself, and her own image. (Weems 1996)

Whilst clearly acknowledging the influence of feminist theories on attitudes to representation, and on art practice specifically, Carrie Mae Weems describes her attempts to do more with photography than merely illustrate theory and makes use of its capacity to present contradictory ideas simultaneously, which is something words cannot do. Described as engaging in a 'politics of anti-colonialism' that contests power structures by challenging viewers to shift their paradigms (hooks 1995: 77), Weems' practice utilises photography to address multiple aspects of cultural identity and feminine subjectivity – in particular, the tension between conflicting conditions, such as: tenderness/power; respect/dominance; identity/stereotype; culture/

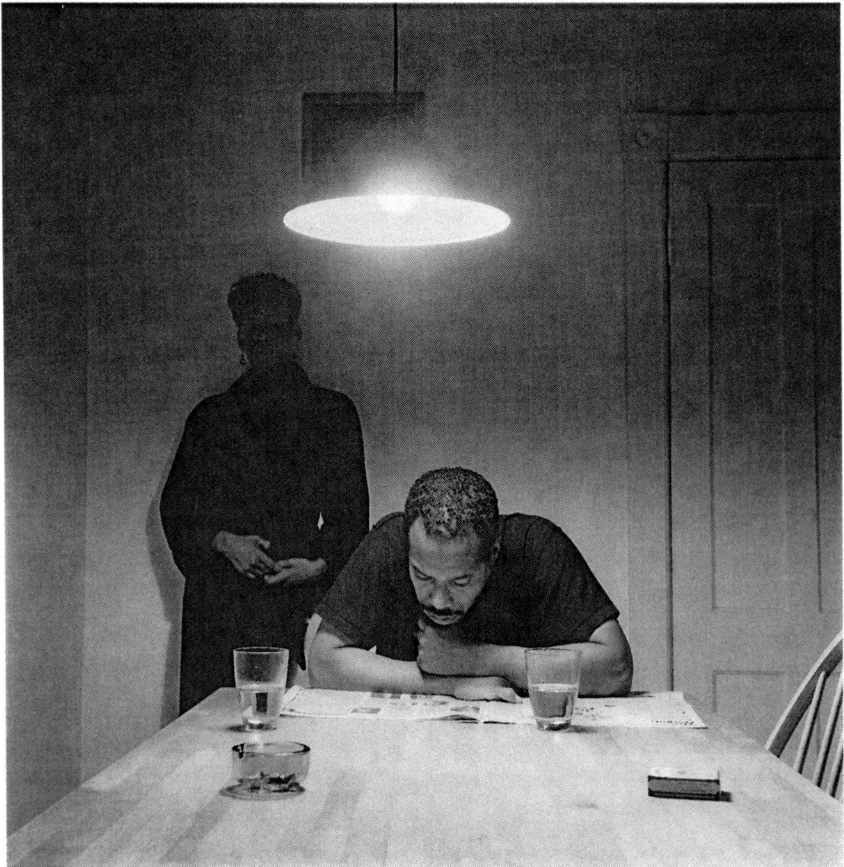

Figure 23.2 Carrie Mae Weems, *Untitled (Man Reading Newspaper)*, from *Kitchen Table* series, 1990.

psychology. Her work is motivated by her fascination with the distances between men and women, and between ethnic groups and nationalities (Friis-Hansen). The *Kitchen Table* series (1990) incorporates a number of issues – gender, desire and power (Figure 23).[10] It presents a series of tableaux relating a range of experiences of one woman (played by Weems). In some she is alone, in others she appears with a child, or with other women or with a man. The black and white format is always the same, with a single hanging lightbulb illuminating the scene, with the man or woman sat at the opposite end of the table to the viewer, as if on a stage. For example, *Mother and Daughter Putting on Make-up* depicts a child imitating her mother who is applying lipstick and looking with concentration at herself in the mirror.

The image Man Reading Newspaper *(Figure 23.2) presents a man sitting confidently and quietly with his arms resting between the table and his chest, chin resting on his left fist. He is reading a newspaper with concentration. There are two glasses of water, a packet of cigarettes*

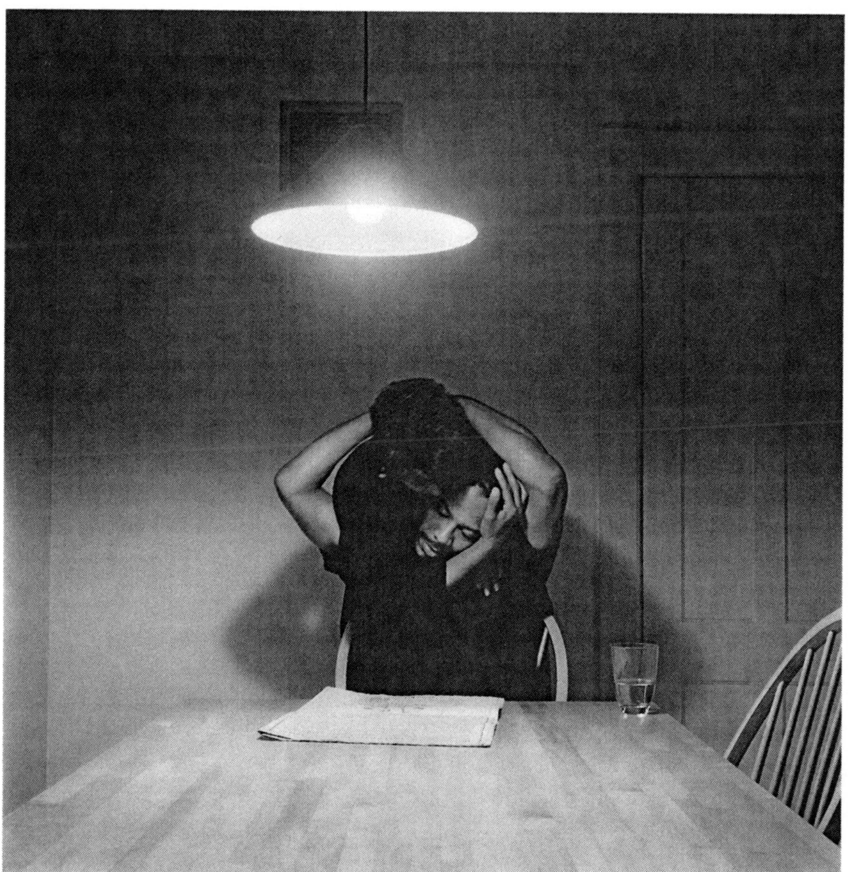

Figure 23.3 Carrie Mae Weems, *Untitled (Man Reading Newspaper)*, from *Kitchen Table* series, 1990.

and an ashtray on the table in front of him. Behind him, standing against the wall in the shadow is the woman; her face is in darkness. Her hands are loosely clasped in front of her. The scene is pregnant with anticipation: watching, waiting, and deciding. What has happened? What will happen next?

Weems describes the difficulty of stepping outside cultural prejudice to address issues that affect us all. She asks: How are black women historically positioned and developed as archetypes? How can that be challenged? And further to this is it possible to see past 'blackness' to discuss more universal concerns? (Weems 2007). As with Simpson, she makes the point that black people are not restricted to concerning themselves with racial issues, just as issues of race are not the sole province of black people. The difficulty in avoiding stereotypical roles identifies a key issue for a visual practice that aspires to argue or point out habitual behaviours and injustice that exist in our culture: a written text can catalogue and establish priority arguments, whilst a visual discourse must present the complexity of assumptions and prejudice simultaneously – rhetorically. In consequence, the viewer has to work that much harder to unravel the many threads of the argument.

The politics of representation: performance

The *Kitchen Table* series demonstrates a number of the features discussed here: rhetorical display, political awareness and fictional construction. Acknowledging her break with the notion of 'capturing' an experience in the tradition of Cartier-Bresson or Eugene Smith, Weems identifies the tension that always exists in photographic realism, between document and fabrication: 'there was something different [from straight documentary] I wanted to explore, work that had the appearance of documentary but was not at all documentary. It was highly fabricated work' (hooks 1995: 81). Strategically, her methods inherit the tradition of narrative construction using 'documentary' as a tool, with the addition of staged fiction, and using humour and irony to force a different perspective. Her methods reflect her desire to understand the significance of cultural difference in relation to her own family, and by extension to the experience of black families in America. She directs a visual narrative loaded with cultural clues, some of which subtly suggest familiar media scenes on screen and television. She assumes a psychoanalytical method of enactment, by putting herself in the position of being looked at, or of victimisation, and simulating the appearance of experience. She thereby gains a degree of personal understanding of the way subjectivity is constructed. She describes the use of her body as a 'social barometer for understanding the way in which women are understood culturally and socially' in order to look at the black body much more critically and to bring it forward from the background to the foreground. With regard to this, she draws a visual analogy with the physical location of the black servant in Édouard Manet's *Olympia* (1863), whose individuality disappears into the dark background, whilst in contrast the illuminated white figure confronts us with a direct gaze. In addition, Weems is interested in the interaction between viewer and image, viewer and text, and the self-awareness that occurs in that looking, which will always be pushed and pulled in relation to the image and text. Using a performative exchange, she engages the viewer in an examination of the relationships between women and women, women and children, women and men, white women and black women, and the question of how subjectivity specifically, and representation more generally, is constructed.

Deacon's use of objects, Simpson's analysis of presentation, Lockhart's democratic portrayal and Weems's psychoanalytical simulation each extend the acknowledgement of 'difference' to an active demonstration, and the mask of presentation to an orchestrated 'performance'. Judith Butler's expansion of the 'performative' subject [1988] has made a significant contribution to feminism's reconsideration of the material body and the construction of identity, by extending the debate concerning looking and being looked at. Her discussion of the fabrication of gender norms uses 'performance' as metaphor for a process whereby we perform as individuals in order to establish ourselves. For example, she describes gender as a 'script' we have learnt to perform. At the same time response from others validates our behaviour and our behaviour reinforces the norm, so that gender is a kind of enacted fiction. Butler argues that the process of sexuality, gender and desire should not be seen as a natural, nor as a consistent, process caused by stable factors. Her premise is that subjectivity is culturally constructed, rather than being grounded in any essential attributes or 'natural' principles. Butler goes further than sociological thought, which describes us assuming different roles, and asserts that the self is not 'outside' but is interiorised, and that gender is as much a concept as it is corporeal (Butler 1993: 32).

Tracey Moffatt's work visually asserts the construction of subjectivity, echoing both Kristeva's 'subject in process' and Butler's expansion of the 'performative' subject. Moffatt develops these concepts through self-consciously fabricated series concerned with race, gender and violence. Composed of various elements that make reference to specific domestic settings, 'performance' and the act of looking in her work operates in two ways – in the construction of enacted 'scenes' and in provoking the viewer to develop narratives from those scenes that only suggest possible cause and effect. The *Scarred for Life* series (1994) addresses power relations in the family (Figure 24). In a series of fabricated cameos, each accompanied by a caption, it visualises the process in psychoanalysis referred to as 'injunction' whereby as children we are constantly taught how to behave in response to other's behaviour – usually implicitly rather than directly. We learn to perform in certain ways because of the rewards that we may receive, whether they be physical attention or material gratification. Like the construction of gender, it is a cyclical process that requires re-enactment and repetition. *Useless 1974* appears with the caption 'Her father's nickname for her was "useless" and shows a young adolescent girl looking at the camera, slyly, cautiously, suspiciously, as if waiting for comment or demonstrating defiance, and determined to impress the viewer with her composure, her self-assuredness, her capability, her usefulness. The presentation of her look directed at the viewer is central to the image:

I am washing the car, but this is not what is important. What is important is my relationship to you, who are looking at me. I really don't care about the car. What I care about is what you think of me.

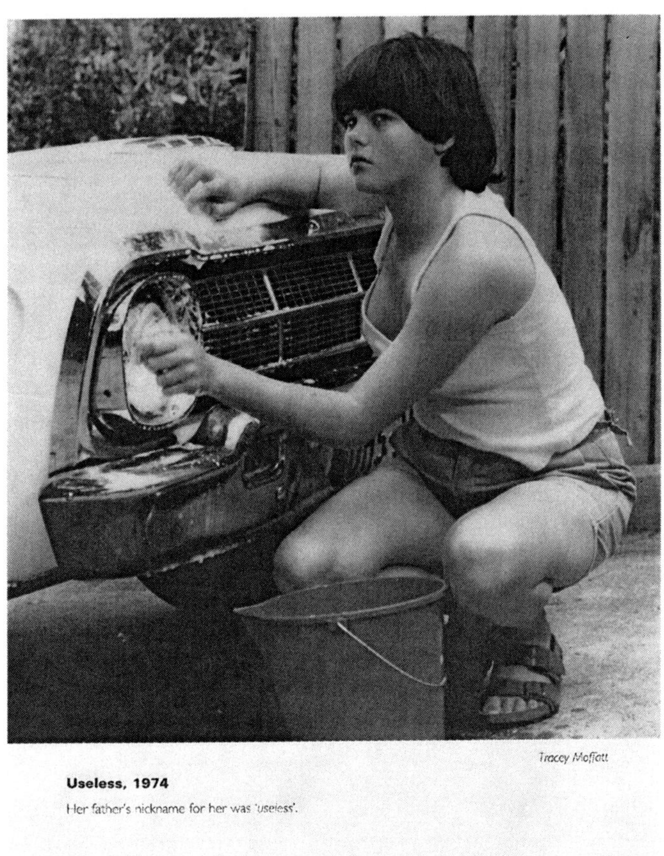

Figure 24 Tracey Moffatt, *Useless, 1974*, from the series *Scarred for Life*, 1994.

The nine images of *Something More* (1989) are placed in a square grid, so that we are able to roam between them – across, up, down – building a number of narratives. This familiar cinematic formula is accentuated by the painted scenic background, which labels them as 'make believe' – another form of performance. The series contrasts glossy colour with black and white images, aspiration with failure, and composure with violence. The first image (top left) is the most complex:

Everyone watches the central female character, who is dressed in a red cheongsam with black flowers and who dominates the scene in the foreground. She looks upward and beyond to somewhere else out of this picture, and to what I imagine to be her future. The two boys are blurred but seem more rooted in reality than the woman, whose expression is wistful or expectant or dreamy and purposeful in the performance of her stance, which is incongruously graceful. Behind her is a slatternly woman in cream silk slip, rucked up at the hip, cigarette in the corner of her mouth, lolling against the doorway in a careless and provocative manner – is she an alter ego or an apparition? Behind them sits a hulky male figure in black vest behind a desk, looking at them both. The whole scene is heavy with past events and full of possibilities.

A number of themes develop between images. For example, the three images which follow focus on 'touching': *The boy's hand reaches out and touches her dress as if to see if it is real: it is a dare, it is exciting; it is delightful; it is fantasy; a young male rests his head in her lap, his right hand rests on her leg and her left hand pats his head; she holds a brocade dress against her body, feeling the surface of the fabric, stroking it, loving it.* 'Violence' is another which builds to a crescendo, ending with her sprawled across the road to Brisbane (bottom right).

Concerned with creating 'reality', rather than 'capturing' it, Moffatt takes a similar stance to Wall's by constructing photographs in response to her own experience. Moffatt's biography lends an undercurrent of cultural displacement and uncertainty to her work, which is full of metaphor that speaks of Australian history, Aboriginal experience, the seizure of land, forced adoptions, colonial repression: 'the images come from inside, from the things I'm familiar with. Things I've seen or experienced. Perhaps it's also an exaggerated version of my own reality' (1999: 20).[11] All her work demonstrates ambivalence – the uncertainty or the possibility of meaning. Each image is rich in dramatic effect, with pregnant pause and potent possibility, which provokes us to guess at what came before, and to anticipate what will follow. Accepting the premise of artifice, her work brings together a number of characteristics typical of this era – uncertainty, implicit critique, memory, and a pluralistic referencing to literature, film, and popular culture past and present.

This chapter has discussed practices that address the political implications of representation, which range from the subversion of appearance (Fani-Kayode) to more provocative demonstration (Deacon). Practices articulate a stage of critique that is self-reflexive in its awareness following the influence of feminist and post-colonial writings. Further than this, they demonstrate a stance that strives to progress understanding of subjectivity – through their use of photography. Nikki S. Lee's work is typical of practice in the last decade of the twentieth century that challenges fixed identity and exposes the fact, as Kruger does, that we constitute ourselves as subjects through other's representations. Lee's work is indicative of an elaborate and conceptually conceived strategy to confront the construction of subjectivity. It can be read from two political perspectives – feminism and post-colonial discourse; in performing a series of woman-as-hispanic or woman-as-yuppie, she subverts the issues of stereotypical female identity and racial difference. The chapter has pointed to the ongoing debate concerning the photograph's exploitation for political comment or expressive use, and whether these have to be alternatives. Weems's work serves here as example of an implicitly political use of photography. As with Jaar's practice, its elegance and composure challenge Sekula's concern about the art-photograph's ability to address a political condition. Most significantly for discussion in the next chapter, these examples of realism assert politics as being an integral component of their aesthetic, and demonstrate the photograph's potential to incorporate a profound critique of representation and to participate in its discourse.

Suggested further reading

Bhabha, H. K. (1994) 'Introduction: Locations of Culture', in *The Location of Culture*, Routledge, London; New York, 1–18

Hall, S. and M. Sealy (2001) *Different: A Historical Context: Contemporary Photographers and Black Identity*, Phaidon, London

hooks, bel (1995) 'Diasporic Landscapes of Longing', in *Art on My Mind: Visual Politics*. The New Press, New York

Levi Strauss, D. (2003) *Between the Eyes: Essays on Photography and Politics*, Aperture, New York

Mulvey, L. (1989) 'Visual Pleasure and Narrative Cinema' [1975], in *Visual and Other Pleasures*, Macmillan, Basingstoke

Rosler, M. (2004) *Decoys and Disruptions*, The MIT Press, Cambridge, MA; London

Sekula, A. (1982) 'On the Invention of Photographic Meaning' [1975], in V. Burgin (ed.), *Thinking Photography*, Macmillan, London, 84–109

Sontag, Susan (2003) *Regarding the Pain of Others*, Hamish Hamilton, London

Tagg, John (1992) *Grounds of Dispute: Art History, Cultural Politics and the Discursive Field*, University of Minnesota Press, Minneapolis

Notes

1 Search Diane Arbus online at Masters of Photography: www.masters-of-photography.com/A/arbus/arbus2.html, accessed 6 September 2012.

2 See Martin Parr's website at www.martinparr.com/index1.html, accessed 6 September 2012.

3 The image *Women of Madagascar* can be seen in the collection at the J. Paul Getty Museum at www.getty.edu/art/gettyguide/artObjectDetails?artobj=50368, accessed 6 September 2012.

4 See Simon Norfolk's website at www.simonnorfolk.com, accessed 6 September 2012.

5 See Meiselas 1997, and akaKURDISTAN, a place for memory and cultural exchange (www.akakurdistan.com, accessed 15 September 2010).

6 See Rotimi Fani-Kayode's work at Happening Africa (www.happeningafrica.com), Autograph-ABP (www.autograph-abp.co.uk) and Victoria & Albert Museum collection (www.vam.ac.uk/users/node/6448), accessed 13 September 2012.

7 See Iké Udé's website at www.ikeude.com, accessed 10 August 2010.

8 Destiny Deacon can be seen discussing her work *Half Light: Portraits from Black Australia* at www.youtube.com/watch?v=UEMPqoORMNE, accessed 10 August 2010. See also images at the Roslyn Oxley9 Gallery website (www.roslynoxley9.com.au/artists/2/Destiny_Deacon/200/33809), accessed 4 September 2012.

9 See Barbara Kruger's work online at the New York University website (www.nyu.edu/library/bobst/research/fales/exhibits/downtown/soho/sohoart/documents/kruger.html) and her own website (www.barbarakruger.com), accessed 4 September 2012.

10 See Carrie Mae Weem's work on her webite at http://carriemaeweems.net/work.html, accessed 15 September 2010. Also, see her discussing her work on YouTube, at an event that took place in the Forum of the Elizabeth A. Sackler Center for Feminist Art at the Brooklyn Museum on 24 January 2009: www.youtube.com/watch?v=WabrgaaRTj8, accessed 15 September 2010.

11 Tracey Moffatt's work can be seen online at the Roslyn Oxley9 Gallery website: www.roslynoxley9.com.au/artists/26/Tracey_Moffatt/profile, accessed 4 September 2012.

8

Discursive realism

Whilst I have used the terms 'discursive' and 'rhetorical' to describe photographic projects that present visual discussion, neither term wholly suffices to describe the sort of practice that can be both ideological and visually compelling. I have described photography that uses its visuality to argue, critique and propose ideas or to force a response as 'rhetorical' – for example, Jaar's 'Rwanda' project or Savadov's tableaux. The Greek origin of 'rhetoric' indicates the skill of persuasion by spoken argument, so its use asserts the photograph's capacity to argue; the term 'rhetorical' is associated with stylistic devices that amplify meaning, which include metonymy and metaphor, personification, the use of irony, repetition, symbol, motif, all of which the photograph utilises; 'rhetorical' describes the photograph's meaning as being dependent on many elements besides the referent, those that cannot be located and which rely on visual impact or association, so that their complex construction resists absolute analysis. The disadvantage in using this term lies with its association with falsity and *empty* rhetorical style, which is seen as distorting the literal and factual. However, several arguments have adjusted our conception of truth and the relationship between the literal and figurative: Lakoff's argument that describes metaphor as deeply embedded in our understanding; Derrida's rhetorical approach (such as *perquisition*) that explores multiple interpretations; Foucault's consideration of discourse that recognises knowledge as being constantly in process. Rhetorical forms refer to the manner in which documents are used and constructed. As figurative documents, photographs can be 'straight' or they can be mannered and fictional – both uses enable them to be critical or persuasive – rhetorically. The term 'discursive' has two almost contradictory connotations: in a philosophical context, 'discursive' relates to knowledge obtained by reason and argument rather than intuition; and in common usage, it implies passing from one topic to another in an unmethodical or digressive way – deriving from the Latin *discursus* – running about. In this sense it suitably describes photography's capacity to refer to a number of ideas simultaneously. In discussing the construction of narrative, Barthes refers to a 'discursive function' that has a circulatory nature, and which 'accelerates, delays, gives fresh impetus to the discourse, ... summarizes, anticipates and sometimes even lead astray' (1977: 95). His discussion of 'texts' and intertextuality describes any 'work' (writing, photograph, film) that generates meaning as initiating a 'field', in which texts are 'dilatory' – deferring decision (1977: 157). This suggests a kind of discursive space, in which ideas and references are exchanged and can be explored (1977: 146). I use 'discursive' therefore to indicate photographic practices that discuss ideas and conditions, which range across disciplines, and which exploit visuality to address complex situations.

This final chapter considers photographic practices that provoke cultural debate, with reference to conceptual and interdisciplinary projects that address geo-political or psychological issues. It outlines the critical realism asserted by Allan Sekula's photographic works, and the impact of Jeff Wall's photo-pictorialism. It discusses the implications of Gilles Deleuze and Félix Guattari's conception of *event* and *sensation* and the consequences for a response to photographs that encompass the cognitive, the virtual and the material. The chapter has two distinct sections: the first establishes the conceptual inheritance of photographic practice, and the second an eventful resonance; both of which contribute to the development of a discursive aesthetic.

Critical realism

Sekula's body of work since the early 1970s has raised a number of issues that question the mythologies of photography: first, the author being objective or disinterested; second, that the photograph represents a kind of truth; third, and above all, that the photograph is a-historical and not context dependent. He sees photography as discourse, as a space of 'information exchange', which has neither universal nor intrinsic meaning residing wholly within the image. Rather it embodies a point of view, not only in its making but also in the context in which it is seen or read. He extends Walter Benjamin's discussion that, as a form of reproduction, photography enables wider access to information and culture and, as a vehicle for argument, can be a powerful political tool. However, because art-photography is perceived as privileged, being framed as 'art' in a gallery setting can obscure its original context and thereby its ideological agenda. Sekula has attempted to understand what he calls the *traffic* of photography that involves social production, circulation and reception, and the way that the discourse of photography is characterised by an oscillation between objectivity and subjectivity (Sekula 1999: 155).

Projects such as Sekula's *Fish Story* (1990–93) and *TITANIC's Wake* (2000) form part of an ongoing cycle of works that weave a network of tangential facts, events and coincidence, which are cross-disciplinary and trans-historical (Figures 25, 26). They exemplify Sekula's thinking concerning expression and the role of context in an alternative practice to that of the 'self-sufficient image'. They constitute an extended documentary that exposes the myth that any one image can reveal essential truth. Referred to as 'critical realism', this photography has contributed to the disassembly of traditional photographic structures and to the evolution of its conceptual use.[1] Sekula's form is a discursive, and implicitly critical, reflection of the conditions under scrutiny. In its interdisciplinary address to a range of concerns it is both photography as art *and* as philosophy, *and* geography, *and* sociology. All importantly, it demonstrates the potential of the photograph to make use of its necessary reference to objects *in* reality at the same time as provoking thought. The pictorial possibilities of critical realism can demonstrate specific and local elements whilst encompassing different conceptual domains, such as political commentary and social anthropology. Critical realism stretches the limits of simple photographic reference because it includes an extensive and horizontal range of content that refers us to implications far beyond any one image.

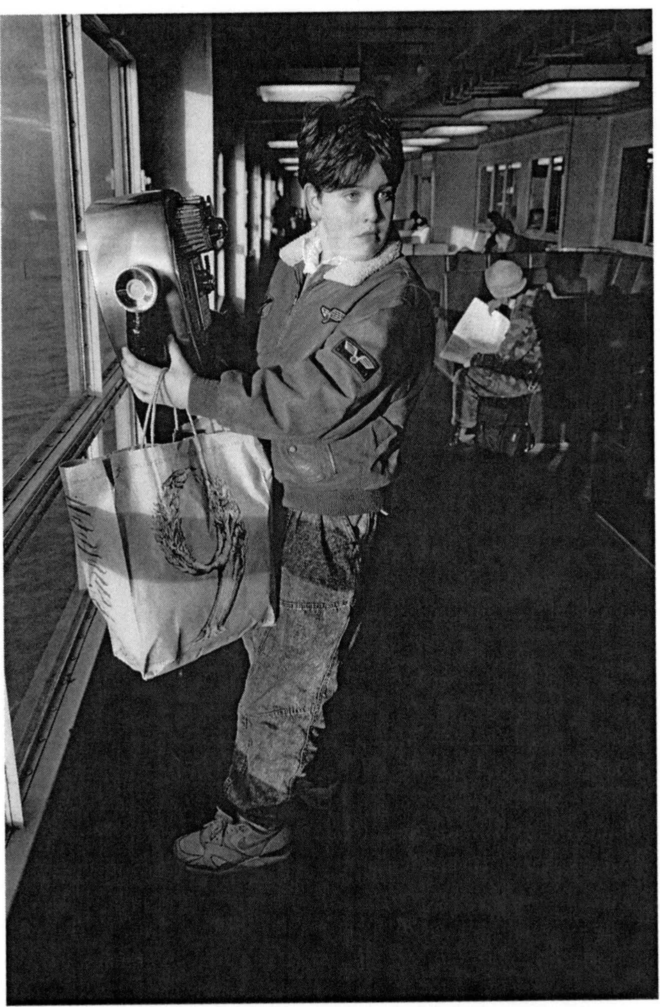

Figure 25 Allan Sekula, *Boy Looking at his Mother, Staten Island Ferry, New York Harbour, February, 1990,* from *Fish Story*, 1990–93.

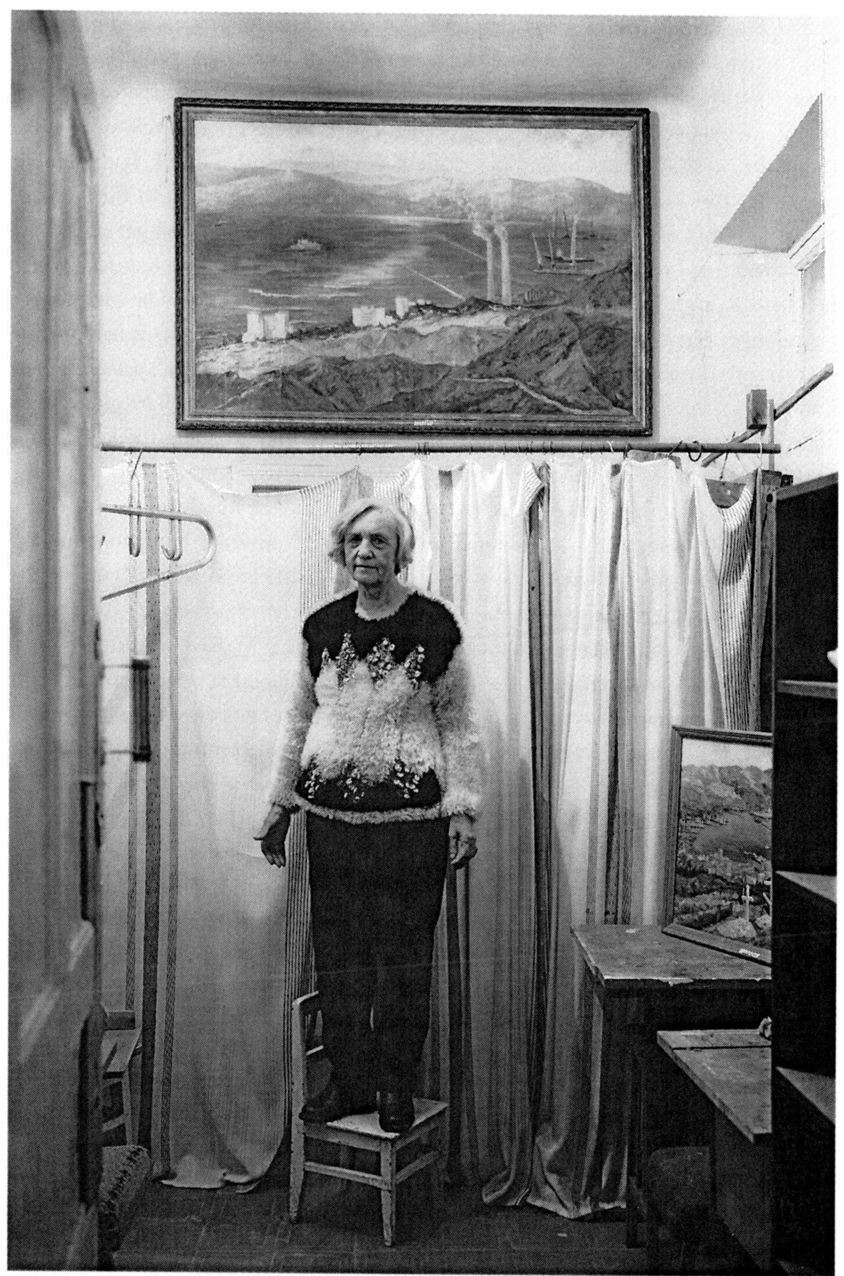

Figure 26 Allan Sekula, *Portrait of the Painter Lioubov Khoudyakova in her Studio, Novorossiysk*, from *TITANIC's Wake*, 1998/2000.

Fish Story is 'a work in seven chapters' that examines the processes of globalisation, which have come to represent the features of late capitalism. Globalisation and mass communication have the effect of compressing the global processes of industry, labour and economy, and extending social, cultural and economic relations across the globe, so that events in one place affect events in another place. For example, migrants have increasingly gravitated to the peripheries of cities in the hope of accessing some of the wealth they witness on global communication networks. *Fish Story* gives focus to the impact of global capitalism on the maritime industry, which he likens to a 'global factory'. It considers the effects of an economy in which there is no longer one city that is central to the world capitalist system, as it has become increasingly dispersed, along with the world's labour force. His essays 'Dismal Science I and II' (in Sekula 1995) track a vertical and a horizontal tale of maritime history and the many contingent operations that it supports, and attribute the key change to the industry as being the containerisation of cargo-movement, which 'reverses the "classical" relationship between the fixity of the land and the fluidity of the sea' (1995: 49). This new fluidity of transnational production and power extends its exploitation across the globe, 'drawing ravenously on the rock-bottom labour costs' of the factories in southern China (48–9).

Sekula's photographic works (since *Aerospace Folktales*, 1973) have consistently been concerned with industries and the people whose livelihood is dependent on their processes. They examine conflicts between the demands of global economic markets, managed by e-communication, and the demands of local communities, which are neglected in pursuit of the former. For example, to enable this 'fluid' market to flourish, dockside labour has been 'tamed', international markets have been deregulated, and crews, predominantly from Asia, have been subjugated to poor working conditions. The photographs focus our attention on what is happening specifically in different locales, by pointing to contrasts and ironies, such as the Chinese Ocean Shipping containers that pour out from Los Angeles seaport (twenty miles south of Downtown) carrying the manufactured goods made in low-wage factories in China, which are drawn by tractors driven by immigrant workers from Mexico and El Salvador, similarly low waged. *Fish Story* gives testament to the detailed circumstances of individual lives:

> David Brown works twelve hours a day for a month at a time, putting in an extra watch at the wheel from noon to 1600, then back at the wheel from midnight to 0400. The extra watch at overtime pay allows him to earn 'just enough to make the trip worthwhile,' considering his family on Jacksonville and the fact that despite his years as a merchant sailor, the scarcity of America-flag ships means that he usually works for only six to nine months out of twelve. (1995: 77)

Rather than elevating the specialness of any one object or moment, Sekula's projects display the many incongruities within one context, such as the magnificence of the *Museo Guggenheim* in Bilbao alongside the demise of that city's maritime industry, or the ironies of Twentieth Century Fox's film set for *Titanic* situated beside the poor fishing village of Popotla and the realities of its mussel-gathering livelihood.

> *Titanic's wake* demonstrates that a simple visual diary of the last two years of the C20 can suggest an epic sweep and resonance of a historical novel, without in any way trying to be a historical novel, and without departing from the pictorial possibilities of careful documentary photography. (Sekula 2003b: 107)

Sekula's analogy with a historical novel adds the significant dimension of fiction to the photograph's capacity to discuss ideas. Sekula's projects incorporate a number of character studies: characters who have no knowledge of each other and yet whose lives and concerns contribute to a bigger story. Referring to the way that so many different people with such varied experience inhabit a shared existential domain, Sekula documents them in action: David Brown telephoning his wife in Jacksonville from a telephone box in the Port of Rotterdam (Sekula 1995: 73); the political activist Kaela Economou who, provoked by a meeting of the World Trade Organisation, protests and is physically beaten by the Seattle police; the Russian painter Lubov Khouyakova, posing in a cramped studio amidst her paintings depicting the industrial landscape and war-time graves of a Black Sea port, Novorossiysk (Sekula 2003b: 107–8). As with the articulation of characters in a novel, the effect of realism is constructed from inconsequential (*integrational*) references, such as the particular chair that Khouyakova is standing on, or the Top Gun jacket worn by the boy on the Staten Island Ferry (Sekula 1995: 11). And as with an epic novel, a number of such interrelated details amount to the visual equivalent of parallel narrative threads. These threads of content work across a number of evolving 'chapters' and 'plots' – for example, one on cargo and industrial capital, another on pollution. They interweave references to Friedrich Engels and economy, the history of Dutch seascape paintings, capitalism and free trade, cartography, the environmental impact of industry, railroad and steam travel, land, sea and weather (Sekula 1995: 41–54).

Sekula's projects highlight the singular differences inherent in very particular concerns so that, in combination, they operate as an elaborate metaphor for human and political processes. *TITANIC's Wake* depicts a range of locations and details across the world, some central and some whimsical, all encompassed by the metaphor 'wake' and its reverberations with the sea, with ships, and with aftermath and death. The principle of generic schema (Lakoff 1993) is demonstrated in an *ensemble* of tableaux, which indicate a diversity of references from the *Titanic* to *Moby Dick*. The global schema of maritime power maps against the specific instance of the image; one physical force – the sea – equates with a political or economic force – capitalism. Both forces assimilate the sea's qualities of magnitude and savagery – 'the liquid womb of the insurance industry' (Sekula 2003b: 116). This project is a complex 'conceptual system' of implications and relationships (Lakoff 1993: 203) that works below the level of consciousness and language, incorporating psychological and cultural associations, which operate non-verbally and interminably. In this process, the sea becomes a mechanism for understanding the far-reaching impact of the general in terms of the very specific – in sub-plots that identify local incidents. The portrait of Lubov Khoudyahova functions as if she were a character in a novel; she is both herself and her *role* in *TITANIC's Wake*, along with the characters of Frank Ghery, who is represented by his architecture, or Bill Gates or Wilmslow Homer, who are present by association but not shown visually. Each character is presented in their locale or by implication and as part of a global network of economies and cultural references. The potential of parallel discourse facilitates a democratic presentation of simultaneous stories, in the sense that they feed off each other, but no one photograph is privileged. Sekula's novelistic method translates reality both literally and conceptually, and accepts the photographic condition of fiction in a way that pushes the cinematic possibilities of the still photograph to its limits. This is a self-conscious, politically aware practice with emphasis on the *ensemble*. Sekula talks of bringing together the 'critic' and the 'visual artist' in a social practice that deliberately invites political dialogue (Sekula 1999: 150). This mode of realism proceeds from the veracity of documentary, but is no longer concerned with individual photographic style or with the success of any one decisive photograph to transcend its content. It situates event beside event and one kind of knowledge beside another kind of knowledge, and challenges a number of the recurring themes of photographic representation: the relationship between documentary and expression; the photographer's responsibility for the inclusion or exclusion of context; the relationship between ideas, sensation and the materiality of the photograph. In particular, Sekula demonstrates two important features: the use of visual pictures as allegory for the extensive *discussion* of geo-politics, and the use of pictures in parallel that, because they lack the formalism of individual photographs, avoid any one direction; they are discursive. Both features engage our cognitive involvement as well as a visceral response to its visual impact.

Allegorical reading

Fish Story and *TITANIC's Wake* are allegories in which one text (set of ideas) is read through another (series of photographs); their focus on the sea, which illustrates complex processes of exchange, provides an allegory for any kind of economic transaction. In 1980, Craig Owens's discussion of postmodernism and allegory asserted the figural aspect that operates within all artworks. His version of postmodern art was one in which practice disassembles modernist forms and redefines its methods. His essay indicates that the 'allegorical impulse' is to be found in strategies of impermanence, accumulation, hybridisation and discursivity (Owens 1980 I: 75). These are more fundamental features than the stylistic effects usually associated with postmodern art, such as pastiche or appropriation, and different from notions of allegory as necessarily being romantic, mythical or fantastical. His recovery of allegory from these historical associations asserts it as a conceptual force that works against the

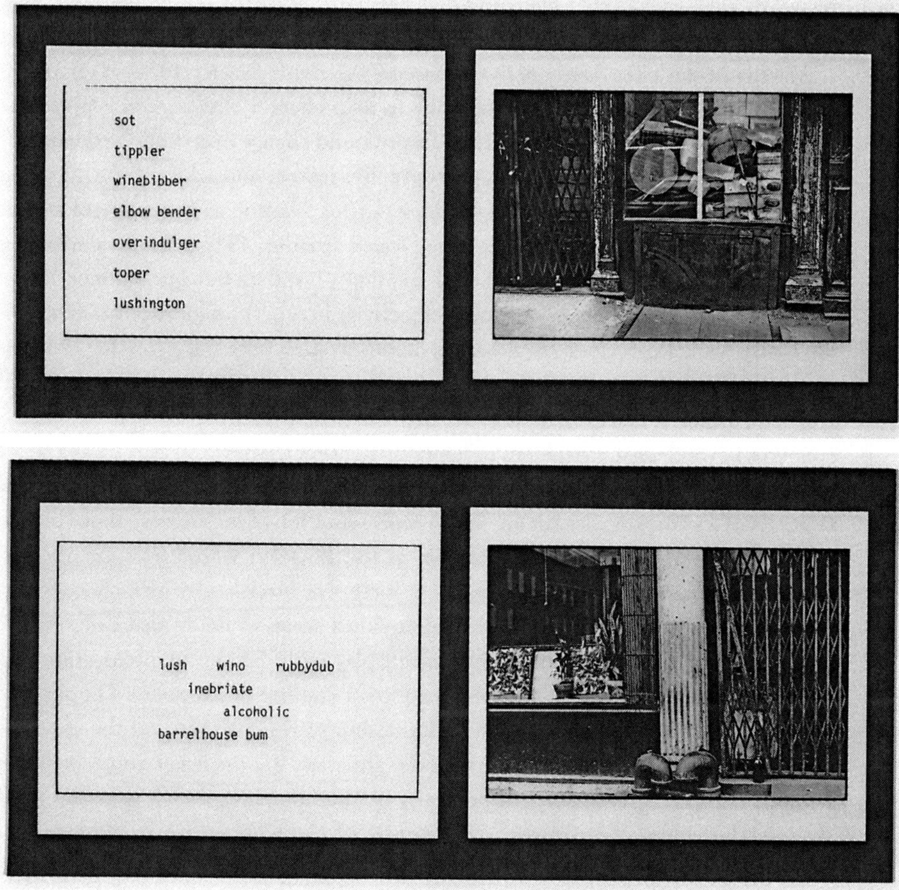

Figure 27 Martha Rosler, details from *The Bowery in Two Inadequate Descriptive Systems*, 1974–75.

'symbolic totalising impulse' that strives to achieve a unity of form with meaning (Owens 1980 II: 80). Owens aligns allegory with Derrida's examination of addition and supplement, and the 'deconstructive impulse' that emphasises a digressive procedure of thought and a *process* of meaning (II: 79). The 'deconstructive impulse' promotes the photograph's potential to extend its relationship with the object depicted, and to exploit and problematise the distinction between the photograph and the referent. What is important in Owens's text for an understanding of critical practice is the acknowledgement of figural reading, which accesses ideology via photographic images. As we have seen, the dynamics of deconstruction (e.g. *parergon*) are largely concerned with the contradictions that accompany absence and supplementation, which we understand as necessary in verbal texts but struggle with in relation to visual texts that keep referring us back to objects in the real world. The revival of allegory asserted ideas and concepts, and liberated the photograph from its reliance on resemblance for its meaning.

Martha Rosler's *The Bowery in Two Inadequate Descriptive Systems* (1974–75) is a form of allegory that appropriates photography to help effect a challenge to representational traditions (Figure 27). Indicative of a profound change of attitude to documentary, it marked a significant point in photography's history and acknowledged a series of historic influences: Evans's straight depiction of location as indicative of condition (*Let Us Now Praise Famous Men: Three Tenant Families*, 1939); Ruscha's arbitrary display avoiding the aesthetics of artful framing (*Twentysix Gasoline Stations*, 1963), and Berndt and Hilda Becher's seeming objectivity in repetitive location (*Watertowers*, 1967–80). Sekula describes *The Bowery* as demonstrating both the signifying richness of metaphor as well as the photograph's failure to adequately describe the material reality to which it refers (Sekula 1984: 62). *The Bowery* uses photographs to discuss concerns beyond what is depicted in referring to homelessness and the city as a set of relationships – 'a geopolitical system' (Rosler 1991: 15). It refers to the structures and relations of a situation without any visual representation of its 'subject' (those people inhabiting the area of Manhattan known as the Bowery) whose lives are affected by such structures. The series comprises forty-five black and white photographs representing a walk down the Bowery, alongside a series of nouns that describe life in the area and adjectives that metaphorically play with the idea of intoxication (e.g. plastered, stuccoed, rosined…). It demonstrates a number of key points: The absence of subject displaces the photograph's relationship to resemblance and the expectations of objective account. It describes the situation in which her subjects reside without composing stereotypical portraits of 'the homeless', which generate what she calls the 'victim photography' symptomatic of much documentary photography. It illustrates that homeless*ness*, much more than a representation of homeless people, is a complexity involving governmental institutions, prejudicial attitudes and the specifics of location. It demonstrates the importance of context and the power of words to influence how one reads an image. It parallels poetic association with that of a 'radical metonymy' (Rosler 2004: 195). It displays the gap between description and what we consider to be the certainty of visual perception. Like Sekula, Rosler is concerned not to allow the aesthetic to distance the image from the reality of human life and to avoid the imposition of expressive authorship (Rosler 1982: 171). She observes that 'the art world embrace of photography can squeeze documentary to death', particularly if it is reduced to a device (Rosler 2004: 240). She suggests that naturalistic realism can lock narrative into a particularly uncritical mode of relating to culture, and that one way to avoid this is to incorporate contradictory representations (Rosler 2004: 7). *The Bowery* aims to avoid the universalism that is characteristic of street photography and which seduces us into believing that we have a shared humanity with those who are photographed, whatever their differences in experience. Instead, Rosler points to the bigger picture and shifts the focus away from the art-object (the photograph) 'to the context, to the process of signification, and to the social process' and asks: 'how can one represent a city's "buried" life, the lives in fact of most city residents? How can one show the conditions of tenants' struggle, homelessness?' (Rosler 1991: 31–3) Rosler avoids stereotypical depiction and focuses instead on her theme, which criticises social conditions. She aims to move away from representations that attempt to be distantly objective and that sanitise the subject (as Sontag suggests). Instead, Rosler is concerned to produce a social document as a form of political activism.

In a later context, Wall explains the separation of the photograph from resemblance to the referent in a discussion of his photograph entitled *Adrian Walker, Artist Drawing from a Specimen in a Laboratory in the Department of Anatomy at the University of British Columbia* (1992). His description, of what appears to be a straightforward and conventional portrayal of someone at his work, correlates the acceptance of fiction with the revival of allegory:[2]

> The fact of it being or not being a 'portrait' of a specific real person, may be secondary in the structure. The title, because it names him, makes it appear that he is such a specific, real person. But it's easily possible that Adrian Walker is simply a fictional name that I decided to make up to create a certain illusion, like 'Emma Bovary'. Even though that's not true and there is such a person, and that is him, I don't think there is necessarily any resonance of that in the structure of the work, generically speaking. The nature of the picture gives no guarantee that that identification matters at all. So, like a lot of pictures, it is a bit of a hybrid. (Wall 1998: 127–8)

Wall's constructions are conceptions rather than portrayals. Because staged photography is both real in its reference and artificial in its construction, it incorporates the photographer's subjectivity, resulting in a hybrid form of fictional realism. Wall's reference to Flaubert's novel *Emma Bovary* suggests a conception of portrayal that incorporates different vistas, different self-contained chapters, which can be read independently and a-chronologically and not only as a narration of facts. Wall's photograph *Adrian Walker* is a chapter in the fiction that is the reality of Adrian Walker. In effect, unless the person is known to us personally, whether it is fact or fiction is only relevant to its resonance if one believes in the existence of essential character or the possibility of truth to reality in 'straight' depiction: 'the fact that someone really is what they appear to be in a picture is not a picture matter' (Wall 1998: 128). Once someone is represented-as-portrait, they are in a picture and *performative*, performing either someone else or a version of themselves. And as we have seen with the dialogical matrix, the photographic-subject assumes a number of roles. As Berger points out (1982: 97), photographs access a different order of truth from that of verification. Wall goes further: pictures (photographs) need not be considered as truth. He questions the assumed goal of truth as being necessary and suggests that fiction may be just as important. His 'portrait' of Adrian Walker is one such example, which demonstrates an indifference to the veracity of subjects. A picture of someone absorbed in an activity is identified less by their personal, empirical, social identity and 'more by their generic identity controlled by the type of picture they're in' (Wall 1998: 128). In this instance, the 'naming' of subject is defined by the title that states Adrian Walker's occupation as 'artist', and 'drawing from a specimen' identifies the conceptual domain of activity in which he participates. The moment of the photograph is extended to an *eventful* and fictional space that assumes the necessary subjective involvement of the viewer in constructing the photographic-subject. The important point here is that the very realistic photograph is, in simple terms, a conceptual operation.

Conceptual realism

In his essay 'Marks of Indifference' [1995], Wall describes the uses of photography by conceptual art as having 'revolutionalised our concept of the picture' (Wall 2003: 44) and 'photoconceptualism's quintessential "anti-object" as being responsible for breaking 'the spell of modernist photography's bid for transcendence' (32–5). Because photography had been bracketed off from the evolution of aesthetics in general art history – at least until the 1960s – it was able to develop, within conceptual art, the procedure of document*ation* alongside its more traditional role of document*ary*. Photography has inherited that experimentation with the anti-aesthetic and reductive amateurism validated by Warhol and Ruscha. The common practice of using photographs to discuss concerns in a cognitive and factual way can be traced back to Ruscha's *Gasoline Stations*, which describes an economic system that is represented by the appearance of its physical structures (Wall 2003: 43). The role of both performance and document-as-parody in late twentieth-century works owes a debt to Bruce Nauman's self-conscious acting out (*Self Portrait as Fountain*, 1966–67),[3] an example that legitimates photographic processes to construct an idea. Photography can simulate reportage without the need for an actual event, narrative or commentary. In photographing ideas, where resemblance is not what is important, Douglas Huebler's *Variable Piece #34* (1970) and *Variable Piece 1A (The Netherlands, United States, Italy, France and Germany)* (1971) reference the world in a way that tests the possibility of removing subject-matter altogether, by centrally positioning the concept instead: the work depicts eight people immediately following their being told: 'you have a beautiful face'. The preconception of the piece determines a reaction in the subjects. Contradicting the modernist premise of 'capturing' reality unawares, photography can assert the project itself (the conceptual idea) as the essential creative element, rather than its visual appearance. Huebler's pieces marked a step away from resemblance and record, and towards a synthetic photographic practice: one which exploits photography's depictive qualities, and *constructs* a situation rather than waiting for one to photograph. In photographing ideas, the photograph becomes a representation of concepts, rather than a representation of absent things.

Conceptual art's use of the photographic reportage of performance and proposition has contributed to the development of those photographic practices that are not dependent on resemblance. In turn, photography has provided the ideal means for changes in art practice more generally: for example, the use of visual intertextual reference and for the critique of representation, both of which can be seen in Rosler's work. *The Bowery* challenges the assumption that photographic representation must depict its subject-matter directly; it parallels the general post-structural critique of essential 'presence', by absenting what is literally central, resulting in a profoundly more figurative use of photography. Later examples by Thomas Ruff effect the same process, but through reference to the subjects themselves. Where Rosler removes the subject and speaks of the subject's circumstances, Ruff, like Huebler, depicts the subject directly whilst addressing something else. Thus the effect of absence is disguised or, in Baudrillard's terms, the absence of reality is masked. Ruff's portraits disguise their detachment from the subject-matter because their apparent 'straightness' collapses the distinctions between the literal and the non-literal. Photography has subsumed the traditional aesthetic and the anti-aesthetic of conceptual art, so that it no longer has to legitimise itself through allegiance to its productive process. Photography can operate in an autonomous way. It can reject its need to emulate painting and at the same time it can present ideas, like painting. Where photographic pictorialism in the nineteenth century is historically allied to idealism and latterly sentimentality, Wall's pictorialism incorporates an implicit conceptualism inherited from conceptual art. The addition of the theatrical uses metaphor, metonym and allegory to construct what John Roberts describes as a 'conceptual realism' (Roberts 1998). Owens's discussion of art and Wall's of the photograph have highlighted the relationship between object and concept, between the photograph naming an object, whilst referring to a concept. Wall's fictional realism plays on this difference; things are named but are principally there to serve a concept. Both Owens and Baudrillard have referred to the easy slippage between the perceptual and conceptual, and Wall's practice proceeds to undermine this relationship entirely, by *inventing* moments of reality. His fictional realism releases photography, hitherto constrained by the ontological relationship between object and representation. *A Ventriloquist* (1990) invites us to explore what else is possible in incongruent or absurdly associated elements that coexist conceptually. Wall's conceptual pictorialism presents photographic literalness *and* conceptual assimilation; it uses themes, ideas *and* the picture. The inheritance of a propositional attitude from conceptual art lends a cognitive element to looking – an emphasis on the viewer being required to participate intellectually as well as passively looking. Modes of photography which depend on thematic conception, or which reference a political concern, become common practice. But it is a premise that is more assumed than acknowledged. Deliberately artificial methods, seen in uses such as Bettina von Zwehl's contrived control or Ulf Lundin's disappearance, demonstrate an implicit assimilation of the principles of conceptual art.

Wall's and Sekula's conceptual realism refuses the characteristics of the modernist aesthetic: the ideal of spontaneity; the poetics of Cartier-Bresson's moment of 'just one thing' (1981 [1952]); the ontology of Bazin's 'real' (1980 [1958]); the instinct of Evans's 'real thing'[4] or Strand's 'unqualified objectivity' (1980 [1917]) or Heidegger's 'thingness of thing' (2000). Wall's practice demonstrates the legacies of pictorialism, realism and conceptualism and reasserts the photograph as not only a sensuous experience dependent on a material object but also an intellectual one. Wall and Sekula, in very different ways, shift the founding premises of the photographic document: Wall by introducing fiction and Sekula by including any number of specific local contexts. Both are forms of allegory that do not aspire to transcendence or visionary insight. And both place poetry and politics on equal terms. Sekula, in particular, is committed to the use of photography to make political comment. Both access meaning rhetorically without resorting to abstraction, visual ambiguity or distortion, so that the photographic space is clearly realistic in its reference and yet clearly figurative in its conception. Sekula and Jaar encourage us to ask questions and direct attention towards the real world rather than towards an escape from it in aesthetic formalism. Both reiterate the post-structural critique of representation and turn situations into studied protests of local concern as focus for extended contemplation. Their complex themes require a more durational viewing than those of the definitive 'moment'. Discourse becomes as important as the sensuous nature of the photograph, but, instead of literally replacing the picture with text, as with *Art & Language*, conceptual discourse offers visual texts that require the kind of considered reading that is associated with verbal text.

Eventful space

This discussion of realism has focused in the main on the nature of content and cognitive response, rather than the materiality determined by the photograph's colour, size or illumination. The significant exploitation of visceral impact in 1980s photography and the post-structural disassembly of mind/body dualism demands consideration of sensation alongside the cognitive. To that end I introduce here some of Gilles Deleuze and Félix Guattari's ideas, which assist consideration of the sensuous nature of photographs.[5] 'Poetic Realism' (Chapter Four) introduced the notion of the photograph as a 'space'. Deleuze suggests a temporal extension to that analogy in his conception of *event* as a space of duration. Passages in *The Logic of Sense* (2003 [1969]) suggest a mobile perspective with which to understand our relationship to visual space. For instance, in its introduction, Deleuze relates Alice's experience (in Lewis Carroll's *Alice Through the Looking Glass*) of becoming smaller and bigger repeatedly, to illustrate the changing condition of becoming this or that and to initiate consideration of a perpetual non-fixed state of *becoming*. And Deleuze's analogy of form, space and event with the physical convolutions of *fold* (1993 [1988]) illustrates a flexible mobility that challenges the Cartesian distinction between mind and body and traditional ways of thinking about subjectivity. *Fold* provides analogies for how we think and for the nature of our response to complex series such as *TITANIC's Wake*, when we might move backwards and forwards between different elements in each *ensemble*. Deleuze's concept of *event* as 'what happens to a thing' is distinctly different from causal event. *Event* encompasses change and the relationships of wholes to parts, or the history of its getting there. Any one *event* includes the sequence of events that leads up to it and the consequences that proceed from it. Deleuze's re-examination of Gottfried Leibnitz's philosophy includes description of a dog being beaten whilst it eats, which serves to illustrate what he means by *event* that incorporates series, consequence and anticipation:

> The movement of the rod does not begin with the blow: carrying his stick, a man has tiptoed up to the dog from behind, then he has raised the instrument in order then to strike it upon the dog's body. Just as this complex movement has an inner unity, so also, in the soul of the dog, the complex change has an active unity: pain has not abruptly followed pleasure, but has been prepared by a thousand minute perceptions – the pitter-patter of feet, the hostile man's odour, the impression of the stick being raised up, in short, an entire, imperceptible 'anxiousness' from which pain will issue. (Deleuze 1993: 56)

Considered as an *eventful space*, the photograph can provoke a similar speculation, which is not necessarily the same as linear narrative because its direction can be digressive and unmethodical. Applying this possibility to Wall's inexplicable photographic *events*, which can be initiated by the slightest gesture or facial expression, I return to *Insomnia* (see Chapter Three, page 73) as an example in which the details of the door being slightly ajar and the artificial light source outside the window suggest psychical possibilities:

My lying on the floor does not begin with my falling from the chair. I have been unable to sleep for weeks. And I find the cool surface of the floor comforting. It started with my anxiety about the night and the fear that my dreams engender. If I sleep I dream horrific tales of claustrophobic proportion in which there is perpetual night, and light is always artificial. I have experienced what lurks in my cellar: have smelt its depths and heard its pounding. I can feel it now behind and beneath me.

This principle of extensive *event* disturbs the habitual mechanisms of logical reasoning. Deleuze argues that reliance on simplistic cause and effect is limited because it does not accommodate the 'infinite difference or variety in the world' (Deleuze 1993: 58). Deleuze's argument with the premise that everything that happens has a reason lies not with the fact that a cause changes the state of things, but with the assumptions that follow – with the rational subject's compulsion to find the cause of things and, logically, *one* cause (1993: 41). Deleuze's *event* requires an a-causal approach to thinking about things. It describes things multi-dimensionally – horizontally, vertically, backwards and forwards. *Event* extends one element to stretch over others that follow, like a vibration. As a process, *event* accommodates a range of particular identities and specific contexts at any one time. The *event* unfolds: it doesn't begin with a cause and finish with a resolution; it endures and includes the time taken to encounter or understand something. The *event* resembles an enclosure that enfolds its capacities within it. For example, 'containment' is the *event* that can happen to a simple drinking glass (*Sonja with Glass*), so that the *possibility* of the glass containing water forms part of the concept of that glass. All that can be assigned to a glass contributes to its qualification, and is part of it (41). Thereby, any attempt to describe a 'glass' can only be a proposition because it is in a constant state of latent possibility. Conceptions of it will be various, simultaneous and subject to individual experience. They encompass its physical qualities – its hard, impervious surface, previous experiences of drinking glasses of water, references to its various uses in art as subject-matter – from Jean-Baptiste-Siméon Chardin's *Glass of Water and Coffee Pot* (1760) to Michael Craig Martin's *An Oak Tree* (1973),[6] to Strba's *Sonja with Glass* – so that the 'glass' is a range of possibilities. In this way of thinking, proposition and speculation defer the possibility of definition indefinitely. Reminiscent of Derrida's description of thought as 'intrinsic multiplicity', Deleuze states what is obvious, but which we tend to forget – that thought is not a constant attribute, but passes endlessly from one thought to another (Deleuze 1993: 53). The concept of any thing can be understood in terms of what happens to it and what makes it happen, or what has brought it to this point, so that the concept of a 'glass', a 'bird' or anything prompted by a photograph provokes a chain of possibilities, which no one essential description can sufficiently explain. Chapter One introduced 'naming' as one of photography's ontological themes. Deleuze's *event* demands consideration of the coexistence of different interpretations, rather than one logical or universal conception (53).

Echoing Derrida's *photogrammar*, Deleuze's use of grammatical analogies – those of the infinitive form of a verb (to fill), the comparative adjective (fuller) and the present participle (filling) – offer subtly different nuances to how we might understand something. Deleuze refers to the perpetual state of *becoming* that is inherent in the sense of the infinitive, and the immanent difference that is implicit in the sense of a comparative adjective, such as 'fuller', 'emptier' or 'murkier'. In contemplating Horn's *Another Water*, we can say that one photograph of the Thames may appear 'murkier' or 'deeper' than another. An adjectival statement which defines its quality as deep is something that has stopped and is fixed at a certain depth, whereas the condition of 'deeper' is in a perpetual state of *becoming* deeper and is therefore never still, because it is always moving toward somewhere deeper (Deleuze 2003: 3–4). Applying the grammatical metaphor further, the infinitive initiates action, which means we can think of something not in a definitive way (e.g. the water *is* disturbed), but as a possibility, which is always at the point of happening: *the water is always about to disturb. The water disturbs me; and it is the water that threatens rather than I, the subject, who imagines the water as threatening possible death.*

Thus resonance (and what Deleuze refers to as *sensation*) reverberates in an infinitive state that is unlocatable. *Sensation* is in a constant state of change, movement and possibility according to possession, location and time – it is, in this sense, virtual and not actual. In encountering photographs, we are caught up in the animation of their stillness and possibilities that are simultaneously different (temporally and spatially).

We can think of a photograph as an event of response, which Yve Lomax describes as eventually breaking with the idea of essential reality:

> What is a photograph? 'Nothing but relations, nothing but affects', we may reply. I'm looking at a photographic image but I'm also listening. Suddenly I am astonished. I see a photograph stretching (and folding) to infinity. Suddenly I see the infamous window on the world not shattering but gently, gently folding. Suddenly I see the frost on the window pane of the frozen moment becoming an intricate pattern of unfolding and enfolding ... The photograph and, and, and. Here then the photograph becomes an event; and finally that tiresome debate of 'reality or representation' becomes a matter of something else. (Lomax 2000: 158)[7]

Photographic events such as Wall's, Mylayne's or Horn's manifest a way of thinking that accords with Deleuze's dynamic of *event*. In Mylayne's photographs, the visual procedure is inverted, so that the *eventful space* is that of the viewer-subject's looking, rather than the world presented for us to look at. Wall's *Insomnia* and Horn's *Another Water* force a contemplation of possibility – *of what has happened or what is happening or what might happen*. As with Derrida, for Deleuze and Guattari the phenomenological conception of the subject is problematic and their discussions offer alternative approaches to thinking about the world, suggesting a useful method with which to respond to photographs. They present an attitude that acknowledges sensation no less than concept, so that consideration of a space includes whatever inhabits that space: the relationships that develop, the remembrance of those in the past and anticipation of those in the future (Deleuze and Guattari, 1994: 210–11). Conceived in these terms, a photograph contains all that has brought it to that present moment, psychologically and ideologically, and anticipates future projections. *Eventful space* signals a direction for a photographic aesthetic that encompasses both ideological propositions *and* imaginative possibilities. For instance, the *eventful space* of *TITANIC's Wake* requires intellectual consideration as well as commanding a response to its visual expression. In this *eventful* encounter, we ask questions of relation rather than definition: What is the relationship of that 'object' to that 'situation' or 'subject'? What impact do they have on each other? 'What new thoughts does it make it possible to think? What new emotions does it make it possible to feel? What new sensations and perceptions does it open in the body?' (Massumi 2007: xv)

Eventful aesthetics: discourse *or* sensation

Despite changes in the way that art represents reality, as for example in behavioural performance art or experiential installation, aesthetic discourse most commonly refers to a primary visual aesthetic. And despite having moved from a Kantian 'disinterested' analysis towards an understanding of seeing, which does not separate the physical space from the psychological *event* that exists within it, translating this conception into the context of a developing aesthetic is more difficult. Deleuze's *becoming* is easier to correlate with performance art, which literally actualises the performative process. When applied to practices such as photography or film, it operates figuratively, suggesting that the relationship between photograph and viewer-subject is one of *exchange*. Deleuze's thesis also presents some confusion regarding materiality, as it suggests an opposition between *sensation* and *discourse*. He asserts the importance of artistic forces, emerging *before* we make sense of things by articulating meaning with words, and which are free from the organising framework of making intelligible and definitive sense. This appears at first to confirm, from a philosophical perspective, Lakoff's pre-linguistic conceptual field. However, in its direct address to art (specifically paintings), the division of *sensation* from other forms of representation and thinking is problematic. Deleuze's *The Logic of Sensation* (2004 [1981]), which scrutinises response to Francis Bacon's paintings, centres the visceral impact of painting's materiality, privileging the metamorphic and *sensation*, and thus bypassing the impact that the notion of *event* might have on images that are filmic or photographic. Deleuze's focus on painterly deformation (as with Bacon's faces) focuses attention on material properties that realistic photographs do not necessarily share. Deleuze and Guattari's philosophy [1991] discusses a dynamic that recognises a created universe of possibility, which suggests an interesting direction for aesthetics that is not restricted to painting. However, direct address by thinkers, such as Deleuze and Guattari, to specific art practices tend to incorporate traditional values and expectations regarding what would be considered as 'art'. In a context in which art practice subsumes conceptual art and incorporates social practice, philosophers' commentary can lose relevance. Their distinctions between different kinds of thinking (art, philosophy, science) move 'art' away from the conceptual field and return us to a form of essential materiality, which is distinct from concept (1994: 167). More relevant for photography and its developing aesthetic, than the response to material attributes in their description of 'art', are Deleuze and Guattari's ideas about a constant dynamic of possibility. In aiming to achieve an alternative means to describe representation from semiotic analysis, which attempts to structure experience and significance, their approach to artworks again separates the senses and *affect* – a more bodily experience –from a cognitive operation.

Dualisms such as this (sensation or conception) suggest one or the other alternative as being superior. So too Lyotard's analogy of discourse with the rational and everything that is 'sayable', and *figure* with what is irrational or not organised, implies that they are mutually exclusive (2011 [1971]). He says, for example: 'The position of art is a denial of the position of discourse', which suggests an opposition between 'reading' and 'seeing' (Readings 1991: 24). We tend to either read a text within the terms defined by semiotic analysis, or we merely *see* it and enjoy it: either it is discourse and a contribution to serious discussion, or it is visual and merely sensational and nothing to do with ideas; either it is documentary and serious reportage, or it is expression and frivolous authorial symbolism, so that discourse is good and the visual not so good – or vice versa. As Foucault points out, visual representations have long since been separated from the discursive, which is understood as being essentially linguistic and translatable (Foucault 1982b: 43). In consequence, aesthetics has traditionally distinguished between *discursive* (communicative) and *non-discursive* symbols that mirror feelings (Langer 1953). And distinctions between rational discourse and the elusive meaning present in photographs can proceed to equate discourse with critical, ideological presentations, and *sensation* with some mysterious visuality that is only accessible via the senses and which excludes the cognitive. There is not enough room here to fully address these distinctions, only to suggest that we can remove some of the over simplistic equations such as: seeing = visuality, or reading = words. We can introduce more diffuse equations such as: seeing = conception, or reading = visuality. We can move away from this good/bad correlation whichever way it figures. A photographic aesthetic requires an approach that does not divide art as a reflection of cultural significance from art as *sensation*.

The photograph possesses both these functions, and this exploration of photography's different dimensions of realism has sought to find alternatives to such divisions. It has encountered a range of post-structural ideas that promote non-dualistic procedures, which avoid oppositions such as fact/fiction or ideology/expression. It has focused on a series of dynamics (Derrida's deconstructive *parergon*, Lyotard's *figure*, Deleuze's *event*), each asserting a way of thinking that promotes a less oppositional relationship between linguistic and visual representation. Each accommodates the photograph's paradoxical condition that refers simultaneously to the objects literally shown and their more elusive and absent content. Derrida and Lyotard attempt a non-dichotomous reasoning, which does not start from the premise of opposition. Derrida asserts difference rather than opposition, so that 'irrational' does not displace 'rational' thought but is recognised as being different and equally valid. Lyotard undermines the oppositional implications of his own terms – *Discours/Figure*, which equate with the textual and visual respectively – by playing with them in a rhetorical way and inserting a chapter titled 'Fiscourse Digure' (Lyotard 1983). Lyotard's *figure* collates a number of the ideas discussed concerning the sort of contribution photographic practice can make, because it accommodates the difficulty in describing an ambiguous visual space, which is resistant to definitive interpretation and is never wholly translatable. *Figure* is present in the nuances of photographic representation – in tone, gesture, texture and endless reference. *Figure* is not the opposite of discourse, but a dynamic that interrupts the possibility of resolution. Photography embodies this interruption of resolved discourse because it digresses and 'leads astray'.

Late twentieth-century photographic practice established a function similar to that of historical allegorical painting, in which the central concern was idea rather than perception. Sekula's photographic projects present an ideological discourse; they encompass allegory and critique, and are rhetorical. Barthes's discussion refers to the relationship between *integrational* elements that lead us to events besides the main focus, and which insert tension in the 'discursive function' (Barthes 1977: 95). Extending this, Sekula speaks of photographic discourse as a 'system of information exchange' and as a 'system of relations'. As such its meaning cannot be separated from its discourse or its spatial or temporal context, which are inter-dependent (Sekula 1982: 84–7). Echoing Foucault's insistence that we should make use of the incommensurable difference between the visual and verbal, Sekula asserts the potential of photography as being 'its dumb resistance to language' because, if it is resistant to language, it can challenge modes of thought and embody argument, visually and rhetorically (Sekula 1999: 150).

Sekula's and Wall's works bring together many of the elements considered in previous chapters that are principally concerned with ideas. 'Dialogical Realism' (Chapter Three) established response to the photograph as an interactive process. This chapter, 'Discursive Realism', presents the photograph as a virtual space to which response must be both cognitive and visceral. It has argued that issues addressed by verbal discourse can also be addressed by visual representation, which will be accentuated by its visceral impact. The visual capacity for a different significance supplements cognitive response. 'Political Realism' claimed Jaar's rhetorical practice approach as an alternative to Sekula's rejection of the 'vaporous and a-historical realm of purely affective expression', and that it is possible for a serious photographic discourse to incorporate intellectual ideas and visual sensation (Sekula 1999b: 118). A conception of discursive photography works within its physical means, as it always has done, but differs from the modernist assertion of a pure and precious visuality. The discursive photograph's power is animated by what it provokes – rather than what it depicts. Photography, as it has incorporated fiction and as considered in the light of post-structural thinking, can be seen as self-reliant and less dependent on its original ontology. Following post-structural critiques of essential 'presence', the world cannot be merely mirrored by transparent copies. Photography can be seen to contain contradictions, rather than reflecting a transparent reality. Discourse establishes the photograph as participating in an ongoing space of enquiry and places debate as central. At the same time, what I have referred to as rhetorical realism includes a response to the photograph as a reverberation of thought that may be provoked by the visual; it can be metaphoric and cognitively unformed. A photograph can be seen as a reflection of, and commentary on, the wider cultural field; it can demonstrate and expand ideas (philosophically, culturally, politically). As discursive practice, it displays a manner of thinking that makes a different, but equivalent, contribution to cultural debate. Photographic realism can be thought of as visual proposition. It can address the same questions as written analysis – the question of capitalism (Sekula's *TITANIC's Wake*) or the question of institutionalised art (Orozco's *Empty Shoebox*) or the question of the heterosexual gaze (Mapplethorpe's *X Portfolio*). This chapter concludes that the visual and verbal, presented as a dichotomy along with the ideological and expressive photograph, need not be alternatives.

Suggested further reading

Elkins, J. (2007) *Photography Theory*, Routledge, London

Fried, M. (2008) *Why Photography Matters as Art as Never Before*, Yale University Press, New Haven; London

Lomax, Y. (2005) *Sounding the Event: Escapades in Dialogues and Matters of Art, Nature and Time*, I. B. Tauris, London; New York

Massumi, B. (2002) 'The Autonomy of Affect' in *Parables of the Virtual: Movement, Affect, Sensation*, Duke University Press, Durham, NC; London, 23–45

— (2007) 'Translator's Foreword: Pleasures of Philosophy', in G. Deleuze and F, Guattari, *A Thousand Plateaus: Capitalism and Schizophrenia* [1980], trans. B. Massumi [1988], Continuum, London; New York, xv–xvi

O'Sullivan, S. (2007) *Art Encounters Deleuze and Guattari*, Palgrave Macmillan, New York

Sekula, A. (2003b) *TITANIC's Wake*, SNEL, Liège

Wall, J. (2003) '"Marks of Indifference": Aspects of Photography in, or as, Conceptual Art' [1995] in Douglas Fogle (ed.), *The Last Picture Show: Artists using Photography*, Walker Art Centre, Minneapolis, 32–44

Notes

1 *Critical Realism in Contemporary Art: Around Allan Sekula's Photography*, Symposium, Lieven Gevaert Research Centre for Photography and Visual Studies, Leuven, Belgium, September 2005, and Buchloh (1995).

2 See Jeff Wall's work online at the MOMA website: www.moma.org/interactives/exhibitions/2007/jeffwall, accessed 13 September 2012.

3 http://whitney.org/Collection/BruceNauman/70509, accessed 5 September 2012.

4 Walker Evans, manuscript notes on 3″ × 5″ index cards, notes for lyric documentary on cards – 'the real thing always has purity, certain severity, rigor, simplicity, directness, clarity, is without artistic pretension, hard + firm as base', in Walker Evans Archive, 1994.250.54, Yale photography notes (11) 25.

5 Ideas introduced by Deleuze and Guattari provide an extension to ideas discussed in earlier chapters, but it must be noted that their texts were generally not available in English until the 1980s and 1990s.

6 www.tate.org.uk/servlet/ViewWork?workid=27072, accessed 20 September 2010.

7 Yve Lomax explores this phenomenon in Lomax (2005). She contemplates 'something' and the subject–predicate distinction in Lomax (2009).

Concluding section: discourse *and* sensation

This concluding section draws two issues towards conclusion: how we consider and respond to the 'post-structural photograph' and the changing attitude to the photographic aesthetic. Chapter Eight identified a central matter in question: how we might reconcile the visual and sensational with the conceptual and ideological in the developing photographic aesthetic. Sekula [1976–78] located the separation of the photograph as an aesthetic idea of the imagination, from that of conceptual knowledge and intellectual reasoning, as originating in Kant's *Critique of Judgement* (Sekula 1999: 118). Kant [1790] articulated the key relationships between understanding and imagining, between what is explicable and what is not. He distinguished between rational concepts (intellectual ideas), which may be imagined and described but can be abstract (e.g. the kingdom of God), and 'aesthetic ideas', which induce so much thought that language can never quite render them completely intelligible (Kant 1952 §49, 175–6). An 'aesthetic idea' is a representation of the imagination (Kant 1952: §57, 209–13) and can supplement unrealisable rational concepts by visualising or providing metaphors for them (as with Langer's *non-discursive* symbols). Rational ideas are concerned with complex concepts of morality, politics and religion, for which photographs can provide an aesthetic symbolisation, as with *Allie Mae*, which presents an idealisation of the human condition. Sekula's logic proceeds to equate Kant's 'aesthetic idea' with idealism and as a kind of indulgence, which he distinguishes from an 'explicit political utterance' that doesn't idealise. In a later context, Wall's photographs complicate this division between the aesthetic and the rational, because as aesthetic ideas they supplement unrealisable concepts by evoking metaphor, *and* they also contribute to intellectual reasoning in discussing ideas or expressing political concerns. Here lies the root of fundamental distinctions between different photographic expectations: 'pure' documentary photographs that do not seek to transcend context; photographs that supplement and transcend rational ideas with individual expression or which symbolise some ideal view; photographs that are ideological or rhetorical. Much of the photography between the 1970s and 2000 was wholly fictional, utilising both aesthetic and rational functions, and presenting the impact of visual appearance together with conceptual or ideological content.

Post-structuralism presents a series of considerations in dismantling such binary divisions: with regard to the visual and verbal, Foucault (2003 [1966]) insists that we should endeavour to keep the infinite relation of language to pictures open. He suggests that the uncertainty of visual digression is useful and that 'the infinity of the task' should be preserved somehow in order to allow the full range of possibilities to emerge. And the *figural*, like Derrida's *différance*, reasserts the rhetoric of the visual. With regard to the material and theoretical, Kristeva insists that theoretical processes are inseparable from the material body and subjectivity. With regard to the irrational and rational, Derrida and Deleuze remind us of the disorder of thought; thought is messy in its interaction with others and objects – and with photographs. In deconstructing the traditional process of logic, Derrida celebrates absurdities that exist within logical constructions as a necessary consequence of their disturbance. And with regard to expression and signification, he reminds us that signs and reference cannot be kept separate from sense and expression – so that photographs can be ideologically expressive. With regard to dissemination and resolved interpretation, Deleuze's *event* suggests a negotiated space that perpetually *develops* meaning, so that the photographic work can be seen as an *event* in which we participate. With regard to visuality and discourse, Lyotard asserts the *dis*order of the *figural* that disturbs an ordered discourse. And his *digure* indicates finding discourse in the figural (Readings 1991: 7) so that the figural and discourse in photographic realism need not be seen as exclusive.

The rapid development of Chinese photography has provided numerous examples of the conflation of discourse (the rational) with a sensual celebration (the aesthetic) using modern digital technologies. For example, Wang Qingsong's work is rhetorical in its use of metonymic extension and metaphoric imagination, and demonstrates attitude and critique efficiently and more immediately than verbal discourse. It is visceral in its sensuous use of colour and dimension that recalls the impact of nineteenth-century photographic tableaux. It establishes the possible coexistence of politics and poetry on equal terms. In the 1980s, China's economic growth, modernisation and exposure to the West precipitated a rapid consumption of both theoretical and photographic influences, demonstrating the effects of globalisation in a particularly vivid way. China's photographic history digested and responded to Western modernism *and* the anti-modernism of conceptual art in close succession. And because its evolution was so rapid, the compressed development in Chinese photography interacted readily with other art forms (installation, performance, new media). Chinese photography displays an absorption of conceptual practice without the complication of an interim legacy of straight photography, and, inheriting the artifice provided by technologies, it assumes fictional theatricality without question (Hung and Phillips 2004). Zhang Huan's work displays many characteristics of this era in that it typically dismisses an essentialist attitude to the medium of practice; his images result from an engagement with the traditions of bodily performance, conceptual art and photography. His career is testimony to the 'globalisation' of art practice towards the end of the century. It is also testament to Chinese art as being an inherently political act, as his activities in the last century were restricted to private venues following his provocative performance of *The Angel* at the National Art Museum, Beijing in 1993. Chinese art declares its history and its process as being necessarily experimental and 'new' and, regardless of its content, Chinese photography and its reference to Chinese history is at once a re-visioning, a critique and a protest.

In drawing points from Part II together here, I have utilised Derrida's differentiation (2010: 5) between analogue and digital photography as being between *recording* an image and *producing* an image, which he suggests results in a 'photographic performativity'. I have deliberately chosen photographs that *invent* reality in very different ways, and which establish a precedent for directions in uses of photography in the twenty-first century: one that records aspects of a performance event (Huan's *To Raise the Water Level in a Fishpond*, 1997, Figure 28), one that constructs a document to simulate looking (Xing Danwen's *Scroll*, 1999–2000) and one that produces a document from a number of complex elements (Qingsong's *Night Revels of Lao Li*, 2000). Each displays elements that could be described as rational *and* aesthetic, and establishes such a division as inappropriate for photographic practice.

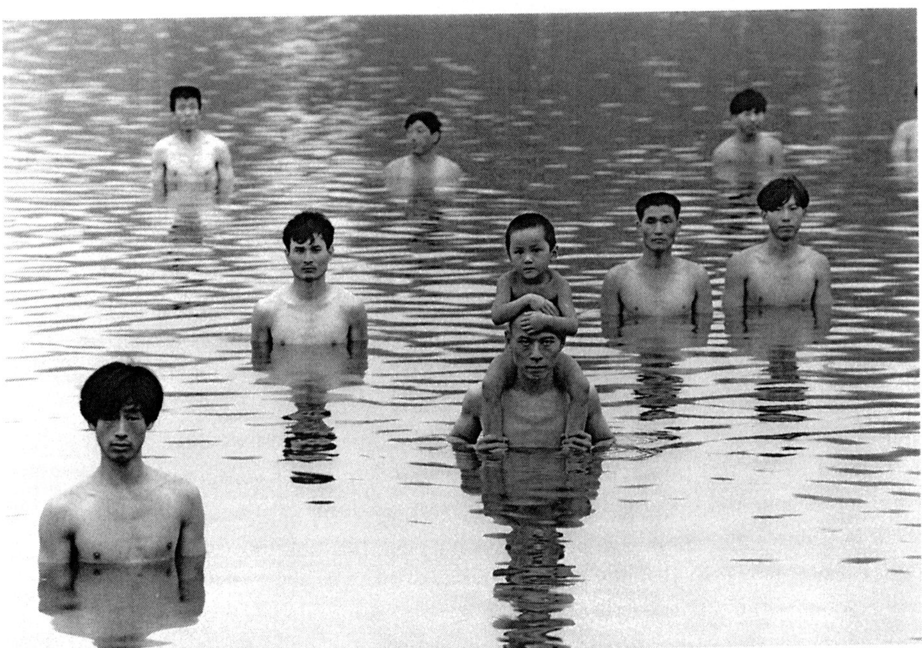

Figure 28 Zhang Huan, *To Raise the Water Level in a Fishpond*, 1997. Performance, Beijing, China.

A number of young men stand chest high in water; it is a lake of some kind. They all look at me, but the central figure appears older and regards me more pointedly. Astride his shoulders sits a small boy who clasps the man's head whilst the man firmly grips the boy's legs against his chest. The boy looks at me too and seems unperturbed by what must be an extraordinary event. I imagine them all to be naked, and summoned to this lake, placed in this position. They are all motionless and entirely focused on this moment. The effect is mesmerising and provokes questions: what is it about this place, these physical circumstances that command them to this place?

As I am familiar with the image *To Raise the Water Level*, it is difficult to separate my engagement with it from my knowledge of it. But attempting to articulate what I see, rather than what I know, confirms for me that, despite the photograph's artificial construction, it retains its singular property that presents us with one place, at one time, from one position: 'this took place, and it took place only once' (Derrida 2010: 3). Huan's image confronts the difficulty in identifying the kind of meaning that dominates – whether it be intertextual play (rational thinking) or physical apprehension (aesthetic sensation). Derrida would say that 'we cannot think outside the text' – we cannot remove ourselves from our time, or language or knowledge to experience 'physical apprehension' without also 'thinking'. The experience of looking will inevitably refer to past experiences, and past photographs that we have seen, so that my attempts at a primary response, in order to describe a photograph as being immediately present, will always fail in this respect. Derrida's interest in the way that words/images produce meaning serves to illustrate the contradiction in my naming photography as 'discursive'; here he aligns 'discourse' with established meaning, so that 'nondiscursive' processes – the non-rational aspects of language – which work in a visually rhetorical or a disruptive or poetic way (as he demonstrates in 'Right of Inspection', 1989 [1985]) are the aspects most useful to discourse:

> So what I do with words is make them explode, so that the nonverbal appears in the verbal. That is to say I make the words function in such a way that at a certain moment they no longer belong to discourse... I am also interested in words, paradoxically, to the extent that they are nondiscursive, for that's how they can be used to explode discourse ... Not always, but in most of my texts there is a point at which the word functions in a nondiscursive manner. All of a sudden it disrupts the order and rules ... I treat [words] as bodies that contain their own perversity ... let's say the regulated disorder of words. As soon as that occurs, language is opened to the nonverbal arts. For this reason it is especially when dealing with painting and photography, for example, that I take risks with such verbal adventures ... It is when words start to go crazy in that way and no longer behave properly in regard to discourse that they have more rapport with the other arts, and conversely this reveals how the apparently nondiscursive arts such as photography and painting correspond to the linguistic scene. (Derrida 1994: 20)

Derrida implies that photographs, which he describes as being 'nondiscursive', work in a similarly intertextual way to words, and contribute to debate by stretching what is considered to be 'meaning', which is generally seen as residing solely in the linguistic domain. As a result, there is an interaction between these two processes – the discursive and the figural. The experience of sensation is always subject to discourse, and discourse is always infected by sensation, so that apprehension incorporates the figural *and* the discursive. Concerned to analyse the different operations involved in experiencing images, Norman Bryson (1981) clarifies the process by distinguishing between the sense generated by those features in the image influenced by language and culturally formed concepts (the discursive), and those generated elements that 'belong-to-the image-alone' (the figural), which are supplementary and lead astray. Bryson aligns those elements in the image that rely on narrative or information with discourse, and distinguishes them from those that do not and are in *excess* of what is necessary for communication:

Looking at To Raise the Water Level, *I can see that it is water by the horizontal ripple effect as the light bounces off the surface. I do not need the vertical and distorted reflections of the men in the water to know that it is water. I can see that they are men because they are bare-chested. The variety of haircut and the steely stare towards me, besides the three at the back who look slightly aslant, are supplementary elements.*

Bryson explains the interaction between those two processes of figure and discourse, which are habitually assumed to be in opposition, as being one of 'subtle mutuality' (1981: 12). It is this mutual interaction between discourse (information, narrative) and the elements that are superfluous to our understanding of what we are looking at – not the resemblance between image and world – which persuade us of its realism (Bryson 1981: 10–12, 27).

We have consistently valued what exceeds the discursive, so that 'aesthetics' is traditionally associated with the properties of transcendence or excess of affect. Because the supposed transparency of photography has been aligned with the discursive, the history of photography has been preoccupied with its capacity for transcendence. Photographs undoubtedly do produce meaning that exceeds the communication of simple things; Jean-Luc Mylayne's birds speak of much more that the appearance or location of birds. And the staged photograph, no less that the 'straight', presents superfluous information in gestures (Wall's *Ventriloquist*) or shadows (Huan's *To Raise the Water Level*). Because we value those indescribable meanings that are difficult to locate, meaning that is 'found' has been privileged throughout modernism over more explicit meanings that may have political purpose.

Huan's photograph presents an interesting conflation of the procedures of recording and producing (Derrida 2010), and of discursive and rhetorical elements. *To Raise the Water Level in a Fishpond* (1997) and *The Anonymous Mountain Raised by a Meter* (1995), inspired by the Chinese idiom 'Beyond the mountain, there are more mountains', are photographs that document a 'performance'. Huan's 'raising' of the water level refers us literally to an artificial event that the photograph has recorded. But its visual impact is dependent on the resulting photograph, which perpetuates response and demonstrates the supplementary meaning that is inserted once it becomes an expansive *photographic event*. This is quite separate from the original performance. Alongside its rhetorical immediacy, the photograph assumes symbolic references (discursive in Bryson's terms); its properties establish an iconic resonance that exists entirely besides the performative event and derives from those supplementary elements that exceed communication. This aspect of photographic meaning that aligns with sensation works independently from prior knowledge or the discursive aspect. Other aspects of meaning develop once we are given more information:

> I invited about forty participants, recent migrants to the city who had come to work in Beijing from other parts of China. They were construction workers, fishermen and labourers, all from the bottom of society. They stood around in the pond and then I walked in it. At first they stood in a line in the middle to separate the pond into two parts. Then they all walked freely, until the point of the performance arrived, which was to raise the water level. Then they stood still. In the Chinese tradition, fish is the symbol of sex while water is the source of life. This work expresses, in fact, one kind of understanding and explanation of water. That the water in the pond was raised one metre higher is an action of no avail.[1]

Additional knowledge such as this inserts a chain of conceptual meaning: the cause and effect of migrant labour; liberty and control; cultural symbolism. The work is propositional in that it visualises a contradiction: the possibility that any group of people can alter the state of things, and that such action is futile. Huan says his performances are about humility – the impossibility for changing the natural state of things: 'Climb this mountain and you will find an even bigger mountain in front of you' (Goldberg 2000). The resulting photographs are essentially statements about time, about cultural values and political change, and about bodily process in interaction with the world. He describes these events as 'fictional ideas', 'stories' that realise possibilities, which in this instance concern the lives of Chinese peasants who come to the expanding cities to work for construction companies or to sell vegetables. He describes their ordeal as a kind of 'self-torture' (Kim 2003). *To Raise the Water Level* contains layer upon layer of implication and reference. Ideationally, the image focuses the conflict between the body and the environment. Symbolically, it accentuates the separateness of individuals whilst pointing to the conditions in which one is placed as a common conflict that everyone experiences in some way or other.

To Raise the Water Level is resonant with reference to China's past, which we learn from Huan's early history living in rural He Nan province; he speaks of the influences of Tibetan Buddhism and the traditional spiritual ceremonies that continued secretly in people's homes during the Cultural Revolution. It is an implicitly political commentary concerning the national Chinese policy of urban expansion and the resulting physical conflict occurring in a particular locale and the problems for its inhabitants. The photograph works on two levels: rooted in his experience of childhood and the experience of others and their changing identity and role. Huan's process works personally and politically by focusing on the body and its contact

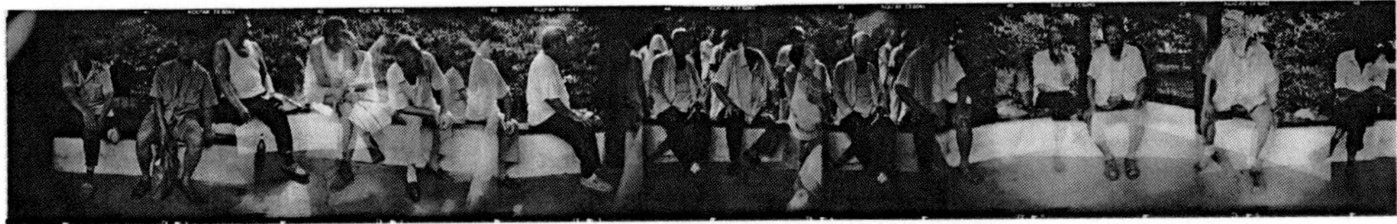

Figure 29.1 Xing Danwen, *Scroll A#1*, 1999–2000; 100 × 8 in. (254 × 20 cm).

with the natural world and others: 'The body is the only direct way through which I come to know society and society comes to know me. The body is proof of identity. The body is language' (Huan, quoted in Heartney 2007). He aims 'to feel and experience the existence of the body under the pressure of different environments'. His endeavour to experience the shift between the mind and the body is an instance of visual thought that attempts the breakdown of that dualism.

To Raise the Water Level coalesces a number of features discussed: the tension between *figure* and discourse and between mind and body; the photograph's condition as an object that references factual reality by recording an event and as an abstract function that produces meaning besides the illustration of verbal discourse. It works *through* its reference to real things to provoke questions. It is a virtual space to which response must be both cognitive and visceral; *it creates a dialogue with me, demanding a relationship, provoked in this instance by the peculiar sensation caused by each of the men appearing to look at me.* Operating as a record, a poem and an ideality, it produces the interrelationship of thought, imagination and perception.

A consistent theme in Xing Danwen's photography is engagement with the world in several registers – the intimate (*I Am a Woman*, 1994–5), the cultural (*Born with Cultural Revolution*, 1995) and the phenomenal (*Scroll*, 1999–2000, Figure 29). Described by Gu Zheng (2006: 91) as encompassing 'the body, memory, sexuality, cultural status, globalisation, dislocation, consumption, desire', the photographic content includes most of the issues addressed in these chapters. The evolution of her work matches a developing post-structural awareness: earlier work demonstrates changing attitudes to the individual subject and its representation, despite being brought up to think of herself as part of a larger unit – the family and the political realm – rather than an independent identity. In the series *I Am a Woman*, she photographs herself and others repeatedly and 'in process' from an array of perspectives. In performing her image, she participates in its construction and addresses the viewer in an intimate dialogue.[2] The series *Born with Cultural Revolution* presents a critical view of her personal reality, influenced by Chinese cultural history and the consequences of the epoch in which she lived. As she was born in 1967 at the start of the Cultural Revolution, Mao was someone she and her friends respected. Following his death and the 1980s period of transition leading to a more mixed economy and the increasing influence from the West, Danwen describes people as still immersed in a culture inherited from Mao, whilst confusedly experiencing contradictory feelings about their expectations for the future. Later works, which reference the violence

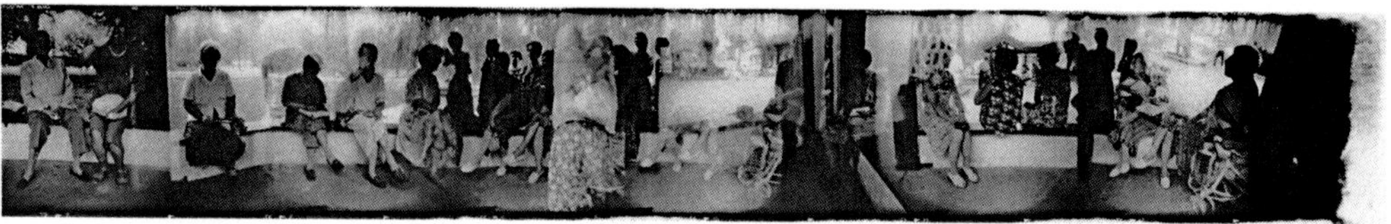

of repressive regimes, the consequences of global capital markets and the ironies of Chinese industry, anticipate the more overtly political agenda in art practice of the twenty-first century (*Duplication*, 2002; *disCONNEXION*, 2004).

Scroll A consists of seven horizontal sequences that return to a relationship with the physical world determined by what the camera can and can't do. Each sequence records people in the manner of a cinematic strip of film – but one that is paradoxically prevented from progressing in time beyond one moment. *A1 #3* points to the significance of this series; it features a boy in white standing quite prominently in the foreground, breaking the sequence, and marking the image as 'photographic'. The other strips confirm *Scroll* as a contradiction that is momentary *and* sequential, a linear sequence of one moment:

> *Scroll A #1 traverses along a wall on which people are sitting, alone or in couples and groups. Some are distracted by what is happening behind and around them, others sit quietly others talk to each other. Nothing remarkable is happening; it is a scene that is recognisable anywhere. The men are dressed similarly in white shirts, t-shirts and shorts in various combinations.*

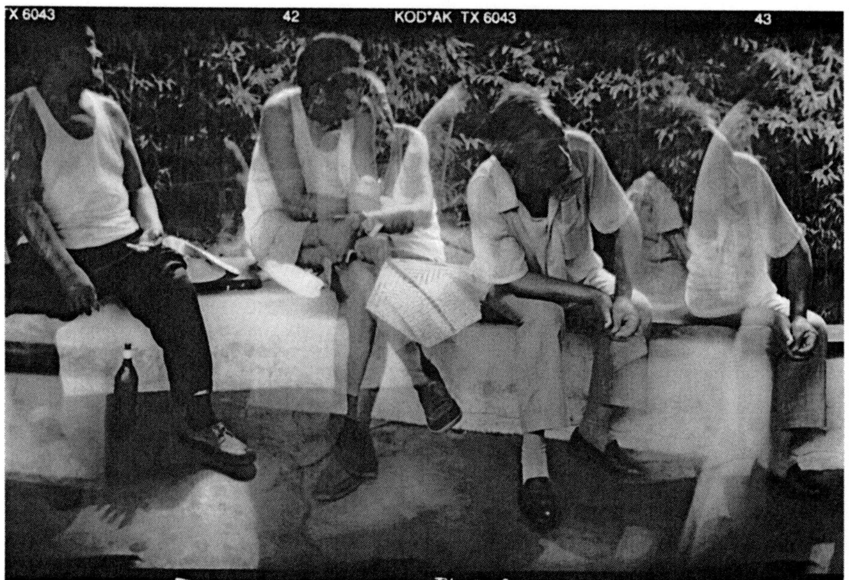

Figure 29.2 Xing Danwen, a section of *Scroll A#1*, 1999–2000.

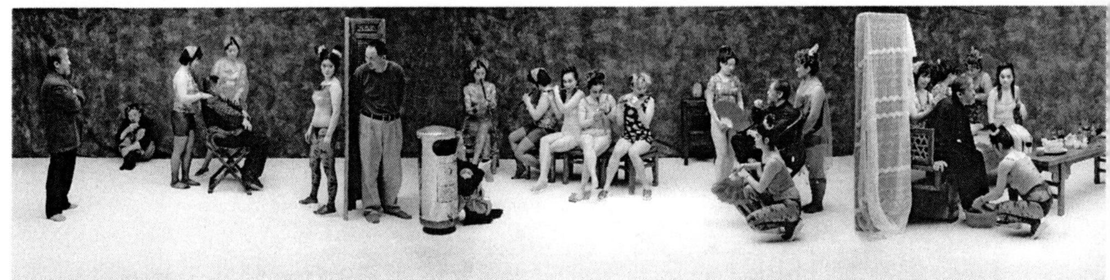

Figure 30 Wang Qingsong, *Night Revels of Lao Li*, 2000.

Individuals appear more than once, so that a small adjustment in position records a moment later. I can see some in more than one position as if caught in quick succession so that someone turns to the person next to them, and then appears engrossed in conversation. It seems like one moment and lots of moments simultaneously. We move along and the atmosphere changes, the light is more diffuse and it is predominantly women who are talking, looking and reading. Their hands are the most noticeable features, resting in their laps or clasping their knees – usually crossed.

Scroll A is a temporal traversal of one moment in time, in the sense that it is concerned with the way time appears to us; it describes one perspective of present life. The observation is transitory and simultaneous and reminiscent of Derrida's critique of phenomenology's conception of the process of thought and its attempt to grasp temporality as a linear process. In a peculiar reversal of the 'straight' photograph, Xing Danwen describes her aim to create an image without manipulation, shooting directly and successively so that the resulting image must rely on the 'original data' without editing. At the same time, the process defers the possibility of the decisive moment by creating a single still image, which encompasses multi-vantage-point perspectives and 'places each recorded moment within a continuous timeline'. Her goal was to create a continuous frame that establishes 'a parallel between the time and the dimension of a subject'. Presenting a photograph that requires a durational viewing, she sums up a characteristic of photography of the period as having 'deliberately broken with the usual way of viewing photography by asking the audience to *read* my work rather than to *look* at my images' (Danwen in Hung 2004: 214). Her work demonstrates several features of work in this period: principally that of the interactive process that forces a dialogue with the image. Her use of the camera's limitations constructs a paradox that references photography's history and contradicts it – simultaneously. It is a representation of looking and thinking.

Wang Qingsong's work displays the most obvious Western influences and is typical in its concern with the rapidly changing social environment in China. His elaborate constructions reference the contrast between traditional mythologies and the absurdity of commercial culture. Images such as *Requesting Buddha No.1* (1999) create a virtual exchange between digital imagery (representing present life) with traditional

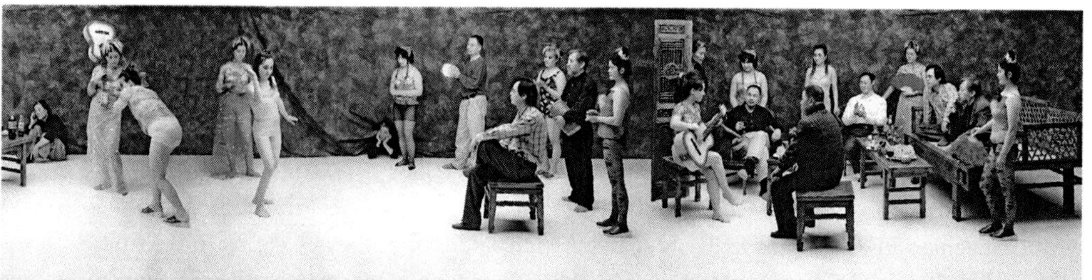

philosophical language (representing past life). They contrast the spiritual with the banal and the serious with the humorous.[3] *Night Revels of Lao Li* (2000) speaks of the contradictory Chinese condition that is attracted to Western ideas and yet is aware of a hiatus in Chinese culture that both embraces and rejects different aspects. It is an attitude that refers with ambivalence to socio-political issues. Whilst Chinese culture is still rooted in Buddhism and expectations of responsibility towards others, it is also seduced by the attractions of material life. Qingsong's work expresses suspicion about the nature of the changes in his society and the extent to which they are accepted or assimilated. *Requesting Buddha* and *Look up! Look up!* (2000) poke fun at the superficiality of consumerism that worships global brands such as Coca Cola or McDonalds, and is highly critical of the consequences of globalisation and its effect on Chinese values. *Night Revels of Lao Li* (Figure 30) articulates these contradictions by referencing the scroll painting *Night Revels of Han Xizai* (Gu Hongzhong, tenth century) and paralleling the position of contemporary artists and intellectuals with those of the post-Tang dynasty. It refers to the story of Han Xizai who, unable to rebel against the government, resorted to a life of indulgence. Qingsong's version refers to the art critic and curator Li Xianting who, like Huan, had fallen foul of the official Chinese position by championing confrontational art works.

Night Revels translates the discursive process into a cinematic adventure – an epic in photographic terms. As with Chinese script, it reads from right to left, disrupting the Western process of narrative construction and the certainty of the moment:

I can look at one point in the sequence or I can try to apprehend them as simultaneous. They can be read as a series of five single photographs identified by the repeated device of a dividing screen, or a sequence of events; it doesn't really matter; characters repeat in the sequence … that is not a sequence; it presents us with a photographic piece of paradox. The moment in time is deferred: there is this event and then this and this… The figure of Li stands at the extreme left of the photograph surveying the 'revels'. The characters are entirely engrossed by what they are doing, and exclude me, except one character (possibly Qingsong) who appears several times, watching intermittently but seemingly indifferent to everyone else: he smokes, he peers from under the curtain, and he speaks to someone on his cell phone outside the present scene.

More than a dialogue, *Night Revels* is a series of simultaneous conversations on different levels and from different perspectives: those of the commentator on power relations between men and women, the amused observer and the social critic. The men look, the women attend to the men; they dance; they play music. It is a wholly contrived and self-conscious fantasy that dispenses with resemblance to the real world altogether. It instigates narrative and yet digresses from narrative, encouraging speculation and doubt. It is also a subtle critique that addresses contrasting issues: the state of Chinese art and its relationship to government, extreme traditionalism and the possibilities offered by material life. It is gaudy and yet restrained; it is entertainment and social commentary; it is discursive and sensual. It demonstrates the facility with which photography can show contradictory conditions simultaneously: poverty/wealth, history/present, tradition/materialism.

Post-structural aesthetics

On being asked [1990] about the relation of thought to the arts, Derrida replies that thought is not the sole province of philosophy, and that practical arts offer other modes of thought that question in a different way:

> It is necessary to say that there is thought, something that produces sense without belonging to the order of sense, that exceeds philosophical discourse and questions philosophy, that potentially contains a questioning of philosophy, that goes beyond philosophy. This does not mean that the painter or filmmaker has the means of questioning philosophy, but what she or he creates becomes the bearer of something that cannot be mastered by philosophy. Thus, there is thought there. (Derrida 1994: 24).

Derrida's alignment of 'art' – and photography – with another mode of thought echoes Sekula's point about the photograph's 'dumb resistance to language' and its potential to provoke thought. This way of considering a photograph affirms it as a conceptual space that does not require translation into language to produce 'sense'. In these terms, the uses of photography discussed here provoke another way of 'thinking', not in a separate province from sensation, but as an expansive or eventful mode in which ideas circulate. In a context in which photography 'thinks', the alignment of aesthetics with the figural, or politics with discourse, is an unsustainable polarity, which the contradiction of the 'discursive photograph' embodies.

The legacy of this era of post-structural theory and practice is signalled here by examples of Chinese photography in the years before 2000. Whilst late twentieth-century uses of photography can be seen to have promoted sensationally demonstrative photographs, an equally significant development has been its conflation of the aesthetic and the rational, or the irrational with the conceptual. Rooted in the aftermath of conceptual art, it incorporated the conceptual, the rhetorical and the critical. No longer obliged to justify itself as art on the basis of 'authentic' use of the medium, it responded to the influence of ideas and steered its aesthetic toward an exchange between the theoretical and the visual contributing to cross-disciplinary concerns, rather than only being relevant within the rarefied context of art-photography. Following the realignment of philosophy *post* post-structuralism, of art history *post* visual studies and the assimilation of the anti-aesthetic *post* modernism, the acknowledgement of 'difference' and the questioning of the nature of the subject, photographic aesthetics progressed from a preoccupation with perception and affect, to incorporate an engagement with the world and discourse. A post-structural photographic 'realism' demands a relationship with it. And a response to the photograph as an event or process requires an active and durational looking, as suggested by Xing Danwen. When the hierarchy between discourse and the figural is removed, photography establishes its capacity also to be discursive, and is more suitably considered in terms of a *representation of thinking* than a representation of the object – a representation that offers an opportunity for social, political and emotional content.

In general terms, aesthetic discourse has not yet assimilated the demands of late twentieth-century practice, or even conceptual art. And photography theory has perpetuated a focus on the photograph's ontology rather than what the content may address (Elkins 2007). Framing discussion around 'what photography is' (Elkins 2010) keeps the debate rooted in the consequences of technological process – hence the significance of digitalisation. Digitalisation has prompted a reappraisal of photographic meaning, because it undermines the original ontological principles on which photographic aesthetics was founded. Roberts (2009: 289) sums up the central issue and divide as caused by the fact that 'post-production' digital manipulation moves photography from a 'neutral transcription of appearances' to a painterly and figural function, and from an 'indexical integrity' to one that promotes fictional construction. Facilitated by the increasing artifice made available by staging and digitalisation, uses of photography have forced a different way of understanding the appearance and condition of 'reality'. However, a digital photograph still presents a version of 'realism'; what has shifted is the use of the referent to include the imaginary, besides the record of objects in the real world. And along with expanded aspirations for its use, the dimensions of photographic 'meaning' have changed. Photographic practice, which incorporates conceptual and political thinking, has exceeded the discourse that struggles to describe it. It has assimilated the principles of conceptual art to the extent that the prevailing focus has shifted from transcendent meaning to conceptual reverberation, so that the need for conceptualisation has replaced the desire for revelation. And once the potential of digital technology is wholly assimilated, photography's discourse will be forced to talk about content as well as its ontology, technique and form. Where photography in the 1980s adopted the postmodern phenomenon as typically photographic, the more profound characteristics that developed between 1980 and 2000 have yet to be described by a universal umbrella term. The dynamics of 'post-structural aesthetics' include the thoughts photography provokes – what the photograph does. Asking: 'what photography does' must move the debate in a different direction.[4]

This book has been concerned with an evolving conceptual framework for uses of photography in art practice, in which, *post* post-structuralism, photography utilises a history of thinking that circulates around conceptions of reality, truth and document. It has explored how the photograph might be both 'unsayable' and ideological. It has given emphasis to the contradictory aspects of the non-literal, besides the reference to real things, which are central to our understanding of photographic realism. It has promoted the possibilities of an interpretative process as self-reflexive, and as a search or a dialogue. It asserts the photograph as a conceptual, poetic and dialogical space that demands our interaction with it. As a representation of thought, and as representation that thinks, the post-structural aesthetic encompasses ideas and ideology, and accommodates the disorder of cognitive resonance as readily as visual effect.

Notes

1 See his work and a number of essays and interviews on his website at www.zhanghuan.com.

2 For more information about Xing Danwen, see www.danwen.com, accessed 15 September 2011.

3 For more information about Wang Qingsong, see www.wangqingsong.com/index.php?lang=en, accessed 8 September 2010.

4 Debate since the 2000s does suggest other directions. For example, Fried (2008) addresses a rethinking of the relationship between the photograph and the viewer with regard to its direct address (theatricality) or the degree of absorption provoked, and Costello and Iversen (2010) reconsider the photograph *post* conceptual art.

Bibliography

Agee, J. (1939) *Let Us Now Praise Famous Men: Three Tenant Families*, photographs by Walker Evans, Houghton Mifflin, Boston

Andrew, D. (1984) *Concepts in Film Theory*, Oxford University Press, Oxford

Aragon, L. (1989) 'The Quarrel over Realism' [1936], in C. Phillips (ed.), *Photography in the Modern Era: European Documents and Critical Writings, 1913–1940*, The Metropolitan Museum of Art; Aperture, New York

Arnaudet, D. (1997) 'Image of a Gift', *Parkett* 50/51, 122–6

Bakhtin, M. (1981) *The Dialogic Imagination* [1975], trans. C. Emerson and M. Holquist, University of Texas Press, Austin

Bal, M. (2001) *Looking In: The Art of Viewing*, G+B Arts International, Amsterdam

— (2002) *Travelling Concepts in the Humanities*, University of Toronto Press, Toronto; Buffalo; London

Balken, D. B. (1999) *Alfredo Jaar: Lament of the Images*, Massachusetts Institute of Technology, Cambridge, MA

Barney, T. (1997) *Photographs: Theater of Manners*, Scalo, Zurich; Berlin; New York

Barth, U. (2000) *In Between Places*, Henry Art Gallery, Seattle, WA

Barthes, R. (1977) 'The Photographic Message' [1961], 'Rhetoric of the Image' [1964], 'Introduction to the Structural Analysis of Narrative' [1966], 'The Death of the Author' [1968], 'The Third Meaning' [1970] and 'From Work to Text' [1971], in *Image: Music: Text*, trans. S. Heath, Fontana Press, London

— (1982) 'The Reality Effect' [1968], in T. Todorov (ed.), *French Literary Theory Today*, trans. R. Carter, Cambridge University Press, Cambridge, 11–17

— (1993a) *Mythologies*, trans. A. Lavers [1972], Vintage, London, 100–2

— (1993b) *Camera Lucida* [1980], trans. R. Howard [1981], Vintage, London

— (1997) *The Eiffel Tower and Other Mythologies*, trans. R. Howard [1979], University of California Press, Berkeley; Los Angeles

Batchen, G. (1999) *Burning with Desire: The Conception of Photography*, The MIT Press, Cambridge, MA

— (2000) 'Vernacular Photographies', *History of Photography*, 24:3 (Autumn), 262–71

— (2009) *Photography Degree Zero: Reflections on Roland Barthes's* Camera Lucida, The MIT Press, Cambridge, MA

Bate, D. (2004) 'After Thought', *Source*, 40 (Autumn), 30–3

— (2009) *Photography: The Key Concepts*, Berg, Oxford; New York

Baudrillard, J. (1983) *Simulations* [1981], trans. P. Foss, P. Patton et al., Semiotext[e], New York

— (1997) 'Objects, Images and the Possibilities of Aesthetic Illusion', in N. Zurbrugg, (ed.), *Art & Artefact*, Sage Publications, London, 7–18

— (1999a) 'Poetic Transference of Situation', in Luc Delahaye, *L'Autre*, Phaidon, London, unpaginated

— (1999b) *Photographies 1985–1998*, ed. P. Weibel, Hatje-Cantz Publishers, Ostfildern

— (2000) 'Photography, or the Writing of Light' [1999], trans. François Debrix at *Ctheory.net*, www.ctheory.net/articles.aspx?id=126, accessed 13 September 2012

— (2004) *Fragments: Conversations with Francois L'Yvonnet*, Routledge, London; New York

Baxandall, M. (1985) *Patterns of Intention: On the Historical Explanation of Pictures*, Yale University Press, New Haven; London

Bazin, A. (1980) 'The Ontology of the Photographic Image' [1958], trans. Hugh Gray in *Film Quarterly*, 13:4 (Summer 1960), in A. Trachtenberg (ed.) *Classic Essays on Photography*, Leete's Island Books, New Haven, 237–44

Benjamin, W. (1980) 'A Short History of Photography' [1931], in A. Trachtenberg (ed.), *Classic Essays on Photography*, Leete's Island Books, New Haven, 237, 199–216

— (2005) 'The Work of Art in the Age of Mechanical Reproduction' [1936], in C. Harrison and P. Wood (eds) *Art in Theory 1900–2000: An Anthology of Changing Ideas*, Blackwell, Oxford, 520–7

Berger, J. and J. Mohr (1995) *Another Way of Telling* [1982], Vintage Books, New York

Bertrand, A. (2006) 'Denkbilder', *Camera Austria*, 93, 18–29

Beyst, S. (2007) 'A Spirit's Eye View' (March), http://d-sites.net/english/gursky.htm. Accessed 8 August 2010.

Bhabha, H. K. (1994) *The Location of Culture*, Routledge, London; New York

Birnbaum, D. (1998) 'A Thousand Words: Gabriel Orozco Talks about His Recent Films', *Artforum* 36:10 (Summer), 114–15

Black, M. (1993) 'More about Metaphor', in A. Ortony (ed.) *Metaphor and Thought*, Cambridge University Press, Cambridge, 19–41

Bois, Y. (2004) 'The Paper Tigress' in C. Macel (ed.), *M'as tu vu(e)? = Did you see me?* Prestel, Munich

Bonami, F. (1985) 'Clean Clusters in a Shopping Mall', *Flash Art*, 183 (Summer), 105–6

Boyce Davies, C. (1994) *Black Women, Writing and Identity: Migrations of the Subject*, Routledge, London; New York

Braidotti, R. (1994) *Nomadic Subjects: Embodiment and Sexual Difference in Contemporary Feminist Theory*, Columbia University Press, New York

Brecht, B. (1977) 'Popularity and Realism' [1938], in 'Against Georg Lukàcs', trans. Stuart Hood, in E. Bloch, T. Adorno et al., *Aesthetics and Politics*, Verso, London, 79–85

Breton, A. (1960) *Nadja*, Grove Press, New York

— (2005) 'First Manifesto of Surrealism' [1924], in C. Harrison and P. Wood (eds), *Art in Theory 1900–1990: An Anthology of Changing Ideas*, Blackwell, Oxford, 447–53

Broker, D. (2003) 'Interview with Destiny Deacon', Satire issue, *Photofile*, 72, 16–21

Bryson, N. (1981) 'Discourse, Figure', in *Word and Image: French Painting of the Ancien Régime*, Cambridge University Press, Cambridge, 1–28

Buchloh, B. (1995) 'Allan Sekula: Photography Between Discourse and Document', in A. Sekula, *Fish Story*, Richter Verlag, Rotterdam, 189–201

— (1998) 'Portraits / Genre: Thomas Struth', in *Portraits: Thomas Struth*, Schirmer / Mosel Production, Munich.

Buñuel, L. (2000) 'Notes on the Making of *Un Chien andalou*', British Film Institute, London

Burgin, V. (ed.) (1982) *Thinking Photography*, Macmillan, London

— (1986) *The End of Art Theory*, Palgrave, Basingstoke; New York

— (2004) *Stillness and Time: Photography and the Image*, Photoforum conference at Kent Institute of Art & Design, Canterbury, 7–8 May

— (2005) 'Socialist Formalism' [1976], in C. Harrison and P. Wood, *Art in Theory 1900–2000: An Anthology of Changing Ideas*, Blackwell, Oxford, 938–42

Butler, J. (1990) *Gender Trouble: Feminism and the Subversion of Identity*, Routledge, New York; London

— (1993) *Bodies that Matter: On the Discursive Limits of 'Sex'*, Routledge, London; New York

— (1997) 'Performative Acts and Gender Constitution: An Essay in Phenomenology and Feminist Theory' [1988], in K. Conboy, N. Medina and S. Stanbury (eds), *Writing on the Body*, Columbia University Press, New York

Cartier-Bresson, H. (1981) 'The Decisive Moment' [1952], in V. Goldberg (ed.), *Photography in Print: Writings from 1876 to the Present*, Simon & Schuster, New York

Castells, M. (2004) 'Space of Flows, Space of Places: Materials for a Theory of Urbanism in the Information Age', in S. Graham, *The Cybercities Reader*, Routledge, London; New York, 82–93

Cazeaux, C. (ed.) (2000) *The Continental Aesthetics Reader*, Routledge, London

Charlesworth, M. (1995) 'Fox Talbot and the "White Mythology" of Photography', *Word & Image*, 11:3 (July/September), 207–15

Colebrooke, C. (2005) *Philosophy and Poststructuralist Theory: From Kant to Deleuze*, Edinburgh University Press, Edinburgh

Cooke, L. (1997) 'Cosmologer', *Parkett*, 50/51, 103–7

— (2007) 'Time Lapse', in *Jean Luc Mylayne*, Twin Palms Publishers, Santa Fe, unpaginated

Costello, D. and M. Iversen (eds) (2010), *Photography after Conceptual Art*, Wiley-Blackwell, Oxford

Coulter, G. (2010) 'The Catastrophe of the Digital and the Fate of Photography', *Kritikos*, 7 (November–December), http://intertheory.org/catastrophe.htm, accessed 13 September 2012

Crimp, D. (1979) 'Pictures', *October*, 8 (Spring), 75–88

— (1980) 'The Photographic Activity of Postmodernism', *October*, 15 (Winter), 91–101

Crome, K. and J. Williams (eds) (2006), *The Lyotard Reader and Guide*, Edinburgh University Press, Edinburgh

Cruz, A., E. Smith and A. Jones (1997) *Cindy Sherman: Retrospective*, Thames & Hudson, London

Danto, A. C. (1998/99) 'Beat Streuli's Gesamtkunstwerk', *Parkett* 54, 126–33

Deleuze, G. (1993) *The Fold: Leibnitz and the Baroque* [1988], trans. Tom Conley [1992], University of Minnesota Press, Minneapolis

— (2003) *The Logic of Sense* [1969], trans. M. Lester and C. Stivale [1990], Continuum, London; New York

— (2004) *Francis Bacon: The Logic of Sensation* [1981], trans. Daniel W. Smith [2003], University of Minnesota Press, Minneapolis

Deleuze, G. and F. Guattari (1994) *What is Philosophy?* [1991], trans. G. Burchill and H. Tomlinson [1994], Verso, London; New York

— (2007) *A Thousand Plateaus: Capitalism and Schizophrenia* [1980], trans. B. Massumi [1988], Continuum, London; New York

Derrida, J. (1973) *Speech and Phenomena* [1967], trans. D. B. Allison [1973], North Western University Press, Evanston

— (1978) 'Violence and Metaphysics' [1964], in *Writing and Difference*, trans. Alan Bass [1978], Routledge, London; New York

— (1982a) *Positions* [1972], trans. Alan Bass [1981], University of Chicago Press, Chicago

— (1982b) *Margins of Philosophy* [1972], trans. Alan Bass [1982], University of Chicago Press, Chicago

— (1987) *The Truth in Painting* [1978], trans. G. Bennington and I. McLeod, University of Chicago Press, Chicago

— (1988) 'The Deaths of Roland Barthes' [1981], in H. J. Silverman (ed.), *Philosophy and Non-Philosophy since Merleau-Ponty*, Routledge, New York

— (1989) 'Right of Inspection' ['Droit de Regard', 1985] with Marie-Françoise Plissart, trans. D. Wills, *Art & Text*, 32, 19–97

— (1993) *Aporias*, trans. T. Dutoit [1993], Stanford University Press, Stanford

— (1994) 'The Spatial Arts: An Interview with Jacques Derrida' [1990], in P. Brunette and D. Wills, *Deconstruction and the Visual Arts*, Cambridge University Press, Cambridge, 9–32

— (2001) *What Is Called Not Thinking*, lecture given at Loughborough University, 10 November 2001

— (2004) *Dissemination* [1972], trans. B. Johnson [1981], Continuum, London; New York

— (2010) *Copy, Archive, Signature: A Conversation on Photography* [2000], ed. Gerhardt Richter, trans. Jeff Fort, Stanford University Press, Stanford

Di Corcia, P. (1998) *Streetwork 1993–97*, Ediciones Universidad de Salamanca, Salamanca

Dion, M. (1997) 'For Jean-Luc Mylayne', *Parkett* 50/51, 113–16

Donald, J. (1999) *Imagining the Modern City*, University of Minnesota Press, Minneapolis

Douglas, M. (1970) *Natural Symbols: Explorations in Cosmology*, Barry & Rockliff; The Crescent Press, London

Easthope, A. (ed.) (1993) *Contemporary Film Theory*, Longman, London; New York

Eco, U. (1982) 'Critique of the Image' [1970], in Burgin, *Thinking Photography*, Macmillan, London, 32–8

Edwards, S. (1989) 'The Snapshooters of History: Passages in the Postmodern Argument', *TEN 8, International Photography Magazine*, 32, 2–21

— (2006) *Photography: A Very Short Introduction*, Oxford University Press, Oxford

Elkins, J. (2007) *Photography Theory*, Routledge, London

— (2010) *What Photography Is*, Routledge, New York; Abingdon

El Lissitsky (1989) 'The Architect's Eye' [1926], in C. Phillips (ed.), *Photography in the Modern Era: European Documents and Critical Writings, 1913–1940*, The Metropolitan Museum of Art; Aperture, New York, 221–6

Emerson, P. H. (1980) 'Hints on Art' [1889], in A. Trachtenberg (ed.), *Classic Essays on Photography*, Leete's Island Books, New Haven, 100–5

Evans, W. (1994a) 'Lyric Documentary', transcript of lecture delivered at Yale University Art Gallery, New Haven, 11 March 1964, in Walker Evans Archive, Metropolitan Museum of Art, New York

— (1994b) 'Categories of Quality' [1969] in Walker Evans Archive, 1994.250.54 (18), Metropolitan Museum of Art, New York

— (1994c) Interview Jonathan Goell, Brookline, Massachusetts, 4 August 1971, Walker Evans Archive, Metropolitan Museum of Art, New York

— (1994d) Interview with Paul Cummings, recorded at his home in Connecticut, 13 October 1971, Walker Evans Archive, Metropolitan Museum of Art, New York

Fani-Kayode, R. (1988) 'Traces of Ecstasy', *TEN 8*, 28, Birmingham, 36–42

Fanon, F. (1991) *Black Skin, White Masks* [1952], Grove Weidenfeld, New York

Ferguson, R. (2001) *Nikki S. Lee: Projects*, Hatje Cantz Publishers, Ostfildern

Fineman, M. (2004) 'The Cypress in the Orchard', in *Gabriel Orozco: Photographs*, Hirshhorn Museum and Sculpture Garden; Smithsonian Institution, Washington, DC / Steidl, Göttingen

Fisher, J. (2003) *Vampire in the Text: Narratives of Contemporary Art*, Institute of International Visual Arts, London

Flusser, V. (2000) *Towards a Philosophy of Photography* [1983], Reaktion Books, London

Fogle, D. (ed.) (2003) *The Last Picture Show: Artists using Photography*, Walker Art Centre, Minneapolis

Foster, H. (1982) 'Re: Post', *Parachute*, 26, 11–15

— (ed.) (1983) *The Anti-Aesthetic: Essays on Postmodern Culture*, Bay Press, Seattle

— (1996) *The Return of the Real*, The MIT Press, Cambridge, MA; London

Foucault, M. (1982a) 'The Subject and Power', *Critical Inquiry*, 8 (Summer), 777–95

— (1982b) *This Is Not a Pipe*, University of California Press, Berkeley; Los Angeles; London

— (1998) 'What is an Author?' [1969], in D. Preziosi (ed.), *The Art of Art History: A Critical Anthology*, Oxford University Press, Oxford, 299–314

— (2003) 'Las Meninas', in *The Order of Things* [1966], [English translation 1970], Routledge, London; New York

Fox Talbot, W. H. (1980) 'A Brief Historical Sketch of the Invention of the Art' [1834], in A. Trachtenberg (ed.), *Classic Essays on Photography*, Leete's Island Books, New Haven, 27–36

— (2011) *The Pencil of Nature* [1844], Hirmer Verlag, Munich

Freud, S. (1991) *On Metapsychology: The Theory of Psychoanalysis*, Penguin, London

— (2002) *The Psychopathology of Everyday Life* [1901], Penguin, London

Friday, J. (2002) *Aesthetics and Photography*, Ashgate, Aldershot

Fried, M. (2008) *Why Photography Matters as Art as Never Before*, Yale University Press, New Haven; London

Gane, M. (1991) (ed.) *Baudrillard's Bestiary, Baudrillard and Culture*, Routledge, London; New York

— (ed.) (1993) *Baudrillard Live: Selected Interviews*, Routledge, London; New York

Gearon, T. (2001) *I Am a Camera*, Saatchi Gallery exhibition, London

Glendinning, S. (ed.) (2001) *Arguing with Derrida*, Blackwell, Oxford

Goldberg, R. (2000) 'Pilgrimage to Santiago: An Interview with Zhang Huan', www.zhanghuan.com/ShowText.asp?id=7&sClassID=3, accessed on 13 September 2012

Goldberg, V. (ed.) (1981) *Photography in Print: Writings from 1876 to the Present*, Simon & Schuster, New York

Goldin, N. (1986) *The Ballad of Sexual Dependency*, Aperture Foundation, New York

— (1996–97) video of interview 'In My Life', Whitney Museum exhibition, New York, shown at Whitechapel Gallery exhibition *The Devil's Playground*, 2002

Goodman, N. (1969) *The Languages of Art: An Approach to the Theory of Symbols*, Oxford University Press, London; Oxford

Greenberg, C. (1986) *Collated Essays and Criticism*, Vol. 2, University of Chicago Press, Chicago
— (2005) 'Modernist Painting' [1960], in C. Harrison and P. Wood (eds), *Art in Theory 1900–2000: An Anthology of Changing Ideas*, Blackwell, Oxford, 773–9
Grosz, E. (1994) *Volatile Bodies: Toward a Corporeal Feminism*, Indiana University Press, Bloomington; Indianapolis
— (1995) *Space, Time and Perversion: Essays on the Politics of Bodies*, Routledge, London; New York
Groys, B. (2008) *Art Power*, The MIT Press, Cambridge, MA; London
Habermas, J. (1985) 'Modernity: An Incomplete Project' [1981], in H. Foster (ed.), *Postmodern Culture* [1983], Pluto Press, London
Hall, S. (1997a) 'Race, the Floating Signifier', lecture at Goldsmiths College, Media Education Foundation, 10 September 2009, www.mediaed.org
— (1997b) 'Representation and the Media', lecture at the Media Education Foundation, www.mediaed.org, www.youtube.com/watch?v=aTzMsPqssOY accessed 10 September 2009
Hall, S. and M. Sealy (2001) *Different: A Historical Context: Contemporary Photographers and Black Identity*, Phaidon, London
Hammond, P. (ed.) (2000) *The Shadow and its Shadow: Surrealist Writings on the Cinema* [1978], City Lights Books, San Francisco
Haraway, D. (1991) *Simians, Cyborgs and Women: The Reinvention of Nature*, Free Association, London
Harrison, J. (2001) *The New Art History*, Routledge, London; New York
Harrison, C. and P. Wood (eds) (2005) *Art in Theory 1900–2000: An Anthology of Changing Ideas*, Blackwell, Oxford
Heartney, E. (2007) 'Zhang Huan: Becoming the Body', www.zhanghuan.com/ShowText.asp?id=30&sClassID=1, accessed 13 September 2012
Heidegger, M. (1968) *What Is Called Thinking?* Lectures delivered at the University of Freiburg during the winter and summer semesters of 1951–52 and translated by J. Glenn Gray, New York, Harper & Row
— (2000) 'The Origin of the Work of Art', in C. Cazeaux (ed.), *The Continental Aesthetics Reader*, Routledge, London, 80–101
Higgs, M. (2004) *Uta Barth*, Phaidon Press, London
Honderich, T. (ed.) (1999) *Oxford Companion to Philosophy*, Oxford University Press, Oxford; New York
hooks, bel (1995) *Art on My Mind: Visual Politics*, The New Press, New York
— (1996) 'Cultural Criticism and Transformation', Media Education Foundation, www.mediaed.org, www.youtube.com/watch?v=zQUuHFKP-9s&feature=fvw accessed 5 October 2009
Horn, R. (2000) *Another Water (the River Thames for example)*, Scalo, Zurich; London
Hughes, A. and A. Noble (2003) *Phototextualities: Intersections of Photography and Narrative*, University of New Mexico Press, Albuquerque
Hung, W. and C. Phillips (2004) *Between Past and Future: New Photography and Video from China*, Smart Museum, Chicago; International Center of Photography, New York
Indiana, G. (1993) 'Five Nights of a Dreamer', *Art Forum*, 31:5 (January), 63–7
Iverson, M. (1994) 'What is a Photograph?', *Art History*, 17:3 (September), 450–64
Jaar, A. (1999) *Laments of the Images*, List Visual Arts Center; Massachusetts Institute of Technology, Cambridge, MA

Jameson, F. (2009) *Postmodernism, or The Cultural Logic of Late Capitalism* [1991], Verso, London; New York

Jay, M. (1994) *Downcast Eyes: The Denigration of Vision in Twentieth-Century French Thought*, University of California Press, Berkeley; Los Angeles; London

Jeffrey, I. (1992) 'Fragment and Totality in Photography', *History of Photography*, 6:4 (Winter), 351–6

Jerslev, A. (2002) *Realism and Reality on Film and Media*, Museum Tusculanum Press, University of Copenhagen

Johnson, B. (2004) 'Translator's Introduction' in J. Derrida, *Dissemination* [1972], trans. B. Johnson [1981], Continuum, London; New York, vii–xxxv

Joselit, D. (2000) 'Gabriel Orozco', *Artforum* 39: 1 (September), 173–4

Joyce, L. and F. Orton (2003) 'Always Elsewhere: An Introduction to the Art of Jeff Wall', in *Jeff Wall, Photographs*, Museum Moderna Kunst, Vienna, 8–33

Kant, I. (1952) *The Critique of Aesthetic Judgement* [1790], trans. J. Meredith, Clarendon Press, Oxford

Karsh, Y. (1968) *Portraits by Karsh*, Museum of Fine Arts, Boston

— (1976) *Karsh Portraits*, University of Toronto Press, Toronto; Buffalo

Katz, L. (1981) 'Interview with Walker Evans' [1971], in V. Goldberg (ed.), *Photography in Print: Writings from 1876 to the Present*, Simon & Schuster, New York, 358–69

Kelly, M. (ed.) (1998) *Encyclopedia of Aesthetics*, Oxford University Press, Oxford; New York

Kim Yu Yeon (2003) 'Intensified Corporeality', www.zhanghuan.com/ShowText.asp?id=20&sClassID=1, accessed 13 September 2012

Kozloff, M. (1987) 'Opaque Disclosures', *Art in America* (October), 144–53

— (1994) *Lone Visions, Crowded Frames*, University of Mexico Press, Albuquerque

Krauss, R. (1985) *L'Amour Fou: Photography and Surrealism*, Abbeyville Press, New York; London / The Corcoran Gallery of Art, Washington, DC

— (1986) 'Poststructuralism and the Paraliterary' [1980], in *The Originality and the Avant-Garde and Other Modernist Myths*, The MIT Press, Cambridge, MA.

Kristeva, J. (1980) 'Word, Dialogue and Novel' [1969] and 'How Does One Speak to Literature?' [1971], in *Desire in Language: A Semiotic Approach to Literature and Art* [1979], trans. T. Gora, A. Jardine and L. S. Roudiez [1980], Basil Blackwell, Oxford

— (1984) *Revolution in Poetic Language* [1974], trans. M. Waller [1984], Columbia University Press, New York

— (1987) 'Stabat Mater' [1977], in *Tales of Love* [1983], trans. L. S. Roudiez [1987], Columbia University Press, New York

— (1996) 'A Question of Subjectivity: An Interview' [1986], in P. Rice and P. Waugh (eds), *Modern Literary Theory Today: A Reader*, Arnold, London, 131–7

— (2000) 'Powers of Horror: An Essay on Abjection' [1980], trans. L. S. Roudiez [1982], in Cazeaux, *The Continental Aesthetics Reader*, Routledge, London, 542–55

— (2001) An interview with Nina Zivancevici, Paris, March–April 2001, http://evans-experientialism.freewebspace.com/kristeva.htm, accessed 4 April 2005

Kuan, C. 'Interview with Wang Qingsong', *Oxford Art Online*, www.oxfordartonline.com/public/page/asiancontinter, accessed 13 September 2012

Lacan, J. (1977) *Écrits: A Selection* [1966], trans. A. Sheridan, Tavistock, London

La Grange, A. (2005) *Basic Critical Theory for Photographers*, Focal Press, Amsterdam; Oxford

Lakoff, G. (1993) 'The Contemporary Theory of Metaphor', in A. Ortony (ed.), *Metaphor and*

Thought, Cambridge University Press, Cambridge, 202–51

Langer, S. K. (1953) *Feeling and Form: A Theory of Art Developed from 'Philosophy in a New Key'*, Routledge & Kegan Paul, London

Langford, M. (2005) *Image and Imagination*, McGill-Queen's University Press, Montreal; London

Levi Strauss, D. (2003) *Between the Eyes: Essays on Photography and Politics*, Aperture, New York

Levin, S. R. (1993) 'Language, Concepts and Worlds' in A. Ortony (ed.), *Metaphor and Thought*, Cambridge University Press, Cambridge, 112–23

Levinas, E. (1969) *Totality and Infinity: An Essay in Exteriority* [1961], trans. A. Lingis, Duquesne University Press, Pittsburgh

— (1986) 'In Dialogue with Richard Kearney', in R. A. Cohen (ed.), *Face to Face with Levinas*, State University of New York Press, Albany

— (1988) 'The Paradox of Morality: An Interview with Emmanuel Levinas', in R. Bernasconi and D. Wood (eds), *The Provocation of Levinas: Rethinking the Other*, Routledge, London; New York

Lippard, Lucy R. (1973) *Six Years: The Dematerialisation of the Art Object from 1966 to 1972*, Studio Vista, London

Lomax, Y. (2000) *Writing the Image*, I. B. Tauris, London

— (2005) *Sounding the Event: Escapades in Dialogues and Matters of Art, Nature and Time*, I. B. Tauris, London; New York

— (2009) 'Talking Theory', in J. Tormey and G. Whiteley (eds), *Telling Stories: Countering Narrative in Art, Theory and Film*, Cambridge Scholars Publishing, Newcastle upon Tyne, 38–49

Lyotard, J. F. (1983) 'Fiscourse Digure: The Utopia behind the Scenes of the Phantasy', trans. Mary Lydon, *Theatre Journal*, 35:3, The Poetics of Theatre (October), 333–57

— (1984) *The Postmodern Condition: A Report on Knowledge* [1979], trans. G. Bennington and B. Massumi [1984], University of Minnesota, Minneapolis

— (2006) 'Taking the Side of the Figural', trans. M. Sinclair and 'The Connivance of Desire with the Figural', trans. A. Knab, from *Discours, figure* [1971], in K. Crome and J. Williams, *The Lyotard Reader and Guide*, Edinburgh University Press, Edinburgh

— (2011) *Discourse, Figure* [1971], trans. A. Hudek and M. Lydon, University of Minnesota Press, Minneapolis

MacCormack, P. (2000) 'Pleasure, Perversion and Death: Three Lines of Flight for the Viewing Body', *TRANSMAT, Resources in Transcendental Materialism*, www.cinestatic.com/trans-mat/MacCormack/PPDintro2.htm accessed 6 September 2012

McFarlane, R. (2004) *Walk and Don't Look Blak*, www.smh.com.au/news/Arts/Walk-and-dont-look-blak/2004/12/13/1102787009591.html accessed 6 September, 2009

Marks, L. U. (2002) *Touch: Sensuous Theory and Multi-Sensory Media*, University of Minnesota Press, Minneapolis

Martin, T. (1999) 'Documentary Theatre', in *Sharon Lockhart: Teatro Amazonas*, Museum Boijmans Van Beuningen, Rotterdam

Massumi, B. (2002) 'The Autonomy of Affect', in *Parables of the Virtual: Movement, Affect, Sensation*, Duke University Press, Durham, NC; London, 23–45

— (2007) 'Translator's Foreword: Pleasures of Philosophy', in G. Deleuze and F. Guattari, *A Thousand Plateaus: Capitalism and Schizophrenia*, trans. B. Massumi [1988], Continuum, London; New York, xv–xvi

Meiselas, S. (1997) *Kurdistan: In the Shadow of History*, Random House, New York

Merleau-Ponty, M. (1962) *The Phenomenology of Perception* [1960], trans. C. Smith, Routledge & Kegan Paul, London; New York

— (1964) *The Primacy of Perception, and Other Essays on Phenomenological Psychology, the Philosophy of Art, History and Politics*, Northwestern University Press, Evanston

— (1968) *The Visible and Invisible* [1964], trans. A. Lingis, Northwestern University Press, Evanston

Mikhailov, B. (1999) *Case History*, Scalo, Zurich; Berlin; New York

Miller, G. A. (1993) 'Images and Models, Similes and Metaphors', in A. Ortony (ed.), *Metaphor and Thought*, Cambridge University Press, Cambridge, 357–400

Mitchell, W. J. T. (1987) *Iconology: Image, Text, Ideology*, University of Chicago Press, Chicago

— (1994) *Picture Theory*, University of Chicago Press, London; Chicago

Moffat, M. (1995) *Tracey Moffatt: Fever Pitch*, Piper Press, Annandale

— (1999) *Tracey Moffatt*, Hatje Cantz Publishers, Ostfildern

Moholy-Nagy, L. (1989) 'Unprecedented Photography' [1927], in C. Phillips (ed.), *Photography in the Modern Era: European Documents and Critical Writings, 1913–1940*, The Metropolitan Museum of Art; Aperture, New York

Mora, G. and J. Hill (eds) (1993) *Walker Evans: The Hungry Eye*, Thames & Hudson, London

Moxey, K. (1994) *The Practice of Theory: Poststructuralism, Cultural Politics and Art History*, Cornell University Press, New York, 83–5

Muir, P. (2004) 'Signs of a Beginning: *October* and the *Pictures* Exhibition', *Word & Image*, 20:1 (January–March), 52–62

Mulvey, L. (1989) 'Visual Pleasure and Narrative Cinema' [1975], in *Visual and Other Pleasures*, Macmillan, Basingstoke

— (1996) 'Dialogue with Spectatorship: Barbara Kruger and Victor Burgin' [1983], in L. Heron and V. Williams, *Illuminations, Women Writing on Photography from the 1850s to the Present*, I. B. Tauris, London; New York, 83–5

— (2004) *Stillness and Time: Photography and the Image*, Photoforum conference at Kent Institute of Art & Design, Canterbury, 7–8 May

Mylayne, J. L. (2007) *Jean Luc Mylayne*, Twin Palm Publishers, Santa Fe, unpaginated

Naef, W. (ed.) (1995) *Handbook of the Photographs Collection*, The J. Paul Getty Museum, Malibu

Nelmes, J. (ed.) (1999) *An Introduction to Film Studies*, Routledge, London; New York

Newhall, B. (1982) *The History of Photography: From 1839 to the Present* [1949], Secker & Warburg, London

— (1993) *In Focus: Memoirs of a Life in Photography*, Bullfinch, Boston

Newman, M. (ed.) (2007) *Jeff Wall: Works and Collected Writings*, Ediciones Poligrafa, Barcelona

Nickel, D. R. (1998) *Snapshots: The Photography of Everyday Life 1888 to the Present*, San Francisco Museum of Modern Art, San Francisco

— (2001) 'History of Photography: The State of Research', *The Art Bulletin*, 83:3 (September), 548–58

Nuyts, J. and P. Pederson (eds) (1997) *Language and Conceptualisation*, Cambridge University Press, Cambridge

Oliver, K. (ed.) (1997) *The Portable Kristeva*, Columbia University Press, New York

Olkowski, D. and G. Weiss (eds) (2006) *Feminist Interpretations of Maurice Merleau-Ponty*, Pennsylvania State University Press, University Park

Orozco, G. (n.d.) PBS interview, *Art 21*, www.pbs.org/art21/artists/orozco accessed 2 August 2009

Ortony, A. (ed.) (1993) *Metaphor and Thought*, Cambridge University Press, Cambridge

O'Sullivan, S. (2007) *Art Encounters Deleuze and Guattari*, Palgrave Macmillan, New York

Owens, C. (1980) 'The Allegorical Impulse: Toward a Theory of Postmodernism', Part I, *October*, 12 (Spring), 66–86; Part II, *October*, 13 (Summer), 58–80

— (1992) *Beyond Recognition: Representation, Power and Culture*, University of California Press, Berkeley; Los Angeles; London

Peirce, C. S. (1955) *The Philosophical Writings of Peirce*, Mineola, NY, Dover

Phelan, P. (2003) 'Performance, Live Culture and Things of the Heart', *Journal of Visual Culture*, 2:3, 291–302

Phillips, C. (1989) *Photography in the Modern Era: European Documents and Critical Writings, 1913–1940*, The Metropolitan Museum of Art; Aperture, New York

Phillips, D. (1998) 'Photo-Logos: Photography and Deconstruction', in M. A. Cheetham, M. A. Holly and K. Moxey (eds), *The Subjects of Art History*, Cambridge University Press, Cambridge, 155–79

Plato (2003) 'Art and Illusion', in *The Republic* [c. 375 BC], Penguin, London

Pollock, G. (1999) *Differencing the Canon: Feminist Desire and the Writing of Art's Histories*, Routledge, London

Readings, B. (1991) *Introducing Lyotard: Art and Politics*, Routledge, London; New York

Rendell, J. (2010) *Site-Writing: The Architecture of Art Criticism: Art, Architecture and Criticism*, I. B.Tauris, London

Renger-Patzsch, A. (1989) 'Aims' [1927], in C. Phillips (ed.), *Photography in the Modern Era: European Documents and Critical Writings, 1913–1940*, The Metropolitan Museum of Art, New York, 104–5

Richter, G. (1995) Interview with B. Buchloh [1986], in G. Richter, *The Daily Practice of Painting: Writings and Interviews 1962–1993*, London: Thames & Hudson

— (2010) 'Between Translation and Invention', in *Copy, Archive, Signature: A Conversation on Photography* [2000], ed. G. Richter, trans. J. Fort, Stanford University Press, Stanford

Ricoeur, P. (1978) *The Rule of Metaphor: Multi-Disciplinary Studies of the Creation of Meaning in Language* [1975], trans. R. Czerny, K. McLaughlin and J. Costello [1977], Routledge & Kegan Paul, London

Rignall, J. (1992) *Realist Fiction and the Strolling Spectator*, Routledge, London; New York

Roberts, J. (1994) *Art Has no History! The Making and Unmaking of Modern Art*. London; New York: Verso

— (1998) *The Art of Interruption: Realism, Photography and the Everyday*, Manchester University Press, Manchester; New York

— (2009) 'Photography after the Photograph: Event, Archive, and the Non-Symbolic', *Oxford Art Journal*, 32:9, 281–98

Robinson, H. P. (1980) 'Idealism, Realism, Expressionism' [1896], in A. Trachtenberg (ed.), *Classic Essays on Photography*, Leete's Island Books, New Haven, 91–8

Rodchenko, A. (1989) 'Downright Ignorance or a Mean Trick?' [1928], in C. Phillips (ed.) *Photography in the Modern Era: European Documents and Critical Writings, 1913–1940*, The Metropolitan Museum of Art; Aperture, New York, 245–8

Rodowick, D. N. (2001) *Reading the Figural, or Philosophy After the New Media*, Duke University Press, Durham, NC; London

Rose, G. (2001) *Visual Methodologies: An Introduction to the Interpretation of Visual Materials*, Sage, London

Rosenheim, J. L. (2002) *Walker Evans: Polaroids*, Scalo, Zurich; Berlin; New York

Rosler, M. (1991) 'Fragments of a Metropolitan Viewpoint', in B. Wallis (ed.), *If You Lived Here: The City in Art Theory, and Social Activism: A Project by Martha Rosler*, Bay Press, Seattle

— (1998) 'Interview with Benjamin Buchloh', in C. de Zegher (ed.), *Martha Rosler: Positions in the Life World*, Ikon Gallery, Birmingham; The MIT Press, London

— (2004) 'For an Art Against the Mythology of Everyday Life' [1979] and 'Post-Documentary: Post-Photography?' [1999], in *Decoys and Disruptions*, The MIT Press, Cambridge, MA; London

Said, E. (1995) *Orientalism* [1978], Penguin, London

— (2003) 'Orientalism' [1978], in B. Ashcroft, G. Griffiths and H. Tiffin (eds), *The Post-Colonial Studies Reader*, Routledge, London; New York

Sartre, J. P. (1965) *Nausea* [1938], trans. Robert Baldick, Penguin, Hamondsworth

— (2001) *Being and Nothingness* [1943], trans. H. E. Barnes, Routledge, London

Saussure, F. de (1983) *Course in General Linguistics* [1916], Duckworth, London

Schapiro, M. (1998) 'The Still Life as a Personal Object: A Note on Heidegger and Van Gogh' [1968], in D. Preziosi (ed.), *The Art of Art History: A Critical Anthology*, Oxford University Press, Oxford, 427–31

Scheer, E. (2006) '"The most delicate of operations": Baudrillard's Photographic Abreactions', *International Journal of Baudrillard Studies*, 3:1 (January), www.ubishops.ca/baudrillardstudies/vol3_1/scheer.htm, accessed 13 September 2012

Seamon, R. (2001) 'The Conceptual Dimension in Art and the Modern Theory of Artistic Value', *The Journal of Aesthetics and Art Criticism*, 59:2 (Spring), 139–51

Sekula, A. (1982) 'On the Invention of Photographic Meaning' [1975], in V. Burgin (ed.), *Thinking Photography*, Macmillan, London, 84–109

— (1984) *Photography Against the Grain: Essays and Photo-works*, The Press of the Nova Scotia College of Art & Design, Halifax

— (1995) *Fish Story*, Richter Verlag, Rotterdam

— (1999) 'Dismantling Modernism, Reinventing Documentary' [1976–78], in *Dismal Science: Photo Works 1972–1996*, University Galleries; Illinois State University, Normal

— (2003a) *Performance Under Working Conditions*, Generali Foundation, Vienna

— (2003b) *TITANIC's Wake*, SNEL, Liège

Shawcross, N. M. (1997) *Roland Barthes on Photography: The Critical Tradition in Perspective*, University Press of Florida, Gainsville

Silverman, K. (1996) *The Threshold of the Visible World*, Routledge, New York; London

Singerman, H. (2002) 'Sherrie Levine's Art History', *October*, 101 (Summer), 96–121

Sobchack, V. (1992) *The Address of the Eye: A Phenomenology of Film Experience*, Princeton University Press, Princeton

Solomon-Godeau, A. (1982) 'Playing in the Fields of the Image', *Afterimage* 10(1–2) (Summer), 11–18.

— (1984) 'Photography after Art Photography' in B. Wallis (ed.), *Art After Modernism*, Museum of Contemporary Art, New York

— (1991) *Photography at the Dock: Essays on Photographic History, Institutions, and Practices*, Minnesota University Press, Minneapolis

Sontag, S. (1979) *On Photography* [1977], Penguin, London

— (2003) *Regarding the Pain of Others*, Hamish Hamilton, London

Soutter, L. (1999) 'The Photographic Idea: Reconsidering Conceptual Photography',

AfterImage, 26:5 (March/April), 8–10
Spence, J. (1986) *Putting Myself in the Picture: A Political, Personal and Photographic Autobiography*, Camden Press, London
Squiers, Carol (ed.) (1991) *The Critical Image: Essays on Contemporary Photography*, Lawrence & Wishart, London
Stieglitz, A. (1980) 'Pictorial Photography' [1899] in A. Trachtenberg (ed.), *Classic Essays on Photography*, Leete's Island Books, New Haven, 115–23
Strand, P. (1980) 'Photography and the New God' [1917], in A. Trachtenberg (ed.), *Classic Essays on Photography*, Leete's Island Books, New Haven, 141–53
Strba, A. (1997) *Shades of Time*, Lars Muller Publishers, Zurich
Streuli, B. (2000) 'Interview with Beat Streuli', in A. Pace (ed.), *Portraits 98–00, La belle estate*, Galleria Civica d'Arte Moderna e Contemporanea, Turin
Sultan, L. (1992) *Pictures From Home*, Harry N. Abrams, New York
Sultan, T. (2007) 'A Matter of Place', in *Jean Luc Mylayne*. Santa Fe: Twin Palms Publishers, unpaginated
Szarkowski, J. (1971) 'Introduction', in *Walker Evans*. Exhibition Catalogue, Museum of Modern Art, New York, 10–17
Tagg, J. (1988) *The Burden of Representation: Essays on Photographies and Histories*, Palgrave Macmillan, Basingstoke; New York
— (1992) *Grounds of Dispute: Art History, Cultural Politics and the Discursive Field*, University of Minnesota Press, Minneapolis
Tormey, J. (2003a) 'Sonja's Voice', in K. Newton and C. Rolph (eds), *Masquerade: Women's Contemporary Portrait Photography*, Ffotogallery, Cardiff
— (2003b) 'Walker Evans' "Counter-Aesthetic"', *Afterimage, The Journal of Media Arts & Cultural Criticism*, 311 (1 July), 10–12
Tormey, J. and G. Whiteley (2009) (eds) *Telling Stories: Countering Narrative in Art, Theory and Film*, Cambridge Scholars Publishing, Newcastle upon Tyne
Trachtenberg, A. (ed.) (1980) *Classic Essays on Photography*, Leete's Island Books, New Haven
Tumlir, J. (2004) *White Blind (Bright Red) Uta Barth*, Site, Santa Fe
Tupitsyn, M. (1998) 'Photography as a Remedy for Stammering', in *Boris Mikhailov, Unfinished Dissertation*, Scalo, Zurich, 218–20
Tynan, S. (2002) 'Underpants', in *Source* 30 (Spring), 13–19
Van Lier, H. (2007). *Philosophy of Photography* [1983], Leuven University Press, Leuven
von Amelunxen, H. (1995) 'Beat Christoph Streuli (II)', *European Photography*, 57 (Spring/Summer), 55–8
Walker, I. (2002) *City Gorged with Dreams: Surrealism and Documentary Photography in Interwar Paris*, Manchester University Press, Manchester
Wall, J. (1998) *Jeff Wall*, Phaidon, London
— (2003) "Marks of Indifference": Aspects of Photography in, or as, Conceptual Art' [1995], in D. Fogle (ed.), *The Last Picture Show: Artists using Photography*, Walker Art Centre, Minneapolis, 32–44
Walton, K. (1984) 'Transparent Pictures: On the Nature of Photographic Realism', *Critical Inquiry*, 11:2 (December), 246–77
Waplington, N. (1998) *The Indecisive Memento*, Booth Clibborn Editions, London
Ward, O. (2011) 'Signs of Struggle', *The Independent* (21 August 2011)
Watney, S. (1982) 'Making Strange: The Shattered Mirror', in V. Burgin (ed.), *Thinking*

Photography, Macmillan, London, 154–76

— (2006) 'Tunnel Vision: Photographic Education in Britain in the 1980s' *AfterImage*, 33:4 (January/Febuary), 32–6

Weems, C. M. (1996) in interview with D. Friis-Hansen, 'From Carrie's Kitchen Table and Beyond', *ChickenBones: A Journal for Literary & Artistic African-American Themes*, www.nathanielturner.com/carriemaeweems.htm accessed 6 September 2009

— (2007) 'All About Eve: Women, Sex, and Desire', *Rudenstine Gallery Artists' Talks*, 15 October, Sackler Hall, 32 Quincy Street, Cambridge MA. http://dubois.fas.harvard.edu/node/255 accessed 6 September 2012

Weiss, G. (1998) *Body Images: Embodiment as Intercorporeality*, Routledge, London

Wells, L. (ed.) (2000) *Photography: A Critical Introduction*, Routledge, London

— (2002) (ed.) *The Photography Reader*, Routledge, London

What Happened here? Photography in Britain Since 1968 (2005) Conferences held at Derby University and Tate Britain

Wittgenstein, L. (2001) *Philosophical Investigations* [1953], trans. G. E. M. Anscombe, Blackwell Publishing, Oxford

Wolf, S. (ed.) (2004), *Ed Ruscha and Photography*, Whitney Museum of American Art, New York / Steidl, Gottingen

Wulffen, T. (1993) 'Thomas Ruff: Reality So Real It's Unrecognisable', *Flash Art*, 168 (January/February), 64–7

Zangwill, N. (2002) 'Are There Counterexamples to Aesthetic Theories of Art?' *The Journal of Aesthetics and Art Criticism*, 60:2 (Spring), 111–18

Zheng, G. (2006) 'Projecting the Reality of China through the Lens: On the Artistic Practice of Xing Danwen', *Yishu* (Spring), 91–6 – www.danwen.com/web/press/pdf/2006_YISHU_en.pdf accessed 6 September 2012

Ziegler, C. (1998) 'Extracts from a Conversation between Annelies Strba and Crista Ziegler, April 1998', *Great 21: The Photographer's Gallery Magazine*

Zurbrugg, N. (ed.) (1997) *Jean Baudrillard: Art & Artefact*, Sage, London

Index